CONSOLIDATED BIBLIOGRAPHY

OF

COUNTY HISTORIES
IN FIFTY STATES IN 1961

Consolidated 1935-1961

Compiled and Consolidated by

Ex. Lieut. Clarence Stewart Peterson, M.A.

GENEALOGICAL PUBLISHING CO., INC.
BALTIMORE   1973

Originally Published
[Baltimore], 1961

Reprinted
Genealogical Publishing Co., Inc.
Baltimore, 1963

Reissued
Genealogical Publishing Co., Inc.
Baltimore, 1973

Library of Congress Catalogue Card Number 73-8036
International Standard Book Number 0-8063-0563-0

INTRODUCTION

This 1961 Consolidated Bibliography aims to list all County histories of at least 100 pages, with few exceptions, and related works as published in the original in 1935 and in the supplements published in 1944, 1946-7, 1950, 1955 and 1960, and earlier works recently found that might be helpful but were not included in the previous publications of this Bibliography of County Histories in the United States.

Ex. Lieut. Clarence Stewart Peterson, M.A.
P.O. Box 342
Baltimore, Maryland

Author of:

Bibliography of County Histories of the 2980 Counties In The 48 States	1935
Governors Lists of The 48 States	1938
The American Pioneer In 48 States	1944
Bibliography of County Histories of The 3050 Counties In The 48 States, 1st Rev. Ed.	1944
Teaching 48 States Histories By Counties	1945
Admiral John A. Dahlgren	1945
America's Rune Stone	1946
Bibliography of County Histories of The 3111 Counties In The 48 States, 2nd Rev. Ed.	1946
First Governors of The 48 States (Set in Braille By Library of Congress)	1947
Governors Lists of The 48 States, 1st Rev. Ed.	1947
American-Scandinavian Diplomatic Relations 1776-1876	1948
Red River Valley Territorial Pioneers	1949
St. Croix River Valley Territorial Pioneers	1949
International Boundary Territorial Pioneers	1949
Meeker County Territorial Pioneers	1949
Stephen Taylor 1757-1857 Only Revolutionary War Soldier Buried In Minnesota	1949
Swift County's First Pioneers	1949
Supplement to Bibliography of County Histories	1950
Last Civil War Veteran In Each State	1950
Known Descendants of Carl Olofsson 1685-1953	1953
Known Military Dead During War of 1812	1955
Supplement to Bibliography of County Histories	1955
Bethesda's First Eighty - Two Years	1956
Known Military Dead During Mexican War 1846-48	1957
Known Military Dead During The Spanish American War and The Philippines Insurrection 1898-1901	1958
Known Military and Civilian Dead In The Minnesota Sioux Indian Massacre in 1862	1958
Known Dead In The Great Blizzard In Minnesota In 1873	1958
Known Military Dead During The American Revolutionary War 1775-1783	1959
1960 Supplement To Bibliography of County Histories In The Fifty States - (Twenty-Fifth Anniversary Supplement)	1960
Last Civil War Veteran In Fifty States	1961
Bibliography of County Histories In The Fifty States In 1961 (Consolidated 1935-1961)	1961

DEDICATED TO

The late Mrs. Ilse Blanche Meyer-Boos
who was the original and constant aid
and inspiration for over a quarter of
a century, in the compilation of the
Original and Final Supplements of this
Bibliography Of County Histories In The
United States.

* * * * * *

* * * * * * *

ACKNOWLEDGMENTS

I wish to thank all, everywhere, who have aided
in any way in the compilation and publication of the
original Bibliography of County Histories In The
Forty-eight States, published in 1935, and the five
Supplements, respectively, 1944, 1946-7, 1950, 1955,
and 1960 and in the ultimate consolidation of all of
these into this final Bibliography of County Histories
In The Fifty States In 1961. Without your kind help
and generous encouragement this work would forever
have remained undone by the author. And thank you to
Mrs. Sadie Leopold for a quiet place to work, and
to Miss Sara Owen for help on the manuscript.

Labor Day
Sept. 4, 1961
Baltimore, Md.

ACKNOWLEDGMENTS (Continued)

Special Acknowledgment is due the librarians of the New York
Public Library, 5th Avenue & 42nd Street, New York; the
Librarians of the New York Historical Society, 79th St. &
Central Park West, New York, and the librarians of the
Harkners Library, Columbia University, New York.

New York, N. Y., December 1935.

* * * * * *

In the revision of this bibliography, I wish to acknowledge
special aid rendered by the staff of the Library of Congress,
The National Archives, Washington, D. C.; the staff of the
West Virginia Dept. of Archives and History, Charleston, W. Va.;
the staff of the Enoch Pratt Library and the Maryland Historical Society Library, Baltimore, Md.; Johns Hopkins Library,
Peabody Library, Maryland University Library, Baltimore, Md.;
and Hall of Records in Annapolis, Md.

Baltimore, Md., August 1944.

* * * * * *

In preparing the 1947 revision of this bibliography of 2988
county histories about 1380 Counties of the 3111 Counties in
the 48 States, I wish first to acknowledge with deep appreciation the kind and generous aid of the county librarians in the
1380 Counties whose combined county histories total the 2988
herein listed. Others who have rendered invaluable aid in this
work and to whom acknowledgments are in order are: the forty-
eight State Historical Society Librarians; State Librarians;
History Departments in the Colleges and Universities in the
forty-eight States; and to all those who rendered aid in 1935
when this county history bibliography was first prepared of the
then 2982 counties and to those who aided in the first revision
in 1944 of this bibliography, the total counties at that time
numbering 3050 in the 48 states.

Baltimore, Md., October 1946.

* * * * * *

ACKNOWLEDGMENTS (Continued)

In preparing this 1950 Supplement to the Bibliography of County
Histories of the 3111 Counties in the 48 States, 1946-1947 Revised Edition, the First Revision 1944 (3050 Counties) and the
Original Bibliography Prepared in 1935 (2982 Counties), I owe
special acknowledgment with deep appreciation for kind and
generous aid to all City, County, State, College and University
Librarians all over this land. Especially valuable assistance
on this 1950 Supplement was very kindly and cheerfully given me
in:- The Library of the National Society, Daughters of the
American Revolution; The National Archives; and Library of
Congress, all of Washington, D. C., and the Librarians of the
Forty-eight State Historical Societies.

* * * * * *

In preparing this 1955 Supplement to the Bibliography of County
Histories of The Counties in the 48 States, first published in
1935, First Revision 1944, Second Revision 1946-47, Third Revision
1950, and now in 1955 this Fourth Revision, I owe special acknowledgment with deep appreciation for kind and generous aid to all
City, County, State, College and University Librarians in all of
the forty-eight States. Especially valuable assistance on this
1955 Supplement was very kindly and cheerfully given me in:- The
Library of The National Society, Daughters of the American Revolution; The National Society, U. S. Daughters of 1812; The National
Archives, and the Library of Congress, all of Washington, D. C.;
The Philadelphia City Library; The University of Pennsylvania
Library in Philadelphia; The Enoch Pratt Free Library; The Peabody
Library; The Johns Hopkins University Library, all in Baltimore,
Maryland; The State Librarians and the Librarians of the forty-
eight State Historical Societies.

* * * * * *

In preparing this 1960 Supplement to the Bibliography of County
Histories In Fifty States first published for the forty-eight
states in 1935 with Supplements in 1944, 1946-7, 1950 and 1955,
I owe special acknowledgment with deep appreciation and gratitude
for kind and generous aid to all City, County, State, College and
University Librarians all over the fifty states and the District
of Columbia. Especially valuable assistance on this 1960 Supple-
ment was cheerfully and helpfully given me in:- The Library of The
National Society of the Daughters of The American Revolution; The
National Archives; and the Library of Congress, all of Washington,
D. C.; and the Librarians, Directors and chiefs of the Fifty State
Historical Societies, State Historical Commissions, and State archives.

Ex-Lieut. Clarence Stewart Peterson, M.A.
Veterans Day, Nov. 11, 1960.

INTRODUCTION TO 1947 EDITION OF
<u>BIBLIOGRAPHY OF COUNTY HISTORIES OF 3111 COUNTIES IN THE 48 STATES</u>

Twenty-nine hundred and eighty-eight (2988) County histories have
been written about thirteen hundred and eighty (1380) Counties of the
Thirty-one hundred and eleven (3111) Counties in the forty-eight (48) States.
This includes only a very few of the County histories that have less than
one hundred pages. A few historical County Atlases are included. These
are all individual histories. State histories or other compilations that
contain a series of histories of one section or of the entire state are not
included in this bibliography. An attempt has been made to maintain a standard of including individual County histories of not less than one hundred
pages, with very few exceptions.

Illinois has most County histories of all 48 States, a total of 483,
while Pennsylvania has 246 or the next highest, Indiana and Iowa both rank
third with 207 County histories each. Connecticut, Illinois, Iowa, Massachusetts and New Jersey have histories about all their Counties. No histories have been written about the Counties in Delaware and Nevada. Only
one history has been written of Arizona's 14 Counties, only one of Montana's
57 and only one of New Mexico's 31 Counties. In thirty-two or less than
half of the States less than half of the Counties have County histories.
In ten States three-fourths or more Counties have County histories.

About ten years ago, one year, a number of County histories were sub-
mitted as M. A. Thesis in the history department in the Universities there.

A dominant characteristic of County histories is that they are rich
in personal reminiscences. They give common everyday detailed experiences
of life, of those who actually lived in the County. They are not classical
works of history produced from scientific research. Neither war nor politics are, as a rule, overemphasized in County histories as they sometimes
are in general histories. They simply give the way of life of the settlers
without adulation. In them, in the main, are discussed the essentials and
the facts of life of the common everyday folks. The study of County histories should create an appreciation of the pioneers. They give a better
understanding of local community growth and experiences.

County histories may in a sense be considered as memorials since it
is a record of the memories of the people of the County. Thus they become
cultural agents and aids in the preservation of civilization. As such
they have their part in inspiring loyalty to the land of the founding
fathers. The County history is a unit of a larger whole.

Some authors of County histories, in their belief that the history
that springs from the land is best have proceeded to include something of
the geology, the animal life, and vegetation of their locality. There are
in existence a surprising number of historical County atlases and County
directories.

As for the authors of these County histories themselves, they are cer-
tainly not of those who are dominated by the profit motive in their labors.
The writing of a County history is a labor of love. They have prepared the
way for those who will follow and write State and National histories.

A bibliography should give the following information regarding a book: the title, the author's name, name of publishers, date and place of publication, number and size of pages, price, edition, descriptive information such as type of publication, and whether photos, maps, illustrations and indexes are included, number of volumes, type of cover such as paper, cloth or leather or other material, and any other information characteristic of the book. The alphabetical arrangement of the material in a bibliography is one of the best. In this bibliography the states, counties, and authors, have been so arranged.

In some few of the forty-eight States splendid work has been done down through the years in preparing bibliographies of their local, county and state histories. But in by far most of the States nothing has been accomplished along this line. Forty years ago appeared an excellent standard bibliographical work, namely, Dr. T. L. Bradford's "Bibliographer's Manual of State, Territory, County and Town Histories", published 1907 by Sam. V. Hempels & Co., Philadelphia. The Federal W.P.A. Technical Series, Research and Records Bibliography No. 7 Rev. April 1943, Washington, D. C., is a creditable effort. Some States have made splendid individual efforts. Otis G. Hammond, Supt. of N. H. Hist. Society has prepared a check list of New Hampshire Local History. The Indiana Magazine History Vol. 6 No. 1 March 1910 and The Indiana State Library Bulletin Vol. 5 No. 2 have bibliographies of Indiana local histories. R. E. and R. G. Cowan have compiled a Bibliography of The History of California 1510-1930. Furthermore there are the following in addition: Illinois History Collections - Travel and Descriptions 1765-1865 by Solon Buck; County Historical Material in The Ohio State Archaeological and Historical Society Library by Clarence L. Weaver and Helen Mills; Texas County History - A Bibliography by H. Bailey Carroll; N. Y. State Lib. Bull. No. 53, Dec. 1900 gives reference list on Conn. local history; N. Y. State Lib. Bull. #56 Feb. 1901 has a Bibliography of N. Y. Colonial History by Charles A. Flagg and Judson T. Jennings; N. Y. State Lib. Bull. #63 June 1901 lists Maine Local History By Drew B. Hall; excellent County History Bibliographies of each of their respective States have been prepared by the State Historical Societies in Iowa, Nebraska, Minnesota, North Carolina and Tennessee.

The W.P.A. took 566 inventories of County Archives in 45 States, omitting Connecticut, Maine, and Rhode Island.

Baltimore, Md., October 1946.

* * * * * *

It is doubtful that any bibliography of the over 3,000 counties in the 48 States will ever be up to date. At least three county histories now in preparation but as yet unpublished, are not included herein. Since this bibliography was first prepared and published in 1935 the Works Progress Administration has done extensive historical research throughout the land in making inventories of the county archives and publication of guides and histories for many States. Additional county histories have been found that had been published in 1935 but had not been found and included when this bibliography first appeared at that time.

It may be of interest here to note that in recent years on one of my visits to England I found in London in the British Museum Library a handbook, published in 1917, to county bibliography, being a bibliography of bibliographies relating to the counties and towns of Great Britain and Ireland by Sir Arthur L. Humphreys, London, published by Strangeways and Sons.

Baltimore, Maryland 1944.

* * * * * *

This Research Survey of County Histories of the Counties of the 48 States throughout the Union, consisting of 2982 counties, which has never before been attempted, has brought out some interesting facts. This Research is incomplete and is being carried on further. It has been found, that the following States have County Histories written of all the Counties: Connecticut, Indiana, Iowa, New Hampshire, New Jersey, New York, Ohio, and Pennsylvania. New Jersey was found to have the best bibliography of local history. New York was found to have more county histories written than any other state in the Union. A partial history has been written of every county in Kentucky and Vermont. In the following States no county history whatsoever could be found: Delaware, Montana, Nevada, New Mexico, except as written and included in State Histories. But there were no separate county histories. Two States, Arizona and Rhode Island, each have only one complete county history. Only two complete county histories were found for North Dakota, Oklahoma and Utah. In Illinois, Massachusetts and Missouri, nearly all counties have county histories. There is a county history for most of the counties in California. About one-half of the counties have been written up in separate county histories in Oregon, Tennessee, South Carolina, Washington, West Virginia and Wisconsin. Due to the vast field covered in this work in order to keep the bibliography of this kind up to date it is necessary to constantly make additions and for that reason it can never be said to be in a complete form.

For the great majority of the 48 States an attempt has been made to give herein a complete bibliography of the county histories for each particular state. However, for a very few states due to lack of time and funds, at present, mention has merely been made of the names of the counties in the state of which county histories have been written. In the very near future it is hoped that the complete bibliography will soon be prepared for each of these.

New York, N.Y., December 1935.

* * * * * *

W.P.A. Historical Records Survey Project

Acting Chief Robert Claus, Division of Interior Department Archives, National Archives states, that "when the W.P.A. Historical Records Survey Project was terminated in June 1942," it had issued in mimeograph form inventories of the archives of at least one county in every state except Maine. The records of the former Work Projects Administration now in the National Archives indicate, however, that none of the series of inventories that was planned for each state was completed. An almost complete list of the published county inventories appears in a publication of the W.P.A. Division of Service Projects, entitled Bibliography of Research Projects Reports: Check List of Historical Records Survey Publications, Research and Records Bibliography No. 7 (Washington, D.C., Revised April 1943), pages 17-31. Surplus copies of published H.R.S. inventories available for distribution have been deposited in the Library of Congress. Inquiries regarding the possibility of obtaining such copies should be addressed to Mr. Clyde S. Edwards of the Government Publications Department of that agency.

"It was usually the practice of the W.P.A. to deposit unpublished manuscript material with the sponsor of the project, and a list of the depositories for unpublished H.R.S. material in the states is included as Appendix V of the bibliography mentioned above."

<u>ALABAMA</u> - 67 Counties

Autauga — Mimms, S. - Hist. of Autauga Co., 23 p.q. Prattville, N.D.

Baldwin
— Carney, Mary O. - The Yanks Take Over The Eastern Shore,
Daphne, Ala., 1949, 20 p.
— Carter, Hodding - Gulf Coast Country. By Hodding Carter and
Anthony Ragusin. New York, 1951, 247 p.
— Comings, Newcomb and Albers - Hist. of Baldwin Co., 91 pp.
Fairhope, 1928, Ala. Rec. Com. Census of Baldwin Co. 1820,
Report 1934, V. 1, p. 2-6.
— McManus, Grace Kelly - Baldwin Co., Ala. 1860 Federal Census
and schedule of deaths copied and indexed by Grace Kelly McManus,
88 pp., Typewritten.

Barbour
— Thompson, Mattie Thomas. History of Barbour County. Privately
printed, 1939.
— Walker, Annie Kedrick. Backtracking In Barbour County, Dietz
Press, Richmond, 1941.

Bibb — Jones, Kathleen Paul, and Pauline Jones Gandrud, Ala. Records,
Huntsville, Ala.

Blount — Elliot, Carl. Annals of Northwest Alabama, including a reprint
of Nelson F. Smith's Hist. of Pickens Co., Ala., 1856.
Tuscaloosa, Ala., 1958, 240 pp. - pp. 137-142, 171-172.

Bullock — McNair, Cecil E. Reconstruction In Bullock Co. - U. of Ala.
1931 Thesis. Ala. Hist. Quart. Vol. 15, 1953.

Butler
— Little, John Buckner. The History of Butler Co., Alabama. From
1815 to 1885, Cincinnati: Elm St. Printing Co., 1885 - 12 mo.
256 pp. map.
— McManus, Grace Kelly. Butler Co., Ala. 1860 Fed. Census and
schedule of deaths copied and indexed by Grace Kelly McManus.

Calhoun — Jones, Kathleen Paul and Pauline Jones Gandrud. Alabama Records,
Huntsville, 1956.

Chambers — Chambers, Nella Jean. A Survey of The Older Church Cemeteries
in Chambers Co., Ala., 1954, and Jefferson A. Chambers, 93 pp.,
mimeographed. (Chattahootchie Valley Hist. Assn., Bull. No. 2).

Cherokee — Stewart, Mrs. Frank Ross, Cherokee Co., Ala. Hist. 1836-56,
Centre 1958.

Chilton — Wyatt, Thomas Eugene. Chilton County and Her People. Union
Banner, Clanton, Ala. $1.00

Clarke
— Ball, Timothy Horton. Clarke Co., Ala., 1546-1877. Chi.Knight
1882.
— Graham, John S., Hist. of Clarke Co., 345 pp., Birmingham, 1923.
— McManus, Grace Kelly, Clarke Co., Ala. Marriage Records, 1814-1891.
From W.P.A. Records, Montgomery, 1955. Mimeog.

2

<u>Colbert</u>   – Jones, Kathleen and Gandrud, Pauline J. Tombstone, Bible and
            Marriage Records of Colbert Co., Ala., 1939. Ala. Rec.Vol.56.
            – Leftwich, Nina. 200 Years of Muscle Shoals. Hist. of Colbert
            Co., 1790-1900, 280 pp., Tuscumbia, 1935.

<u>Connecuh</u> – Riley, Connecuh County. Pub. by J. Gilbert, Columbus, 1881.
            XI. 233 pp.

<u>Coosa</u>   – Howard, Ola M. Tombstone Inscriptions in Talladega and Coosa
            Counties, Ala.

<u>Crenshaw</u> – Ala. Gen. Rec. Com. Marriage Records 1912-15 Montgomery, 1935.

<u>Dale</u>   – Fleming, May Love (Edwards), Dale Co. and Its People During The
            Civil War Reminiscences. p. 61-110. (Ala. Hist. Quart.
            Vol. 19, 1957).

<u>Dallas</u>   – Ala. Gen. Rec. Com. Inhabitants of Dallas Co. 1820 Rep. 1934 Vol. 1,
            pp. 10-24, Dallas Co. Pensions, Tombstone Inscriptions, 1937,
            Ala. Rec. V. 46.
            – Jackson. Hist. of Selma and Dallas Counties.

<u>Elmore</u>   – Porter, Elizabeth Gamble and Madora Lancaster Smith. Hist. of
            Wetumpka Methodist Church. Centennial 1854-1954 Wetumpka, Ala.
            1954. 56 pp.

<u>Etowah</u>   – Martin, Will I. If Memory Serves. Banner Print, Cleveland, Tenn.
            1951. 83 pp.

<u>Fayette</u> – Newell, Herbert Moses. Hist. of Fayette Co. Ala. Fayette, 1960.
            – Newell, Herbert Moses. Fayette Co. Ala. Cemetery Records, 1959.

<u>Franklin</u> – James, Robert L. Distinguished Familes of Franklin Co. 111 pp.

<u>Greene</u>   – Jones, Katherine P. and Gandrud, Pauline J., Cemetery Records,
            Revolutionary and 1812 Pensions of Greene Co. 1941, Ala. Rec.
            v. 69. Same authors: Wills, Deeds and Marriages of Greene Co.
            Ala. Rec. v. 87.

<u>Henry</u>   – Scott, Clyde (Stovall). Tombstone Inscriptions and Obituary
            Notices of Henry Co., Ala. By Mrs. Marvin Scott, 261 p. Mimeo.

<u>Jackson</u> – Gandrud, Pauline (Jones). Federal Census of 1850 For Jackson Co.,
            Ala. Copied by author, with notes added on families. Nov. 1953.
            284 p. Typewritten.
            – Jones, K. P. and Gandrud, P. J. Wills, Estates, Deeds, Marriages.
            Ala. Rec. 1934. v. 19, pp. 1-80.
            – Kennamer, John Robert. Hist. of Jackson Co. 1935. Southern
            Printing and Pub. Co. Winchester, Tenn.

ALABAMA (continued)

Jefferson — Farrell, Mrs. Thomas Franklin. Jefferson Co. Birmingham, Ala.
Book 2 By Wright. Marriages For The Years, 1841-42-43, 1847-
48-49. General Sumther Chap. D.A.R. 18 pp. Typed.
— Jones, Kathleen Paul and P. J. Gandrud. Ala. Rec. Huntsville,
1957.
— History of Jefferson Co. and Birmingham, Ala. Teeple & Smith,
Pub. 1887. 575 pp.

Lamar — Elliott, Carl. Annals of Northwest Ala., including a reprint of
Nelson F. Smith's Hist. of Pickens Co. Ala. 1856. Tuscaloosa,
Ala. 1958.

Lawrence — D.A.R. Ala. Some Ala. Marriage Records. Compiled by Ala.
Socy. D.A.R. 1954. Typed. 7 V. (See Vol. 4).

Lee — Hollifield, Mollie. Auburn, Loveliest of the Plain, Auburn,
1955. 124 p.

Limestone — Jones, K. P. and Gandrud, P. J. Limestone Co., Ala. Rec. 1934.
v. 21, pp. 1-64, 91-100.
— McClellan, R. A. Early Limestone Co., 24 pp. 1881.

Lowndes — Catts, Samuel Walker. Some Forgotten Incidents In Lowndes Co.
(Ala. Hist. Guard. Vol. 14, 1952).

Macon — Reynolds, Mrs. W. E. Census of Warrior Stand Cemetery, Macon
Co., Ala. Tuskegee, Ala. 1959. 41 pp. Handwritten.

Madison — Carter, Clarence E. Census of Madison Co. 1809. Ter. Papers
of U.S. 1937, v. 5, pp. 684-92.
— D.A.R. Ala. Some Ala. Marriage Records Comp. By Ala. Socy.
D.A.R. 1954. 7 V. Typed (See Vol. 5).
— Houston, Martha Lou. Index of Madison Co., Ala. Wills 1808-
1870. Comp. By Genealogical Rec. Com., Twickenham Town Chap.,
D.A.R. Ann Arbor, Mich.
— Record, James R. Report on Madison Co., its hist. operation, and
finances, Compiled by James R. Record, County Auditor. 1951.
104 pp.
— Taylor, Thomas Jones. Early History of Madison Co. 1800-1840.
By a Reliable Scribe 1883.
— Jones, Kathleen Paul and Gandrud, Pauline Jones. Ala. Records.
Huntsville, 1956.

Marengo — D.A.R. Some Ala. Marriage Records, Comp. by Ala. Socy, D.A.R.
1954. 7 v. Typed (See v. 1 and 3).

Marion — Elliott Carl. Annals of Northwest Ala. with Reprint of Nelson
F. Smith's Hist. of Pickens Co., Ala. 1856. Tuscaloosa, Ala.
1958. 240 pp.
— Marion Co. Ala. Teachers Assn., Hist. of Marion Co. Ala.
Hamilton, 1959.

ALABAMA (continued)

__Marshall__   - Jones, Kathleen Paul and Gandrud, Pauline Jones. Ala. Records.
Huntsville, 1956. V. 167.

__Mobile__   - D.A.R. Ala. Some Ala. Marriage Records, Comp. by Ala. Socy.
D.A.R. 1954. 7 V. Typed. (See Vol. 1 and 3).
- Mobile, Ala. Public Schools: A History Reader For the Fourth
Grade. Mobile, 1954. 73 pp.
- Walter, Francis X. The Naval Battle of Mobile Bay. Thesis for
English 2A at Spring Hill College, Ala. April 1951. pp. 5-48.
(Ala. Hist. Quart. Vol. 14, 1952).

__Montgomery__ - D.A.R. Ala. Some Ala. Marriage Records. Comp. by Ala. Socy
D.A.R. 1954. 7 V. Typed. (See Vol. 3 and 7).
- Jones, Kathleen Paul and Gandrud, Pauline Jones. Ala. Records.
Tuscaloosa, 1957. V. 135 and 172.
- Montgomery County History. (Ala. Hist. Quart. V. 18, 1956).
- Robertson, W. G. - Recollections of Early Settlers of Montgomery
Co. and Their Families. Montgomery, 1892. Excelsior Printing Co.
157 pp.

__Morgan__   - D.A.R. Ala. Some Ala. Marriage Records. Comp. by the Ala. Socy.
D.A.R. 1954. 7 V. Typed. (See Vol. 1).

__Perry__   - D.A.R. Ala. Some Ala. Marriage Records. Comp. by the Ala. Socy.
D.A.R. 1954. 7 Vol. Typed. (See Vol. 1)
- England, F. D. Cemetery Descriptions From Perry Co. Ala. 1955.
- England, F. Notes of Some Families of Perry Co., Ala. 1956.
- Townes, Samuel A. The Hist. of Marion and Life in Perry Co., Ala.
Printed By D. Dykons, 1844. p. 171-229. (Ala. Hist. Quart.
Vol. 14, 1952).

__Pickens__   - Elliott, Carl. Annals of Northwest Ala. with reprint of Nelson
F. Smith's Hist. of Pickens Co., Ala., 1856. Tuscaloosa, Ala.
1958. 240 pp.
- Smith, Nelson F. Pickens Co. 1817-56, 272 pp. 1856. Carrollton.

__Pike__   - Farmer, Margaret Pace. Hist. of Pike Co., Ala. Troy, Ala.
(Edwards Bros., Inc., Ann Arbor, Mich.) 1953. 144 pp.

__Russell__   - Cherry, Francis Lafayette. The Hist. of Apelika and Territory
More Particularly Lee and Russell Counties by Rev. F. L. Cherry,
1883. pp. 176-537. (Ala. Hist. Quarterly). Vol. 15, 1953.
- Walker, Anne Kendrick. Russell Co. In Retrospect, An Epic of
the Far Southeast. Richmond Dietz Press. 1950. 423 pp.

__St. Clair__ - McGuire, Fannie Jobe. Marriages of St. Clair Co Ala. 1952.
Typed and Indexed by Pauline Jones Gandrud, 103 pp.

__Shelby__   - D.A.R. Ala. Some Ala. Marriage Records. Comp. By Ala. Socy.
D.A.R. 1954. 7 Vol. Typed. (See Vol. 6 & 7).

ALABAMA (continued)

Talladega — Blackford, Randolph F. Fascinating Talladega Co., Ala.
Brannon Pub. Co. 1957.
— D.A.R. Ala. Marriage Records. Comp. by Ala. Socy. D.A.R.
1954. 7 Vol. Typed. (See Vol. 1).
— Kimball, Solon Toothaker. The Talladega Story in Community
Process by S. T. Kimball & Marion Pearsall. University,
Univ. of Ala. Press. 1954. 259 pp.
— Vandiver, Wellington. Pioneer Talladega, its minutes and
memories. pp. 9-297. (Ala. Hist. Quart. Vol. 16, 1954).

Tallapoosa — Coley, C. J. The Battle of Horseshoe Bend by Judge of Pro-
bate, Tallapoosa Co. pp. 129-139. (Ala. Hist. Quart. Vol. 14,
1952.)
— Ingram, William Pressley. A Hist. of Tallapoosa Co.,
Birmingham, Ala. 1951. 119 pp.

Walker — Cemetery Records of Walker Co., 34 pp. 1947. Type.
— Biggerstaff, Inez (Boswell) Records of Walker Co. Ala.
Guttery. Okla. City, 1959.
— Dorbhart, John Martin. History of Walker Co. Its Town and
People. Thornton, Ark. Cayce Pub. Co. 1937, 382 pp.
— Elliott, Carl. Annals of Northwest Ala. with reprint of
W. F. Smith's Hist. of Pickens Co., Ala. 1856. Tuscaloosa,
1958. 240 pp.
— Guttery, F. K. Records of Walker Co. Ala. 1959.
— Johnston, Hewitt. Salmagundi. A Century and a Half. Glade
House. 1957. 386 pp.

Winston — Elliott, Carl. Annals of Northwest Ala. with Reprint of
N. F. Smith's Hist. of Pickens Co., Ala. 1856. Tuscaloosa,
Ala. 1958. 240 pp.
— Fact and Fiction of The Free State of Winston, 1950. 15 pp.
Brief Histories of All Alabama Counties Found in History of
Ala. and Dictionary of Ala. Biography by Thomas M. Owen.
Pub. 1921 by S. J. Clarke, Chicago.

ALASKA

Alaska has neither counties nor County histories according to
information received from the state government at Juneau,
Alaska.

ARIZONA - 14 Counties

GRAHAM — Graham County, by Graham County Guardian, Saffar, Arizona.
— George Kelly's Legislative History 1926, gives a brief
history of counties in Arizona.

6

Arkansas — Burton, W. H. Halli. History of Arkansas Co. from 1541 to 1875. DeWitt. Privately Printed. 1903. 190 pp.

Ashley — Y. W. Ethridge. Hist. of Ashley Co., Ark. Press Argus. Van Buren, Ark. April 1959. 173 pp.

Baxter — Frances H. Shiras. Hist. of Baxter Co. Mountain Home. Daniel and Shiras. 1939. 159 pp.

Benton — Hist. of Benton, Washington, Carroll, Madison, Crawford, Franklin and Sebastian Counties, Ark. 1382 pp. Goodspeed. Chi. 1889.

Boone — Ralph R. Rea. Boone Co. and Its People. Van Buren, Press - Argus. C 1955. 224 pp.

Cherokee — Stewart, Mrs. Frank Ross. Cherokee Co. Hist. Ark. 1836-56.

Clay — Robert T. Webb. Hist. and Traditions of Clay Co. Shiras Bros. Print Shop. Mountain Home, Ark. 1933. 85 pp.
— Webb, Robert and Brown, Bruce. Hist. of Clay Co. Shiras Bros. Print Shop. Mountain Home, Ark. 185 pp.
— Wright, Victor C. Hist. of Our County Seat. Corning, Ark. Clay Co. Courier. 1956.

Columbia — Nettie (Hicks) Killgore, Hist. of Columbia Co. Magnolia Printing Co. 1947. 231 pp.

Conway — Historical Reminiscences and Biographical Memoirs of Conway Co. Ark. Little Rock. Hist. Pub. Co. 1890. 129 pp.

Craighead — Williams, Harry Lee. Hist. of Craighead Co. Parke-Harper Co. Little Rock. 1930. 648 pp.

Crawford — Clara B. Eno. Hist. of Crawford Co. Ark. Van Buren Press Argus. 1951. 499 pp.

Cross — Robert W. Chowning. Hist. of Cross Co. 1955 With Genealogical and Memorial Records of Prominent Families and Personages. Wynne Progress. 1955. 132 pp.

Faulkner — Lincoln, L. C. Editor. Faulkner Co. Records.
— Alexander McPherson. The Hist. of Faulkner Co., Ark. Conway Times Plant. 1927. 104 pp.

Greene — Vivian Hausbrough. Hist. of Greene Co. Ark. Little Rock. Democrat Print & Litho Co. 1946. 201 pp.

Independence — Stockard, S. W. Hist. of Lawrence, Jackson, Independence and Stone Counties. 204 pp. Little Rock. 1904.

ARKANSAS (continued)

Izard — Shannon, K. Hist. of Izard Co. 158 pp. 1947 Little Rock.

Jackson — W. E. Bevens, Makers of Jackson Co. Short Stories of Early
Pioneers and Old Jacksonport. 49 pp.

Jefferson — Jefferson County. 1888.

Johnson — Ella Molly Langford. Johnson Co., Ark. The First Hundred
Years. Clarksville. The Author, 1921. 210 pp.

Lawrence — Walter E. McLeod. Centennial Memorial Hist. of Lawrence Co.
Russellville Print Co. 1936. 163 pp.

Lonoke — R. L. Young. Hist. of Lonoke Co., Ark. Lonoke, 1917. 15 pp.
(Second Edition) Lonoke 1924. 54 pp.

Miller — Barbara Overton Chandler and J. Ed. Howe. Hist. of Texarkana
and Bowie and Miller Co., Tex. - Ark. Texarkana. J. Ed. Howe.
1939. 375 pp.

Mississippi — Fox, J. A. Editor. Mississippi County, Garden Spot of Mississippi Valley.

Newton — Walter Fowler Lackey. Hist. of Newton Co. Ark. Independence,
Mo. Zions Print & Pub. Co. 432 pp. 1950

Ouachita — Ouachita Co. and Camden 1883. Pub. by County Immigration Soc.

Pope — Bullock. Pope County, Hist. of Militia War 1865-1874.
— West, D. Porter. Early History of Pope Co. Russelville, 1906.
53 pp.

Randolph — Lawrence Dalton. Hist. of Randolph Co. Ark. Little Rock.
Democrat Print. & Litho. Co. 1946. 359 pp.

St. Francis — Robert W. Chowning. Hist. of St. Francis Co. Ark. Forrest
City Times Herald Pub. Co. 1954. 156 pp.

Scott — P. M. Claunts. From Memory's Scrap Book. Hist. of Early Scott
and Sebastian Co., Ark. Waldron. The Advance Reporter.
1938. 86 pp.
— Norman, Goodner. Hist. of Scott Co. Ark. Siloam Springs,
Bar D. Press. 1941. 89 pp.
— Henry Grady McCutchen. Hist. of Scott Co., Ark. Little Rock.
H. G. Pugh & Co. 1922. 74 pp.

Sebastian — DuVal, B. T. Hist. of Sebastian Co. Historial Address at Fort
Smith, July 4, 1876. Ft. Smith. 1877. 8 Vol.
— Weaver, F. F. Sebastian Co. and Fort Smith In History and
Commerce. Sebastian County and Fort Smith, Cutter and Mowlin
Publishers.

ARKANSAS (continued)

Union
- Hist. of Union County. By Juanita Whitaker Green. 1954. El Dorado. Ark. 201 pp.

Washington
- W. J. Lemke. Historic Wash. Co., Ark. Fayetteville Print Co., 1952. 30 pp.

White
- Hist. of White Co. (In Biog. & Hist. Memoirs of Eastern Ark. 1890. pp. 113-271.)

Yell
- Wayne Banks. The Hist. of Yell Co., Ark. Van Buren Press - Argus. 1959.
- Biographical and Historical Memoirs of Arkansas, Eastern, North-east, Southern, Western Counties, also Pulaski, Jefferson, Tonoke, Faulkner, Grant, Saline, Perry, Garland and Hot Springs Co. 1889. The Goodspeed Pub. Co., Chicago and St. Louis.

CALIFORNIA - 58 Counties

Alameda
- Calif. Genealogical Rec. Com. Cemetery Records In Alameda Co. (Vital Record 1936, V. 3, pp. 1-49). Typed.
- Baker, Joseph Eugene. 1874-1914 Ed. Past & Present of Alameda Co. Calif. Chi. S. J. Carke Pub. Co. 1914 22. Front, Plates, parts, map. Vol. 2 Biographical Cover-Title: Hist. of Alameda Co. Calif.
- Halley, William. The Centennial Year Book of Alameda Co. Calif. From Discovery of Calif. Biog. Illus. Oakland Pub. by Wm. Halley, 1876. 586 pp. Front, plates, ports.
- Merritt, Frank Clinton. Hist. of Alameda Co. Calif. Illus. Biog. S. J. Clarke Pub. Co. 1928, 2 Vol. 1 vol. Illus. Ports, 2 Vol. Biog.
- Oakland Tribune Calif. Alameda Co. The Eden of the Pacific, Illus. A Hist. of Alameda Co. From Its Formation to the Present. 1898. Cover-Title: Alameda County Illustrated.
- Lays, George ed. Historical sights and Landmarks of Alameda Co., Calif. W. P. A. Project, Oakland, 1938, 349 pp.
- Thompson and West, pub. Official and Historical Map of Alameda Co., 1878. Hunter, Phila. 170 pp. Illus. Maps.
- History of Alameda Co., Oakland. Thompson, 1881.
- Wood, Myron W. Pub. Hist. of Alameda Co. Geology Soil Record of Spanish Grants, American Pioneers, Officers of County since its formation, township histories. Biog. Oakland. Mr. W. Wood, 1883, 1001 pp. Front, Parts.
- W.P.A. Hist. of Rural Alameda Co. in 2 Vols. sponsored by Alameda Co. for its Library. Prepared under the direction of W. E. McCann and Edgar J. Hinkel, Oakland, 1937. 2 Vol.

Amador
- Pierce, Maurice. Hist. Pictures of Amador Co. (reprint).
- Sargent, Elizabeth (Quinn) ed. Amador Co. Hist. American Feder-ation of Women's Clubs, 1927. (127 pp. illus.)

CALIFORNIA (continued)

Amador
(cont'd)
- Schacht, Frances Comp. Camara History of Amador Co. (reprints and texts) Foster & Futernick Bindery. 1937. 120 pp.
- Hist. of Amador Co., with illus. & biog. sketches of its prominent men and pioneers, Oakland, Calif. Thompson & West, 1881. 344 pp. Plates.

Butte
- Mansfield, George C. Hist. of Butte Co. with Biog. Sketches from Early Days. Los Angeles. Historic Record Co. 1918. 1331 pp. Illus.
- Wells, H. L. & Chambers, W. L. Publishers, Butte Co. Hist. 1513 to 1882, 2 Vol. San Francisco, 1882.
- History of Butte Co. Oakland, Thompson & West 1887, 4 to.

Colusa
- McCornish, Charles, Davis, & Lambert, Mrs. Rebecca T. Hist. of Colusa & Glenn Co. Historic Record Co., Los Angeles, Calif. 1918. 1074 pp.
- Rogers, Justus H. Colusa County. (Note: Glenn used to be part of Colusa Co.) Orland, Calif. 1891. 473 pp.
- Colusa Co. Illus. Des. Hist. Sketch of the County San Francisco, 1880.

Contra Costa
- Cheatham, Wilma Gladys. The Story of Contra Costa Co. For Boys and Girls. San Francisco, Harr Wagner, 1942. 229 pp. Illus.
- Historic Record Co. Hist. of Contra Costa,Co., Los Angeles. 1926, 1102 pp. Illus.
- Hulaniski, Frederick J. ed. The Hist. of Contra Costa Co. Berkeley, Elms, 1917. 635 pp.
- Purcell, Mae (Fisher) Hist. of Contra Costa Co. Berkeley, Gillick Press. (1940) 742 pp. Illus).
- Smith & Elliott. Illus. of Contra Costa Co. With Hist. Sketch. Oakland, Smith & Elliott, 1878. 54 pp. with Illus.
- Hist. of Contra Costa Co. (no author) San Francisco Slocum, 1882. 710 pp. Illus.

Del Norte
- Bledsoe, A. J. Hist. of Del Norte Co. With Business Dir. & Travellers Guide. Eureka: Humboldt Times Print (Wyman & Co.) 1881. 8 Vol. 68 pp.
- Del Norte. Hist. of Del Norte Co. By Esther Ruth Smith. Holmes Book Co. Oakland, Cal. 1953.
- Hist. of Del Norte Co., Calif. 1953. Fresno Co. Calif. By O. B. Lewis. Centennial Almanac 1956.
- Del Norte. Hist. of Del Norte Co. By Esther Ruth Smith. Holmes Book Co., Oakland, Cal. 1953.

El Dorado
- Sioli, Paulo - Hist. of El Dorado Co., pub. by Author 1883, 272 pp.
- Upton, Chas. E. Pioneers of El Dorado Co. Pub. By Authors 1906. 201 pp.
- Upton, Will O. Churches of El Dorado Co. 59 pp. Hangtown Press. Placerville.

<u>CALIFORNIA</u> (continued)

Fresno
- Hist. of Fresno Co. Illus. Des. Biog. Sketches, San Francisco. Elliott. 1882. 246 pp.
- Mem. & Biog. Hist. of Fresno, Tulare and Kern Counties. 822 pp. Chi. 1892. Lewis.
- Eighty Years of Fresno Co. 1856-1937. Dedication of Hall of Records, Fresno Co. April 3, 1937. Fresno Co. Hist. Socy. 1937, 8 pp.
- A Memorial and Biog. Hist. of The Co. of Fresno, Tulare, and Kern. Illus. From Earliest Period. Biog. Lewis Pub. Co. Chi. 1892. 822 pp.
- Thompson, T. H. Official Hist. Atlas Map of Fresno Co. Tulare, 1891. 122 pp.
- Vandor, Paul E. Hist. of Fresno Co. Biog. Sketches From Early Days. Los Angeles. Hist. Rec. Co. 1919. 2 Vol.
- Walker, Ben Randal. The Fresno Co. Blue Book, Past & Present. Biog. Fresno. Cawston, 1941. 555 pp.
- Winchell, Lilbourne Alsip. Hist. of Fresno Co. and The San Joaquin Valley, Narrative & Biog. Edited by Ben R. Walker, Fresno. Cawston, 1933. 323 pp.

Humboldt
- Irvine, L. H. Hist. & Humboldt Co. Biog. 1920 pp. Los Angeles, 1915.

Imperial
- Black, S. F. San Diego and Imperial Co. 2 V. Chi. 1913.
- Farr, F. C. Hist. of Imperial Co. 526 pp. Berkeley, 1918.

Inyo
- Chalfant, Willie Arthur. The Story of Inyo. 1922. 358 pp. Rev. ed. 1933. 430 pp.

Kern
- Crites, Arthur S. Pioneer Days in Kern Co. Calif. Los Angeles. Ritchie. 1951.
- Comport, Herbert G. Where Rolls The Kern; A History of Kern Co. Calif. Enterprise Press, Moorpark, Calif. 1934.
- Hist. of Kern Co. San Francisco. W. W. Elliott & Co. 1883. Folio.
- Miller, Thelma B. Hist. of Kern Co., 2 Vols. S. J. Clarke Pub. Co. Chi. 1929.
- Morgan, Wallace M. Hist. of Kern Co. Hist. Rec. Co. Los Angeles, 1914.
- Mem. & Biog. Hist. of Fresno, Tulare, and Kern Counties. 822 pp. Chi. 1892. Lewis

Kings
- Brown, James L. Story of Kings Co., Berkeley, Lederer Strett & Zens, 1941. 126 pp.
- Brown, Robert R. Hist. of King Co. Cawston 1940. 385 pp.
- Menefee, E. L. and Dodge, F. A. Hist. of Tulare and Kings Co's. 820 pp. Los Angeles, 1913.
- Smith, Larry. Hist. of King's Co. Chi. Clarke - 1926. 2 Vols. 625 pp. (Vol. 1 Small's Hist. of Tulare Co.)

CALIFORNIA (continued)

Lake
- Lewis, Ruth M. and Others. Stories of Legends of Lake Co.
- Palmer, Lyman L. A. M. Hist. of Napa and Lake Counties, Pub. by Slocum, Bowen & Co. San Francisco, Calif. 1881. 291 pp.

Los Angeles- No author - (From Bradford's Bibliographers Manual Vol. I pp 159. An historical sketch of Los Angeles Co., Calif. From the Spanish Occupancy By The Founding of the Mission San Gabriel Archangel, Sept. 8, 1771 to July 4, 1876. Pub. by Louis Lewin & Co. Los Angeles: Mirror Print, 1876. 8 Vol. 12 pp. An Illus. Hist. of Los Angeles Co., Calif.
- From The Earliest Period of Its Occupancy to the Present Time, Chicago. 1891. 4 to Lewis. 835 pp.
- Los Angeles Co. Chamber of Commerce: Research Dept. Los Angeles Co. Communities, wealth, history, features, economic trends, 1938 and 1939. 76 pp.
- McGroarty, John Stephen, Editor. Hist. of Los Angeles Co. Biographical, Chicago & N. Y. American Hist. Socy., Inc. 1923, 3 Vol.
- Spalding, William Andrew. Hist. and Reminiscences, Los Angeles City & Co., Los Angeles, Finnell Pub. Co. 1931. 3 Vol.
- Walker, Edward Francis. Five Prehistoric Archaelogical Sites in Los Angeles, Calif. Southwest Museum Found. 1952.
- Warner, J. J., Haydes, Benjamin, Widney, J. P. an Historical Sketch of Los Angeles Co., Calif. Centennial Celebration. Mirror Print, 1876. 8 Vol. 88 pp. Reprinted by O. W. Smith 1936, 159 pp.
- Wilson, John Albert. Hist. of Los Angeles Co. Illus. Des. Oakland, Thompson & West. 1880. 192 pp.

Madera
- Madera Co. Bd. of Educ. Hist. of Madera Co. To accompanying Course of Study For Madera Co. Schools. Mimeo. 95 pp. 1929.

Marin
- Fraser, J. P. Munro. Hist. of Marin Co., Calif. San Francisco; Alley Bowen & Co. 1880. Illus. 8 vols.

Mariposa
- Hist. of Merced, Stanislaus, Calaveras, Tuolumne and Mariposa, 408 pp. Lewis, Chi. 1892.

Mendocino
- Palmer, Lyman L. Hist. of Mendocino Co., San Francisco. Alley, Bowen & Co. 1880. Portraits. Illus. 676 pp.

Merced
- Hist. of Merced Co. with Illus. Biog. Elliott and Moore Pub. San Francisco. 1881
- Outcalt, John. Hist. of Merced Co. Biog. Hist. Record Co., Los Angeles, 1925. 913 pp.
- Radcliffe, Corwin. Hist. of Merced Co. (Narrative & Biog.) Pub. A. H. Cawston, Merced. 1940. 414 pp.

Monterey
- Butler, A.W. Resources of Monterey Co. Calif. San Francisco. 1875 - 8 Vol.

CALIFORNIA (continued)

Monterey
(cont'd)
- Quinn, J. M. Hist. & Biog. Record of Monterey and San Berlito Counties. 2 V. L. A. 1910.
- Watkins, R. G. Monterey & Santa Cruz Co. 2 V. Chi. 1925

Napa
- Gregory, T. J. Hist. of Solona & Napa Counties. 1912.
- Gunn, H. L. Napa Co., 1926, 2 Vol. Clarke. Chi.
- Kanaga, Mrs. Tillie. Hist. of Napa Co. 1901.
- Minnefee, C.A. Hist. & Des. Sketch Book of Napa, Sonoma, Lake and Mendocino. 1873.
- Palmer, L. L. Hist. of Napa and Lake Counties. 1881. Slocum, Bowen & Co., Portraits, Illus. 8 vol.

Nevada
- Bean, Edwin F. Hist. & Dir. of Nevada Co. Calif. Nevada: 1867.
- Lardner, W. B. & Brock, M. J. Hist. of Placer and Nevada Counties. Biog. 1225 pp. L. A. 1924.
- Sargent, Aaron Augustus. Hist. Sketch of Nevada Co., Calif. San Francisco. 1856. 8 Vol. 45 pp.
- Hist. of Nevada Co. Calif. with Illus; Illus. of its Scenery, Residences, Pub. Bldgs., etc. Oakland Thompson & West, 1880. Folio.

Orange
- Armour, Samuel ed. Hist. of Orange Co., Los Angeles Historical Record Co. 1921. 1669 pp.
- Ball, C. D. Orange Co. Medical Hist. Ball. 1921. 205 pp.
- Orange Co. Hist. Socy. Papers. Santa Anna High School & Junior Coll. 1930. 3 Vols.
- Pleasants, A. B. Hist. of Orange Co., J. R. Finnell, Los Angeles, 1931. 3 Vols.
- Illus. Hist. of San Diego, San Bernardino, Los Angeles and Orange Counties. 898 pp. Chi. 1890. Lewis.
- W.P.A. Project. Hist. of Orange Co. 1936. 30 Mimeo. Folders.

Placer
- Hist. of Placer Co. Calif. Illus. Biog. Oakland, Calif. Thompson & West. 1882. 416 pp.

Plumas
- Illus. Hist. of Plumas, Lassen and Sierra Co. From 1530 to 1750. Farris & Smith, San Fran. 1882. 323 pp.

Riverside
- Gabbert, John Raymond. Hist. of Riverside City and County. Riverside Record Pub. Co. 1935. 615 pp.
- Greene, Earl M. Hist. & Govt. of the County of Riverside. Riverside City Schools, 1938. 76 pp.
- Holmes, Elmer Wallace and Others. Hist. of Riverside Co. California Biog. From The Early Days. Los Angeles, Hist. Record Co. 1912. 783 pp.

CALIFORNIA (continued)

Sacramento - Davis, Winfield J. An Illus. Hist. of Sacramento Co. From
Earliest Period. Port. Biog. Chi. Lewis, 1890. 808 pp.

- Reed, G. Walter, ed. Hist. of Sacramento Co. Biog. Los Angeles.
Hist. Record Co. 1923. 1004 pp.

- Thompson & West. Hist. of Sacramento Co. Illus. Des. Sketches.
Oakland 1880. 294 pp.

- Willis, William Todd. Hist. of Sacramento Co., Calif. Biog.
Los Angeles, Hist. Rec. Co. 1913. 1056 pp.

- Wright, George F. Reproduction of Thomson & West's Hist. of
Sacramento Co. Calif. Orig. 1880. Berkeley, Howell-North, 1860.

San Benito - Quinn, J. M. Hist. & Biog. Record of Monterey and San Benito
& Monterey Counties and Hist. of State of Calif. Biog. 2 Vol. Hist. Rec.
Co. Los Angeles, 1910. 764 pp.

San
Bernardino - Brown, John, Jr. and Boyd, James. Hist. of San Bernardino and
Riverside Counties. Biog. The Western Historical Assn. Chi.
Lewis. 1922. 3 Vol. 1538 pp.

- L. A. Ingersoll's Century Annals of San Bernardino Co. 1789.
1904. Biog. Portraits. Los Angeles, 1904. 887 pp. Calif.
W.P.A. Writers Prog.

- Illus. Hist. of Southern Calif. embracing Counties of San Diego,
San Bernardino, Los Angeles, Orange, and Lower Calif. Port.
Biog. Chi. Lewis. 1890. 898 pp. Pen Pictures.

- Hist. of San Bernardino Co. Calif. Illus. San Francisco. W. W.
Elliott & Co. Pub. 1883. 204 pp.

- The Old West. Pioneer Tales of San Bernardino Co. By Arrowhead
Parker No. 110, Native Sons of the Golden West. San Bernardino,
Calif. Pub. by Sun. 1940. 53 pp.

San Diego - Black, S. T. San Diego Co. Calif. 2 Vols. Illus. Chi.
Clarke. 1913.

- Heilbron, C. H. ed. Hist. of San Diego Co. by W. Davidson, A. H.
Cawston, R. F. Heilbron, B. Biewener. Illus. Part. maps. San
Diego Press Clubs. 1936.

- McGrew, C. A. San Diego and San Diego Co. 2 V. Chi. 1922.

- City & County of San Diego. Illus. Biog. San Diego, Libenthon,
1888.

- Mills, Jas. Hist. Landmarks of San Diego Co. Calif. Hist. Socy.
1960.
- Hist. of San Diego Co. Calif. Illus. Des. Biog. Maps. San
Francisco; W. W. Elliott & Co. 1883.

CALIFORNIA (continued)

**San
Francisco** - Byington, Lewis, Francis and Oscar, eds. The Hist. of San
Francisco, Chi-San Fran. Biog. Clarke. 1931. 3 Vols.

- Eldredge, Zoeth Skinner. Beginnings of San Francisco. from anga
1774 to City Charter of April 15, 1850. San Fran. 1912. 2 vols.

- Millard, Bailey. Hist. of San Francisco Bay Region. 3 Vols. Chi.
San Fran. N. Y. Amer. Hist. Socy Inc. 1924.

San Joaquin- Gilbert, F. T. Col. Hist. of San Joaquin Co. 1879. Oakland.
Thompson & West Pub.
- Illustrated Hist. of San Joaquin Co. 1890 Chi., Lewis 666 pp.
- Hist. of San Joaquin Co. California. Oakland. Thompson & West. 1879
- Tinkham, George G. Hist. of Stockton with sketch of San Joaquin
Co. 1880. 391 pp. W. M. Hinton & Co. San Fran.

- W.P.A. Hist. of Stockton and San Joaquin Co. 1938.

**San Luis
Obispo** - Angel, Myron. Hist. of San Luis Obispo Co., Calif. Illus. Biog.
Oakland. Thompson & West. 1883. 391 pp.

- Gidney, Charles Montville. Hist. of Santa Barbara, San Luis Obispo,
and Ventura Counties, Calif. Asst. by Benj. Brooks, Edwin M.
Sheridan, Illus. Biog. Chi. Lewis. 1917. 2 Vol.

- Jespersen, Christjan Nelsen ed. Hist. of San Luis Obispo Co. Its
People and Resources, ed. by Sen. C. N. Jespersen and H. M. Meier.
Illus. 318 pp.

- Morrison, Annie L. Hist. of San Luis Obispo Co. & environs. Biog
Asst. by John H. Haydon, Illus. Los Angeles Hist. Rec. Co. Illus.
1917. 1038 pp.

- Storke, Mrs. Yda Addis. A Memorial & Biog. Hist. of Counties of
Santa Barbara, San Luis Obispo, and Ventura, Calif. Illus. Biog.
Chi. Lewis. 1891. 677 pp.

San Mateo - Hist. of San Mateo Co., Calif. San Francisco: B. F. Alley, 1883.
Illus. 8 Vols.

- Stanger, Frank M. Hist. of San Mateo Co., A. H. Cawston Pub.
San Mateo. 1938. 425 pp.

- Cloud, R. W. Hist. of San Mateo Co. 2 Vo. Chi. 1928.

**Santa
Barbara** - Gidney, Charles M. History of Santa Barbara, San Luis Obispo and
Ventura Counties. Lewis. Chi. 1917. 2 Vols. 1357 pp.

- Mason, Jesse D. Hist. of Santa Barbara Co. Illus. Thompson,
Oakland. 1883. 477 pp.

- O'Neill, Owen H. Ed.-In-Chief. Hist. of Santa Barbara Co. S. B.
Union Print. Co. 1939. 496 pp.

- Perkins, J. J. Santa Barbara Co. 1884. Santa Barbara. 35 pp.

CALIFORNIA (continued)

Santa
Barbara   – Phillips, Michael J. Hist. of Santa Barbara Co. Clerk. Chi.
(cont'd)   1927. 2 Vol. 925 pp.

           – Storke, Yda Addis. Memorial and Biog. Hist. of Counties of
             Santa Barbara, San Luis Obispo and Ventura. Lewis. 1891.
             677 pp.

           – Hist. of Santa Barbara and Ventura Co. Illus. Biog. 477 pp.
             Oakland. 1883.

Santa Clara – Foote, H. S. Pen Pictures From the Garden of the World or Santa
             Clara Co. Lewis. Chi. 1881. 671 pp.

           – Munro - Fraser, J. P. Hist. of Santa Clara Co. Allen, Bowen &
             Co. Pub. San Fran. 1881. 798 pp.

           – San Jose Mercury. Santa Clara Co. Its Resources. Eaton Press.
             San Jose. 1896. 323 pp.

           – Sawyer, Eugene T. Hist. of Santa Clara Co. Biog. Sketches.
             Hist. Research Co. Los Angeles. 1922. 1692.

           – Thompson & West, compilers and pub. Hist. Atlas Map of Santa
             Clara Co. San Fran. 1876. 110 pp.

Santa Cruz – Hist. of Santa Cruz Co. Illus. San Fran. 1879. 102 pp.

           – Hist. of Santa Cruz, By E. S. Harrison, Pub. by author. Pacific
             Press. 1892. 379 pp.

           – Martin, E. Hist. of Santa Cruz. Biog. 357 pp. L.A. 1911.

           – Watkins, R. G. Monterey and Santa Cruz Cos. 2 V. Chi. 1925.

Siskiyou   – Wells, H. L. Hist. of Siskiyou Co. Calif. Oakland: Thompson &
             West 1881. Folio.

           – Hist. of Siskiyou Co. Illus. By H. L. Wells. Stewart. Oakland.
             1881. 218 pp.

Solano   – Fraser, J. P. Munroe. Hist. of Solano Co. Pub. by Wood, Alley
             & Co. San Fran. E. Oakland, 1879. Illus. 503 pp.

           – Hist. Atlas Map of Solano Co. Compiled by Thompson & West.
             San Fran. 1873. Illus. Maps. 68 pp.

           – Hunt, Marguerite. Hist. of Solano Co.

Sonoma   – Hist. of Sonoma Co. with geol. Topography, Mts. etc. Alley &
             Bowen & Co. Pub. San Francisco 1880. 717 pp.

           – Finley, Ernest L. ed. Hist. of Sonoma Co., Calif. Its People,
             Resources. Press Democrat Pub. Co. Santa Rosa, Calif. 1937.
             453 plus 384 pp. Index.

           – Gregory, Tom. Hist. of Sonoma Co. Calif. Biog. Hist. Rec. Co.
             L. A. Calif. 1911. 1112 pp.

           – Illus. Hist. of Sonoma Co. Calif. Lewis. Chi. 1889. 737 pp.

CALIFORNIA (continued)

Sonoma
(cont'd)
- Murphy, Celeste G. Story of Sonoma. W. L. & C. G. Murphy, Sonoma, 1935. 266 pp.
- Thompson, R. A. Hist. & Des. Sketch of Sonoma Co. Phila. 1877. Everts. 104 pp. 8 Vol.
- Tuomey, Honoria. Hist. of Sonoma Co. Calif. S. J. Clarke Chi. S. F. L. A. 2 Vol. 1926 v.1 - 784 pp. V. 2 Biog. 958 pp.

Stanislaus
- Elias, Sol P. Stories of Stanislaus, Hist. and achievements, Modesto, Cal. Elias. 1924. 344 pp.
- Hist. of Stanislaus Co. Calif. Illus. Des. Biog. San Francisco. Elliott & Moore. 1881. 254 pp.
- A Memorial and Biog. Hist. of Counties of Merced, Stanislaus, Calaveras, Tuolumne and Mariposa, Calif. Chi. Lewis. 1892. 408 pp.
- Tinkham, George H. Hist. of Stanislaus Co. Calif. From Early Days. Biog. Los Angeles. Hist. Rec. Co. 1921. 1498 pp.

Sutter
- Hist. of Sutter Co. Oakland, Thompson & West. 1879.

Trinity
- Cox, Isaac. The Annals of Trinity Co. Pub. 1858 Com. Book & Job Steam Printing. San Fran. Editions by J. W. Bartlett, Pub. 1926 and 1940. pub. by U. of Ore. Press. 452 pp.

Tulare
- Elliott, Wallace W. Hist of Tulare Co. San Francisco, Elliott. 1883. 226 pp.
- Lewis Pub. Co. Chi. Memorial & Biog. Hist. of Counties of Fresno, Tulare & Kern, Calif. 822 pp.
- Menefee, Eugene L. Hist. of Tulare and Kings Counties. L. A. Calif. Hist. Rec. Co. 1913. 889 pp.
- Small, K. E. Hist. of Tulare Co. Calif. Chi. S. J. Clarke Pub. Co. 1926. 2 Vol. Co. Hist. Scrap Book.
- Smith, Larry. Hist. of Kings Co. Clarke, 1926. 625 pp.
- Stewart, G. W. Comp. Tulare Newspaper Clippings, 1933.
- Thompson, Thomas H. Official Hist. Atlas. Map of Tulare Co. Calif. 1892. Folio Maps, 147 pp.

Tuolumne
- A. Hist. of Tuolumne Co., Calif. San Fran. Pub. by B. F. Alley, 1882. 48 pp.

Ventura
- Ritter, Elizabeth Kreisher. Hist. of Ventura Co. E. M. Sheridan and Mary Windsor, editors. Meier Pub. 1940. 403 pp.
- Robinson, William Wilcox. The Story of Ventura Co. Los Angeles. TitleIns. 1955.
- Sheridan, Solomon Neill. Hist. of Ventura Co. Chi. Clarke. 1926. 2 Vols. 1034 pp.

CALIFORNIA (continued)

Yolo
- Illus. Hist. of Yolo Co. 1825-80. Statistics, Portraits. DePue & Co. 1879. San Fran. 105 pp. Western Shore Gazetteer & Com. Dir.
- Gregory, Town Hist. of Yolo Co., Biog. 889 pp. L. A. 1913.
- Russell, William O. Ed. Hist. of Yolo Co. Resources and People. Illus. Woodland. 1940. 573 pp.
- Western Shore Gazeteer & Com. Dir. For Calif. Yolo Co. 1 Vol. being devoted to each Co. in the state with brief hist. thereof. Pub. by C. P. Sprague & H. W. Atwell, Woodland, Yolo Co. 1870. 602 pp.

Yuba
- Chamberlain, William H. & Wells, Harry L. Hist. of Yuba Co. Oakland. Thompson & West. 1879.
- Delay, Peter Joseph. Hist. of Yuba & Sutter Co. L. A. Hist. Rec. Co. 1924.
- Ellis. William Turner. Memories; My Seventy-Two years In the Romantic Co. of Yuba. John Henry Nash. 1939.
- Williams, C. E. Yuba and Sutter Counties, Calif. San Fran. Bacon & Co. 1887. 120 pp. Maps. Illus.
- A Bibliography of The History of California 1510-1930 By R. E. and R. G. Cowan, San Francisco, Printed by John Henry Nash, 1933.

COLORADO - 63 Counties

Histories have been written of the following Colorado Counties: Araphol, Boulder, Clear Creek, Custer, Delta, Eagle, El Paso, Gilpin, Jackson, Jefferson, Lake, Las Animas, Logan, Mesa, Montezuma, Pueblo and Weld.

Araphoe
- Baskin, O. L. & Co. Hist. of Denver, Araphoe Co. & Colo. 652 pp. Chi. 1880.

Boulder
- Stewart, Jennie E. Pioneers of Boulder Co. Boulder, 1948.

Clear Creek - Morgan, Mary Edith. Historical Souvenir of Clear Creek Co. Colo. 1948.

Custer
- Hist. & Des. of Freemont and Custer Counties. 136 pp. Canon City. 1879.

Gilpin
- Marshall, Thomas M. Early Records of Gilpin Co. 1859-61. 313 pp. Boulder 1920.

Jackson
- Bailey, Adah B. History of Jackson Co. Colo. Star. 1946.

Lake
- Dill, R. G. Hist. of Lake Co. (In Baskin O. L. & Co. Ark. Valley, Colo.) 1881. pp. 207-414.

18

COLORADO, (continued)

Larimer — Watrous, Ansel. Hist. of Larimer Co. Colo. Courier Printing & Pub. Co. Fort Collins. 1911. 511 pp.

Las Animas — Beshoar, M. Trinidad and Los Animas Counties. 118 pp. Denver. 1882.

Logan — Conklin, Emma B. Hist. of Logan Co. 354 pp. Denver, 1928.

Mesa — Rait, Mary. Hist. of Early Mesa Co. 156 pp. Grand Junction. 1933 Typed.

Montezuma — Freeman, Ira S. A Hist. of Montezuma Co. Boulder. Johnson Pub. 1958.

Pueblo — Ark. Valley Chap. D.A.R. Church and Cemetery Records of Pueblo Co. 263 pp. Pueblo 1947. Typed.

Washington — Washington Co. Colo. Museum Assn. The Pioneer Book of Washington Co. Akron. 1959.

Weld — Jeffs, Mary L. Under Ten Flags; A Hist. of Weld Co. Colo. Greeley. 1938. McVey.
— Krakel, Dean Fenton. South Platte Country. A Hist. of Old Weld Co. Colo. 1739. 1900 Laramie. Powder River 1959.
— Griswold, D. Colorado's Century of Cities. 1958.

CONNECTICUT — 8 Counties

A New York State Library Bulletin No. 53 Dec. 1900, gives a Reference List on Conn. Local Hist., compiled by Charles A. Flagg.

Hist. of Eastern Conn. embracing the Counties of Tolland, Windham, Middlesex and New London by Pliny LeRoy Harwood, - Chicago, New Haven, The Pioneer Hist. Pub. Co. 1931-2.

Fairfield — Geneological Resources of Southwestern Fairfield Co. Conn. Pub. Stamford Geneal. Soc. 1959.
— Fairfield Co. Conn. 1348 pp. Chi. 1899.
— Hurd, Duane Hamilton. Hist. of Fairfield Co. Conn. with Illus. and Biog. Sketches, Phila. Lewis, 1881. 878 pp.
— Wilson, Lynn Winfield. Hist. of Fairfield Co. 1639-1938. 3 Vols. Illus. Chicago, Hartford, Clarke, 1929.

Hartford — Burpee, Charles Winslow. Hist. of Hartford Co. 1633-1928. Vols. 1, 2 & 3. pp. 2751. 1928. Chicago. Clarke.
— Trumbull, J. Hammond. The Memorial Hist. of Hartford Co. 1633-1884. Boston, Osgood. 1886. 704 pp. Projected by Clarence F. Jewett. Vol. 1, 704 pp. Vol. 2, 570 pp.

CONNECTICUT (continued)

Litchfield — Church, Chas. Just. S. Litchfield Co. Centennial Aug. 13-14, 1851. Hartford, Hunt. 1851. 8 Vol. 212 pp.

— Goodenough, A. Clergy of Litchfield Co. 242 pp. Norfolk, 1909.

— Hoskins, Stewart. The Pleasure Book of Litchfield Co. Conn. Lakeville. 1951.

— Kilbourne, Payne Kenyon. Biog. Hist. of Co. of Litchfield, Conn. N.Y. Clark, Austin & Co. 1851. 413 pp.

— Illus. & Biog. Hist. of Litchfield Co. Pub. by J. W. Lewis & Co. Phila. 1881. 730 pp.

— Honor Roll of Litchfield Co. Revolutionary Soldiers compiled by Mary Floyd Tallmadge Chap. D.A.R.

Middlesex — Conn. Tercentenary Com. North Middlesex, edited by N. F. Aitken. The Commission 1935. 43 pp.

— Beers, J. B. & Co. Middlesex Co. Biog. 579 pp. N.Y. 1884.

— Harwood, P. L. Eastern Conn. Counties of Tolland, Windham, Middlesex, New London, 3 V. Chi. 1931.

— Field, David D. A statistical account of the County of Middlesex in Conn. Pub. by Conn. Academy of Arts & Sciences, Middleton, Conn. Printed by Clark & Lyman, April 1819. 8 Vol. 154 pp.

— Field, David D. Centennial Address with Historical Sketches of Cromwell, Portland, Chatham, Middlesex, Haddam, Middletown, By Wm. B. Casey, 1853. 295 pp.

New Haven — Hill, Everett G. A Modern History of New Haven and Eastern New Haven Co. 2 Vol. N. Y.

— Mitchell, Margaret Hewitt. Hist. of New Haven Co. 3 Vol. Chicago. Pioneer Hist. Pub. Co. 1930. Vol 1, 963 pp. Vol. 2 & 3 Biog.

— Rockey, J. L. ed. Hist. of New Haven Co. Conn. 2 Vol. N. Y. W. E. Preston & Co. 1892. Vol. 1, 74 pp. Vol 2, 827 pp.

— Leading Business Men of New Haven Co. and a Hist. Review of The Principal Cities, Boston, Mercantile Pub. Co. 1887. 270 pp.

— New Haven Co. Biog. 1563 pp. Chi. 1902.

— D. A. R. Cemetery and Church Records of Windham and New Haven Counties. 181 pp. 1939.

— Revolutionary Soldiers Buried In Tolland Co. D.A.R. Rep. 1905. 171 pp.

New London — Geneal. and Biog. Record of New London Co. 957 pp. Chi. J. H. Beers & Co. 1905.

— Hurd, Duane Hamilton. Hist. of New London Co. Conn. with Illus. and Biog. Sketches. Phila. J. W. Lewis & Co. 1882. Roy. 8 Vol. 768 pp.

<u>CONNECTICUT</u> (continued)

New London   - Marshall, B. T. Modern History of New London Co. 3 Vols. N.Y.
(cont'd)   Lewis Hist. Pub. Co. 1922.
              - Life Sketches of Leading Citizens of New London Co. 477 pp. Pub.
                by Boston Biog. Review. 1898.

Tolland   - Commemorative Biog. Record of Tolland and Windham Co. with Biog.
                Sketches of Some Prominent Citizens and Early Settlers. Illus.
                J. H. Beers & Co. Pub. 1903, 1358 pp.
              - Cole, J. R. Hist. of Tolland Co. Pub. W. W. Preston 1888. 992 pp.

Windham   - Bayles, R. M. Windham Co. 1204 pp. N. Y. 1889.
              - D.A.R. Cemetery & Church Rec. of Windham & New Haven Counties.
                181 pp. 1939. Typed.
              - Larned, Ellen Douglas. Hist. of Windham Co. Conn. 2 Vols. Pub. by
                Author. 1880. Worcester, Hamilton.
              - Latham, Robert Rev. Historic Gleanings In Windham Co. Conn.
                Providence, R.I. 1899. 258 pp.
              - Lincoln, Allen B. ed. A Modern History of Windham Co. Illus. 2 Vol.
                1827 pp. Clarke. Chi. 1920.
              - Business Directory of Windham Co., Conn. With a History of Each
                Town. West Killingly. 1861. 12 mo.

<u>DELAWARE</u> - 3 Counties

              - J. Thomas Scharf. Hist. of Delaware. Pub. By L. J. Richards & Co.,
                Phila. 1888.
              - Wilson, Lloyd Bevan, ed. Hist. of Del., Past and Present. Lewis
                Hist. Pub. Co. Inc., N.Y. 1929.

Kent   - Hart, Mathilda S. Marriage and Birth Records of Kent Co. 155 pp.
                Rehoboth Beach. 1939.

New Castle   - Baptismal Records of New Castle Co. Pub. Archives Com. Wills, New
                Castle Co., 1682-1800. Col. Dames. 1911.

Sussex   - Orphans Court Records, Sussex Co. 1744-51, Dover. 1940 Photo.
              - Hart, M. S. Wills, Sussex Co. 1694 - 1799. Wilmington. 1934.
              - Turner, C. H. B. Records of Sussex Co. 387 pp. Phila. 1909.
                No County Histories were Published in Del. during 1955-60.
              - Historical Society. Some Aspects of Del. Co. Hist. 1954.
              - Anderson, Florence S. The Delaware River & Valley. Phila. Franklin
                Pub. 1960.
              - Westlager, Clinton Alfred. Delaware's Forgotten River.
              - The Story of The Christina. Wilmington. Hambleton. 1947. Calendar
                of Kent Co. Del. Probate Records. 1680-1800. Dover Pub. Archives,
                1944.

FLORIDA - 67 Counties

Alachma
- Hist. of Alachma Co. by Prof. F. W. Buchholz. Record Co. St. Augustine. 1929. 430 pp.

Brevard
- Marriage Records 1879-96. 218 pp. 1946. Typed.
- Brevard Co. 1891.
- Central Fla. Guide to Central Counties of State Road Dept. 1950. Tallahassee.

Collier
- Tebean, Charlton, West Fla. Last Frontier. Hist. of Collier Co. Coral Gables. U. of Miami Press. 1957.

Columbia
- Columbia Co. 1883.

Dade
- Blackman, E. V. Dade Co. 225 pp. Wash. D.C. 1921.
- Hollingsworth, Tracy. Hist. of Dade Co. Fla. Miami Post. Illus. 151 pp. 1936.
- D.A.R. Marriage Records of Baker, Brevard, Dade, and Marion Counties. 218 pp. 1947. Typed.

Duval
- Marriage Records 1823-1901. 7 Vols. Jacksonville. 1940. Typed.
- Gold, Pleasant Daniel, 1876. Hist. of Duval Co. with Early Hist. of East Fla. 234 pp. St. Augustine. Record Co.
- Gold, Pleasant Daniel, 1876. Hist. of Duval Co. Biog. 693 pp. San Augustine. Record Co. 1928.

Escambia
- Armstrong, Prof. H. Clay, Editor. Robinson, Celia Myrover. Biog. ed. Hist. of Escambia Co. 482 pp. St. Augustine. The Record Co. 1930.
- D.A.R. Marriage Records. 1860-70 and Polk Co. 1861-1902. 254 pp. 1948. Typed.

Hardee
- Hardee County. 1929.

Hernando
- Whitehurst, Mary K. Hernando Co. 1936.

Hillsborough
- Burns, Annie Walker. Hist. Records of Hillsborough Co. Tampa, Fla. Compiled From U.S. Census 1830-70 Wash. 1852.
- Robinson's, Ernest L. Hist. of Hillsborough Co. Pub. by The Record Co. St. Augustine, 1928.

Jackson
- Stanley J. Randall. Hist. of Jackson Co. Fla. Hist. Socy Marianna, Fla. 1950.

Lake
- Lake Co. 1929. Kennedy, Wm. T. Lake Co., Fla.

Leon
- D.A.R. Records of Leon Co. 160 pp. 1940. Typed.

Manatee
- Manatee Co. The Lure of Manatee. McCuffie. 1933.

FLORIDA (continued)

Marion
- D.A.R. Marriage Records of Escambia, Lake, Marion and Nassau Counties. 216 pp. 1946.

No. Fla.
- Guide to Northern Counties of State Road Dept. Tallahassee. 1952.

Orange
- Blackman, William Freemont. Hist. of Orange Co. Biog. Deland. Painter Print Co. 1927.
- Howard, Clarence E. Early Settlers of Orange Co. Biog. Orlando. 1915.

Osceola
- Willson. Osceola Co. 1935.

Pasco
- Hendley. Pasco Co. 1940.

Pinellas
- Bethel, Pinellas Co. 1914.
- W. L. Straub. Pinellas Co. 1929.

Polk
- D.A.R. Marriage Records of Marion, Nassau, Polk and Wakulla Co. 1941. Typed.
- Hetherington, M.F. Hist. of Polk Co. 379 pp. 1928.
- Brooksville and Hernando Co. Ed. & Comp. By Mary K. Whitehurst. Authors: Edith Fulton, Mary E. Coogler, and Mary B. Springstead, 1936. Brooksville Sun. 77 pp.

Putnam
- Putnam Co. 1885.

Sarasota
- Grismer, K. H. Sarasota. Russell. Sarasota. 1946. 376 pp.

So. Fla.
- Guide to Southern Counties of State Rd. Dept. Tallahassee. 1950.

Volusia
- Daytona Beach Observer. Forty Years of Progress 1901-41. Volusia Co. Fla. Fitzgerald. 1941. Daytona.
- Fitzgerald, T. E. Volusia Co. Daytona. Observer 1937. 222 pp.
- Gold, P. D. Volusia Co. 1927.

Walton
- McKinnon, John L. Walton Co. Fla. 1911.

Ft. Meyers
- Fort Meyers And The Caloosahatchie (Lee County Partly). By Thomas A. Gonzalez.

GEORGIA - 159 Counties

Baldwin
- Beeson, Leola S. Stories of Milledgeville & Baldwin Counties, Ga. 202 pp. Macon. 1943.
- Cook, Mrs. Anna M. Green. Hist. of Baldwin Co. 1925. Keys Hearn Printing Co. Anderson, S.C. 484 pp.

GEORGIA (continued)

Baldwin   - Nancy Hart Chap. D.A.R. Tombstone Records of Baldwin Co. 78 pp.
(cont'd)   Typed. Milledgeville.
            - Tunnell, Katherine G. Baldwin Co. 1820 & 1850 Census. 86 pp.
              Typed. Milledgeville.

Bartow   - Cunyus, Lucy J. Bartow Co. Formerly Cass. 344 pp. 1933.
              Tribune. Cartersville.

Bibb   - D.A.R. Bibb Co. Ga. Marriage Records Prior 201660. Typed.

Brooks   - Huxford, Folks. The Hist. of Brooks Co. 1858-1948 D.A.R.
              Athens. McGregor. 1949.
            - McMichel, Mrs. J. R. and Davidso n, Mrs. J. L. Records of
              Brooks & Jackson Counties. 1924. Typed.

Bryan   - Wilson, C. P. Court Records. 16 pp. Savannah. 1929.

Burke   - Baldwin, Nell H. An Intelligent Student's Guide To Burke Co.
              Ga. Hist. Waynesboro, Baldwin. 1956.

Butts   - Lane, Rosa T. Tombstone Records. 115 pp. 1931. Typed.

Camden   - Vocelle, J. T. Camden Co. 156 pp.
            - Cook, L. G. Campbell Co. Marriage Records. 1829-67. 139 pp.
              Atlanta. 1947. Typed.

Catoosa   - McDaniel, Susie Blaylock. Official Hist. of Catoosa Co. Ga.
              1853-1953. Dalton. Gregory. 1953.

Charlton   - McQueen, A. S. Charlton Co. 269 pp. Atlanta. 1932.

Chatham   - Lafar, M. F. and Wilson, C. P. Wills 1773-1817. 251 pp. Wash.
              D.C. 1936.

Chattahoochie-Rogers, N. K. Chattahoochee Co. 397 pp. Columbus, 1933.
              Office Supply.

Cherokee   - Cherokee Co. L. G. Martin. 1932. Brown Pub. Atlanta.

Clarke   - Strahan, C. M. Clarke. 88 pp. Athens. 1893.
            - Rowe, Hugh J. Hist. of Athens & Clarke Co. 180 pp. McGregor.
              1923.

Clinch   - Huxford, F. Clinch Co. 309 pp. Macon. 1916.

Cobb   - Temple, Mrs. Mark. Cobb Co. 901 pp. Brown. Atlanta. 1935.

Coffee   - Ward, W. P. Coffee Co. 354 pp. Foote & Davis Co. Atlanta. 1930.

Colquitt   - Covington, W. A. Colquitt Co. Foote & Davis Co. Atlanta. 1938
            - Coyle, M. O. Colquitt Co. 62 pp. Moultrie. 1925.

GEORGIA (continued)

Columbus   - Worsley, Etta B. Columbus On The Chattahoochie. 513 pp. 1951.
              Office Supply Co.

Coweta   - Jones, Mary G. & Reynolds, Lily. Coweta Co. Chronicles. 869 pp.
              Stein. Atlanta (Adopted Nov. 1933 by Grand Jury as Official
              History.)

Crawford   - Nottingham, C. W. 1850 Census of Crawford Co.- 89 pp. Thomaston.
              1945. Typed.

Crisp   - W. P. Fleming. Crisp Co. 1933. Ham. Print Co. Atlanta.

Decatur   - DeKalb Hist. Socy. Decatur Collections. 1952. Bowen Press.
              V. 1 Year Book

Dodge   - Cobb, A. D. Dodge Co. 256 pp. Atlanta. 1932.

Dougherty   - D.A.R. Thronateeska Chap. Dougherty Co. 411 pp. Albany. 1924.
              Herald.

Elbert   - McIntosh, John H. Hist. of Elbert Co. 554 pp. 1935. Stephen
              Heard. Chap. D.A.R.
              - McIntosh, John H. Hist. of Elbert Co. McGregor. Athens. 1940.

Floyd   - Battey, Dr. George. Hist. of Floyd Co. Vol. 1. 640 pp.
              1922. Webb & Vary Co. Atlanta.

Franklin   - D.A.R. Franklin Co. 1850 Census. 349 pp. 1941. Typed.

Fulton   - Cooper, W. G. Fulton Co. 912 pp. Atlanta. 1934.
              - Knight, Lucian Lamar. Hist. of Fulton Co. Biog. 514 pp. Atlanta.
              Cawston. 1930.

Gilmer   - Ward, George G. Hist. of Gilmer Co., Ga. Typed. M.S. 3V.

Gordon   - Pitts, Lulu. Gordon Co. 480 pp. 1933. Calhoun Times.

Gwinnett   - Flanigan, J. C. Vol. 1. Gwinnett Co. 1944 Tyler. Hopeville
              Bd. of Co. Com. 454 pp. 1944.

Habersham   - Several authors. Hist. and Resources of The Hills of Habersham
              County. 53 pp. Cir. Bull. #1. Dept. of Educ. Clarksville.

Hall   - D.A.R. Marriage Records of Talbot, Upson, Spalding, Ebert,
              Newton and Hall Co. 290 pp. 1948. Typed.

Hancock   - Houston, M. L. Marriages of Hancock Co. 79 pp. Wash. D. C. 1947.

Hart   - Baker, J. W. Hart Co. 426 pp. Atlanta. 1933.

GEORGIA (continued)

Irwin — Clements, J. B. Irwin Co. 539 pp. Atlanta. 1932.

Jackson — Hardman, Thomas Colquitt. Hist. of Harmony Grove. Commerce, Jackson Co., Ga. 1810-1949. Athens. McGregor Co. 1949.
— Wilson, G. J. N. The Hist. of Jackson Co. 1914. Pub. by White Jefferson.

Jefferson — Thomas, Mrs. Z. V. and Grice, W. and Phillips, W. L. Jefferson County. 144 pp. Macon. 1927.

Jones — Houston, M. L. 1850 Census. Jones County, 108 pp. Wash. D. C. Typed.
— Williams, Carolyn White. Hist. of Jones Co., Ga. 1807-1907. Macon, J. W. Burke Co. 1957.

Lamar — Lambdin, Mrs. Augusta and Fish, Mrs. E. A. Lamar Co. 1932. Barnesville News Gazette.

Laurens — Hart, Bertha Sheppard. Official Hist. of Laurens Co. 1807-1941. Ed. & Pub. by John Laurens Chap. D.A.R. Dublin, Ga. 1941. 546 pp. Indexed.

Lincoln — Perryman, Clinton J. Hist. of Lincoln Co., Ga. 1933. Typed M.S.

Lowndes — D.A.R. Lowndes Co. 1825-41. 400 pp. Valdosta. 1941.

Lumpkin — Cain, A. W. Lumpkin Co. 1832-1932. 506 pp. 1932. Atlanta. Stein Print Co.

Macon — Hays, Mrs. J. E. Macon Co. 1933. Stein. Atlanta.
— Hays, L. F. Macon Co. 803 pp. Atlanta. 1933.
— Young, Ida. Hist. of Macon, Lyon, Marshall & Brooks. 1950.

Marion — Powell, Nettie. Marion Co. 178 pp. Columbus, 1931. Hist. Pub. Co.

Monroe — Worsham, Nannie M. Hist. of Stroud Community In Monroe Co., Ga. 1858.
— Worsham, Nannie M. Early Hist. of Culloder, Ga. In Monroe Co. 1959. Typed M.S.

McDuffie — McCommons, Mrs. W. C. Comp. Hist. of McDuffie Co., Ga. 1870-1933. Typed ms.

Mitchell — Spence, Mrs. John M. Mitchell Co., Ga. Hist. 1933. Typed.

Paulding — Roberts, Lucien E. A Hist. of Paulding Co., Ga. Dallas. 1933. Typed.

GEORGIA (continued)

Pickens   -Tate, Luke E. Hist. of Pickens Co. Atlanta.
W. W. Brown Pub. Co. 322 pp. Illus. 1935.

Pike   - Mitchell, Lizzie R. Hist. of Pike Co. 1822-1932. Pub. In Pike
Co. Journal. 1932.

Pulaski   - D.A.R. Pulaski Co. Atlanta. Brown. 1935.
- D.A.R. Ga. Hawkinsville Chap. Hist. of Pulaski and Bleckley
Counties, Ga. 1808-1956. V. 1 & 2. Macon. J. W. Burke Co.
1957-8.

Rabun   - Ritchie, Andrew Jackson. Sketches of Rabun Co. Hist. 1819-1948.
no pp. Foote and Davies Co. Atlanta.

Schley   - Williams, Mrs. H. J. Hist. of Schley Co. 48 pp.

Telfair   - Hist. of Telfair Co. 1812-49. By F. P. Mann. Burke.

Taliaferro   - Lunceford, Alvin Mell. Early Records of Taliaferro Co. Ga.
Crawfordville. 1956.

Tift   - Williams, Ida Belle. Tift Co. 1948. Burke. Macon.

Troup   - Smith, C. L. Troup Co. 323 pp. Atlanta. 1933.

Turner   - Pate, J. B. Turner Co. 198 pp. Atlanta. 1933. Stein.

Upson   - D.A.R. Marriage Records of Upson, Pike, Spalding, Newton and
Troup Counties. 165 pp. 1947. Typed.
- Nottingham, Mrs. C. W. and Hannah E. Upson Co. 1122 pp. 1930.

Walker   - Sartain, J. A. Walker Co. Vol. 1. Dalton. 1932. Showalter.

Ware   - Walker, Mrs. L. J. Ware Co. 1934. 547 pp. Macon. Burke.

Warren   - 1850 Census. Warren Co. Microfilm.

Washington   - Mitchell, E. Washington Co. 171 pp. Atlanta. 1924.

Whitfield   - Herron, Sr., Mrs. R. M. Whitfield Co. 1936. Showalter. Dalton.
- Whitfield Co., Hist. Com. Official Hist. of Whitfield Co., Ga.
1930. Dalton. 238 pp. Showalter.

Wilcox   - Washburn, N. D. Geneal & Hist. Rec. Wilcox Co. 4 V. Rochelle.
1942-5. Typed.

Wilkes   - Bowen, Eliza A. The Story of Wilkes, 1889. Pub. by Wash.
Reporter. W.P.A. Writer's Program.
- The Story of Washington, Wilkes. 136 pp. Univ. of Ga. Press.
Athens. 1941.

GEORGIA (continued)

Wilkinson
- Victor Davidson. Wilkinson Co. 645 pp. 1930. Burke Co. Macon.
- Huxford, Folks. Pioneers of Wiregrass, Ga. 3V. Adel, Patten,1951.

Worth
- Grubbs, Mrs. Lillie Martin. 1934. Worth Co. 1854-1934. 594 pp. Macon. 1934.
- Sketches of Georgia Counties, Towns, etc. W.P.A. Inventory of County Archives, Candler, Allen D.
- Garrett, Franklin M. Atlanta and Environs. 3 V. N. Y. Lewis. 1954.
- Martin, John H. Columbus, Ga. 1827-65. Columbus. Gilbert. 1874.
- Telfair, Nancy. Hist. of Columbus, Ga. 1828-1928. Columbus Pub. Co. 1929.
- Worsley, Etta Blanshard. Columbus On The Chattahoochee. Columbus Office Supply Co. 1951.
- U. S. Works Progress Administration. Augusta (American Guide Series). Tidwell Print Supply Co. 1938.
- Melton, Quimby, Jr. Hist. of Griffin. Daily News. 1959.
- Chattahoochee Valley Hist. Socy. West Point. Bull. #3. 1957.
- W.P.A. Ga. The Story of Washington. Wilkes. (American Guide Series). Athens. U. of Ga. Press. 1941.
- Huxford, F. Pioneers of Wiregrass, Ga. 1957.

HAWAII

The State of Hawaii has four counties: Honolulu (Oahu), Hawaii, Mavi and Kanai, all organized since 1907. There are no individual histories of these counties.

IDAHO - 44 Counties

Alturas
- Hall, Lucile Hathaway - Memories of Old Alturas County, Idaho. Denver. Big Mountain Press. 1956.

Bannock
- Saunders, Arthur C. The Hist. of Bannock Co. Pocatello, Tribune Co. Ltd. 1915.

Blaine
- MacLeod, Geo. A. Hist. of Alturas and Blaine Counties. Rev. ed. The Bailey Times, Ida. 1938. 192 pp.

Bonneville
- Clark, Bargilla Worth. Bonneville Co. Idaho In The Making. Idaho Falls. 1941. 140 pp. 8 Vol. Cloth.

Caribou
- Shupe, V. I. Caribou Co. Chronology. 63 pp. Colo. Sprgs. 1930.

IDAHO (continued)

Elmore — Grolfsema, Mrs. Olive DeEtte Jensen. Elmore Co. Caxton. Caldwell. Its Historical Gleaning. Idaho. 1949.

Franklin — Franklin Co. (Partly). The Trail Blazer, Hist. of Dev. of Southeastern Idaho. By Daughters of The Pioneers 1930.

— The Passing of the Redman - By Franklin Co. Hist. Socy. 1910. Prepared for first "Idaho Days" Celebration at Franklin, Ida. June 14 & 15, 1910. Gov. James H. Brady in 1911 Proclaimed June 15 to be observed each year as "Pioneer Day".

Idaho — Elsensohn, M. Alfreda. Pioneer Days In Idaho Co., Ida. Caldwell. Caxton Ltd. 1947-51. Vol. 2 ms. 1951.

— Facts and Statistics (Hist of Idaho Counties) by James L Onderdonk, 1885.

Nez Perces — McBeth, K. C. Nez Perces. 272 pp. N.Y. 1908.

Owyhee — Owyhee Co. Hist. Des. and Com. Dir. L. A. York, Pub. 1898.

Shoshone — Hobson, Geo. C. ed. Gems of Thought and Hist. of Shoshone Co. by Allied Fraternities Council Shoshone. Kellogg. 1940- 84 pp.

Teton — Teton Co., Hist. of Teton Valley by Driggs. 1936.

— All of Idaho Histories contain short accounts of each county in the state, of these, there are the following:

— Hailey's Hist. of Idaho. 1910. One vol.

— Hawley's Hist. of Idaho. 1920. Four Vols.

— Early Hist. of Idaho by McConnell. 1913. One Vol.

— Elliott's Hist. of Idaho Territory. 1884. One Vol.

— French's Hist. of Idaho Territory. 1914. Three Vol.

— Idaho, The Gem of The Mountains. 1819. Lewis. One vol.

— Hist. of North Idaho, Nez Perce, Idaho, Latah, Kootenai and Shoshone Counties. 1903. W. Hist. Pub. One Vol.

— Hist. of the State of Idaho by C. J. Brosnan. 1918. One vol.

— Idaho, The Place and Its People, A Hist. of The Gem State from Prehistoric to Present Days. By Byron Defenbaugh. 1933. 3 Vol.

— Inventory of County Archives of Idaho.

ILLINOIS - 102 Counties

— Practically a complete list of Ill. County Histories can be secured by consulting Buch's "Travel and Description 1765-1865."

— Hughes, E. J. Counties of Illinois. 67 pp. Springfield. 1934.

ILLINOIS (continued)

County
Archives   - Pease, T. C. Ill. Co. Archives. 730 pp. Springfield. 1915.

Adams   - This Is Adams Co. by John Drury. 1955. Co. Hist. Aerial Series.

   - Port. & Biog. Record of Adams Co., Ill. 598 pp. Chicago.
Chapman Bro. 1892.

   - Collins, W. H. & Perry, C. F. Past & Present of The City of
Quincy and Adams Co. Ill. 1124 pp. Chi. Clarke. 1905.

   - Hist. of Adams Co. 971 pp. Chi. Murray Williamson & Phelps. 1879.

   - Standard Atlas of Adams Co., Ill. Plats of Villages, Maps.
Dir. Pub. by Geo. A. Ogle & Co., Chi. 1901, 117 pp.

   - Wilcox, D. E. and Others. Quincy and Adams Co. Hist. and Biog.
2 Vol. Chi. Lewis. 1919.

   - Atlas Map of Adams Co., Ill. Lyter. Davenport, Iowa, 1872. 169pp.

Alexander   - Perrin, William Henry, ed. Hist. of Alexander, Union and
Pulaski Counties, Ill. Chi. Baskin. 1883. 338 pp.

Bond   - Bateman, Newton & Selby, Paul, eds. Ill. Hist. Bond Co., Biog.
ed. by Warren E. McCaslin, Chi. Munsell, 1915. 2 Vol.

   - Perrin, Wm. Henry, ed. Hist. of Bond & Montgomery Co. Baskin.
Chi. 1882. 752 pp.

   - Port. & Biog. Record of Montgomery and Bond Counties, Ill.
Biog. Chi. Chapman. 1892. 518 pp.

   - Standard Atlas of Bond Co., Ill. Plats. Dir. Comp. & Pub. by
Geo. A. Ogle & Co., Chi. 1900. 43 pp.

   - Atlas of Bond Co. Ill. Maps. Chicago. Warmer & Beers, 1875.
93 pp.

Boone   - Port. & Biog. Record of Winnebago and Boone Counties, Ill.
Chi. Biog. Pub. Co. 1892. 1325 pp.

   - Hist. Encyclopedia of Ill. and Hist. of Boone Co. 2 Vols. 942 pp.
Pages 661-942 (V. 2). Cover Boone Co. and was edited by Richard
V. Carpenter. First vol. and part of V was edited by Newton,
Bateman, and Paul Selby. Munsell Pub. Co. Chicago, Illus.

   - Past and Present of Boone County, Ill. 414 pp. Illus. Chicago.
1877. By H. F. Kett & Co.

   - Illus. Atlas of Boone Co., Ill. Maps. Chicago, Sauer, 1886.
pp 45.

   - Illus. Atlas of Winnebago and Boone Co., Ill. Maps. Plats.
Chicago. Page. 1886. 120 pp.

   - The Rock River Valley: Its Hist., Traditions, Legends and Charm
in 3 Vols. Illus. Vol. 1 - 752 pp. V. 2-616pp. V. 3-646 pp.
Royal Brunson Way of Beloit College, sup. ed. 1926. Covers four
counties in Wis.-Jefferson, Dodge, Dane and Rock; and eight
counties in Ill.-Winnebago, Stephenson, Boone, Ogle Lee,
Whiteside, Henry and Rock Counties. Pub. by S.J.Clarke Pub. Co.
Chi.

<u>ILLINOIS</u> (continued)

<u>Brown</u>
- Combined Hist. of Schuyler and Brown Counties, Ill. Illus. Biog. Phila., Brink. 1882. 412 pp.
- Standard Atlas of Brown Co., Ill. Plats. Dir. Comp. & Pub. by George A. Ogle & Co., Chicago, Ill. 1913. 47 pp.
- Biog. Rev. of Cass, Schuyler & Brown Co. 624 pp. 1892.
- This Is Brown Co. by John Drury. 1955. Co. Hist. Aerial Series.

<u>Bureau</u>
- Cushing, Mrs. E. B. & Smith, G. A. Comp. Early Hist. of Paureau Co., Bureau Co., Centennial 1828-1928. Com.
- Bradsby, N. C. Hist. of Bureau Co., World Pub. Co. Chi. 1885. 710 pp.
- This Is Bureau Co., by John Drury. 1955. Co. Hist. Aerial Series.
- Doris Parr Leonard. A Pioneer Tour of Bureau Co., Ill. Princeton. Bureau Co. 1954.
- Sketches of Early Settlement and Present of Princeton, Ill. with a sketch of Bureau Co., Princeton, 1857. 96 pp.
- Atlas of Bureau Co., Ill. and U.S. Chi. Warner & Beers 1875. 77 pp.
- The Voters and Tax-Payers of Bureau Co., Ill. Biog. Dir. Officers of Societies. Chicago. Kett. 1877. 411 pp.
- The Biog. Record of Bureau, Marshall and Putnam Counties, Ill. Chicago. Clarke. 1896. 737 pp.
- Ford, Henry A. The Hist. of Putnam and Marshall Counties, and Formation of Bureau and Stark Counties. Appendix. Officers. Lacon. 1860. 160 pp.
- Harrington, George B. Past & Present of Bureau Co. Biog. Pioneer Pub. Co. Chicago. 1906. 968 pp.
- Matson, N. Map of Bureau Co., Ill. with Sketches of Its Early Settlement, Chicago. G.H. Fergus. 1867. 26 Maps. 88 pp.
- Matson, N. Reminiscences of Bureau Co. Illus. Princeton, Ill. 1872. 406 pp. Tiskilwa Print. Office. 1937.

<u>Calhoun</u>
- Carpenter, George W. Hist. of Calhoun County.
- Portrait and Biographical Album of Pike and Calhoun Counties, Ill. Port. Biog. Chi. Biog. Pub. Co. 1891. 808 pp.

<u>Carroll</u>
- Hostetter, Chas. L. ed. Historical Encyclopedia of Ill. ed. by Newton Bateman, Paul Selby. Chi. Munsell. 1913. 2 V.
- Port. & Biog. Albums of Jo Daviess & Carroll Cos. Ill. Port. Biog. Chi. Chapman. 1889. 1019 pp.
- The Hist. of Carroll Co., Ill. Biog. Port. Map. Chi. Kett. 1878. 501 pp.
- Hist. of Carroll Co. Its Cities. Biog. Dir. Chi. Murray, Williamson & Phelps. 1878. 8 V. 501 pp.
- Standard Atlas of Carroll Co., Ill. Comp. & Pub. by Geo. G. Ogle & Co., Chi. 1908.

ILLINOIS (continued)

Cass
- Bateman, Newton & Shelby, Paul Edw. Hist. Encyclopedia of Ill. & Hist. of Cass Co., ed. by Charles E. Martin, Chicago, Munsell, 1915. 2 Vol.
- Illus. Atlas Map of Cass Co., Ill. From Personal examinations and Surveys. Phila. Brink. 1874. 99 pp.
- This Is Cass Co. by John Drury. 1955. Chicago. Loree Co.
- Gridley, J. N. & others. Hist. Sketches of Cass Co. Vol. 1. Virginia, Ill., Enquirer. 1907. 445 pp.
- Henderson, John G. Early History of The "Sangamon Country", now comprised within the limits of Morgan, Scott & Cass Counties, Davenport, Iowa, Day, etc. 1873. 33 pp.
- Perrin, William Henry, ed. Hist. of Cass Co., Ill. Chicago. Baskin. 1882. 357 pp.
- Shaw, J. Henry. Hist. Sketch of Cass Co., Ill. July 4, 1876. Oration at Beardstown, Messenger, 1876. 53 pp.
- Hist. of Cass Co., ed. by Charles A. E. Martin. Munsell Pub. Chi. 1915. 986 pp. (Vol. II Bateman and Selby, Hist. Encyclopedia of Ill.)
- Standard Atlas of Cass Co., Ill. comp. & pub. by Geo. A. Ogle & Co. Chicago. 1899. 80 pp.

Champaign
- Hist. Encyclopedia of Ill. ed. by Newton Bateman, Paul Selby & Hist. of Champaign Co., ed. by Joseph O. Cunningham, Chicago. Munsell. 1905. 2 Vol.
- Hist. of Champaign Co., Ill. Illus. Des. Biog. Phila. Brink, etc. 1878. 195 pp.
- Plat Book of Champaign Co., Ill. Comp. & Pub. by Geo. A. Ogle & Co., Chicago. 1893. 93 pp.
- Port. & Biog. album of Champaign Co., Ill. Chi. Chapman. 1887. 980 pp.
- Cunningham, J. O., A Hist. of The Early Settlement of Champaign Co., Ill., and Mathew Busey Family. Urbana, Champaign Co. Herald, 1876. 24 pp.
- Cunningham, J. O. Hist. of Champaign Co. In Vol. 2 of Hist. Encyclopedia of Ill., ed. by N. Bateman & P. Selby, 1905. Munsell Pub. Co.
- This Is Champaign Co. by John Drury. 1955. Chicago Loree Co.
- Lothrop, J. S. Champaign Co. Dir. 1870-01. Hist. of Co., Chi. 1871. 456 pp.
- Mathews, Milton W. & McLean, Lewis A., ed., Early Hist. of Pioneers of Champaign Co., Ill. Illus. Biog. Urbana, Champaign Co. Herald. 1886. 126 pp.
- Standard Atlas of Champaign Co., Ill. Plats, Directory, Chicago. Ogle. 1913. 163 pp.

<u>ILLINOIS</u> (continued)

Champaign
(cont'd)
- Stewart, J.R.A. Standard Hist. of Champaign Co., Ill. with Family Lineage and Memoirs. Chicago. Lewis Pub. 1918. 2 Vol.
- Port. & Biog. Album of Champaign Co., 980 pp. Chi. 1887.
- Record of Champaign Co., 655 pp. Chi. 1900.

Christian
- Bateman, Newton & Selby, Paul eds. Hist. Encyclopedia of Ill. and Christian Co., ed. by H. LeFowkes, Chicago, Munsell, 1918. 2 Vol.
- Hist. of Christian Co., Ill. Illus. Des. Biog. Phila. Brink. 1880. 259 pp.
- Port. and Biog. Record of Christian Co., Ill. Biog. Chicago. Lake City Pub. Co. 1893. 460 pp.
- Fowkes, H. L. Christian Co. 623-1014 pp. Chi. 1918.
- McBride, J. C. Hon. Past and Present of Christian Co., Ill. Chicago. Clarke. 1904. 582 pp.
- Standard Atlas Christian Co., Ill. Plats, Dir. Comp. and Pub. by Geo. A. Ogle & Co., Chicago. 1911. 115 pp.
- (No author) - Hist. of Christian Co. Illus. Biog. Phila. 1880 275 pp.

Clark
- Historical Encyclopedia of Ill., Newton Bateman, ed.-in-chief. Paul Selby, Assoc. Ed., and Hist. of Clark Co., by Hon. H. C. Bell, Chicago. Munsell for Mid-West Pub. Co. 1907.
- Plat Book of Clark Co., Ill., comp. and pub. by Geo. A. Ogle & Co., Chicago. 1892. 73 pp/
- Perrin, William H., ed. Hist. of Crawford and Clark Counties, Chicago. Baskin. 1883. 470 pp. Ill.
- Wheeler, G. S. Clark Co. 130 pp. Evanston. 1946. Typed.

Clay
- Biog. & Reminiscent Hist. of Richland, Clay and Marion Counties, Ill. Indianapolis, Bowen. 1909. 608 pp.
- Hist. of Wayne and Clay Counties, Ill. Chicago. Globe. 1884. 242 pp.
- An Atlas of Clay Co., Ill. actual surveys by B. N. Griffing. Phila. Lake. 1881. 50 pp.

Clinton
- Hist. of Marion and Clinton Counties, Ill. Illus. Des. Biog. Phila. Brink. 1881. 316 pp.
- Port. & Biog. Record of Clinton, Washington, Marion, and Jefferson Counties, Ill. Biog. Chicago. Chapman, 1894. 285 pp.
- Plat book of Clinton Co., Ill. Comp. & Pub. by Occidental Pub. Co., Ogle. Prop. Chicago. 1892. 72 pp.

Coles
- Hist. Encyclopedia of Ill. ed. by Newton Bateman, Paul Selby, and Hist. of Coles Co., ed. Charles Edward Wilson. Chicago. Munsell. 1906. 886 pp.

ILLINOIS (continued)

Coles
(cont'd)

- Port. & Biog. Album of Coles Co., Ill. Chi. Chapman, 1887. 577 pp.
- Hist. of Coles Co., Ill. Dir. Port. Statistics. Map. Chicago. LeBaron. 1879. 699 pp.
- Plat Book of Coles Co., Ill. Comp. & Pub. by The American Atlas Co., Chicago, Ogle. 1893. 80 pp.

Cook

- Andreas, A. T. Hist. of Cook Co., Ill. From Earliest Period. Chi. Andreas. 1884. 888 pp.
- Hist. Encyclo. of Ill. ed. by Newton Bateman, Paul Selby. Cook Co. edition. Chi. Munsell. 1905. 2 Vol.
- Album of Geneal. & Biog. Cook Co. Port. Biog. Calumet Book'& Engraving Co. 1895. 614 pp.
- Hist. of Cook Co., Ill. with Hist. of Chi. From First Settlement. Editors: W. A. Goodspeed, Daniel D. Healey, Chi. Goodspeed. 1909. 2 Vol.
- Geneal. and Biog. Record of Cook Co., Ill. Chi. Lake City Pub. 1894. 501 pp.
- Hist. Rev. of Chi. and Cook Co. Biog by A. N. Waterman. Chi. and N. Y. Lewis. 1908. 3 Vol.
- Johnson, Charles B. Growth of Cook Co., Ill. Chi. Bd. of Comm. Cook Co. 1960.
- D.A.R. Cook Co. Geneal. Record. 175 pp. Evanston. 1945. Typed.

Crawford

- Ill. Historical. Editors Newton Bateman, Paul Selby. Crawford Co. Biog. Contributors: Wm. C. Jones, E. Callahan & others. Chi. Munsell. 1909. 846 pp.
- Hist. of Crawford & Clark Counties, Ill. ed. W. H. Perrin. Chi. Baskin. 1883. 374 pp.

Cumberland

- Counties of Cumberland, Jasper and Richland, Ill. Hist. and Biog. Chi. Battey. 1884. 839 pp.

De Kalb

- Hist. of De Kalb Co. Bois-Bassett. 1868. 530 pp.
- Port. & Biog. Album of De Kalb Co., Ill. From Earliest Settlement. Chi. Chapman. 1883. 901 pp.
- Biog. Record of De Kalb Co. Clark. 1898. 559 pp.
- Past & Present of De Kalb Co., Ill. By Prof. L. M. Gross, H. W. Fay, G. E. Congdon, F. W. Lowman and Judge C. A. Bishop. Pioneer. Chi. 1907. 2 Vol.
- The Voters and Tax Payers of De Kalb Co., Ill. Biog. Dir. Maps. Chi. Kitt. 1876. 342 pp.
- Standard Atlas of De Kalb Co., Ill. Comp. & Pub. by Geo. A. Ogle & Co., Chi. 1905.
- Atlas Map of De Kalb Co., Ill. by Thompson & Everts, Geneva. 1871. 57 pp.
- Plat book of De Kalb Co., Ill. Surveys, Records, Chi. Ensign. 1892. 131 pp.

<u>ILLINOIS</u> (continued)

DeWitt
- Hist. of DeWitt Co., Ill. Illus. Des. Biog. Brink, Phila. 1882. 338 pp.
- Port. & Biog. Album of DeWitt & Piatt Co., Ill. Chi. Chapman. 1891. 992 pp.
- The Biog. Record of DeWitt Co., Ill. Chi. Clarke. 1901. 218 pp.
- Plat Book of DeWitt Co., Ill. Comp. & Pub. by G. A. Ogle & Co. (Amer. Atlas Co.) Chi. 1894. 57 pp.
- Hist. of DeWitt Co., Ill. Biog. Chi. Pioneer. 1910. 2 Vol.
- Atlas of DeWitt Co., Ill. Maps. Chi. Warner & Peers. 1875. 93 pp.
- Hist. of DeWitt Co., Biog. Port. Phila. 1882. 338 pp.
- Port. Biog. Album of DeWitt & Pratt Co., 1891. Chapman.
- This Is DeWitt Co., Ill. By John Drury, Chicago. Loree. 1955.

Douglas
- Ill. Historical; editors N. Bateman, P. Selby. Douglas Co. Biog., ed. John W. King, Chi. Munsell, 1910. 837 pp.
- County of Douglas, Ill. Hist. and Biog. & Sketch of N.W. Ter. & Ill. Chi. Batttey. 1884. 563 pp.
- An Illus. Hist. Atlas Map of Douglas Co., Ill. Phila. Brink. 1875. 107 pp.
- Hist. & Biog. Record of Douglas Co., Ill. Comp. by John Gresham, Logansport, Ind. Wilson. 1900. 299 pp.
- Hist. of Douglas Co., Ill. For Centennial Anniversary of American Independence, July 4, 1876 by Henry C. Miles. Tuscola. Converse & Parks. 1876. 79 pp.

Du Page
- N. Bateman and Paul Selby. Hist. of DuPage Co. Hist. Biog. Chi. Munsell. 1913. 2 Vol.
- Hist. of Du Page Co., Ill. by R. Blanchard. Chi. Baskin. 1882. 247 pp.
- Blanchard, Rufus. Hist. of DuPage Co., 1882. Pub. by Author.
- Port. & Biog. Record of Cook & Du Page Co., Chi. Lake City Pub. Co. 1894. 640 pp.
- McDonough & Co., DuPage Co., Dir. 1924-5. Port. & Biog. Record of DuPage Counties. Chi. & Lake City. 1894.
- 20th Century Atlas of DuPage Co., Ill. Maps, Chi. Mid-West Pub. Co. 1904. 89 pp.
- Richmond, C. W. & Valette, H. F. Hist. of The County of Du Page, Ill. and Several Towns, Stat. Chi. Scripps. 1857. 212 pp.
- Hist. of Du Page Co., Ill. Comp. by Bd. of Supv. 1876 by C. W. Richmond, Aurora, Knickerbocker & Hodder. 1877. 250 pp.
- Combination Atlas Map of DuPage Co., Ill. Thompson Bros. & Burr. Elgin. 1874. 71 pp.

ILLINOIS (continued)

DuPage
(cont'd)
- Hattie G. Glos. Wayne Township, Du Page Co., Ill. Glen Ellyn, Ill. Du Page Hist. Rev. 1950.
- Frederick S. Weiser. Post Offices and Postal Routes In Du Page Co., Ill. in 1850. Glen Ellyn, Du Page. Hist. Rev. 1950.
- DuPage Hist. Rev. Vol. 1-3, Ja. 1950 - Dec. 1952, Fed. Writing Project.
- DuPage Co. Des. & Hist. Guide. Wheaton, Ill. DuPage Title Co.1951.

Edgar
- Plat Book of Edgar Co., Ill. Comp. & Pub. by The American Atlas Co., Chi. 1894. 58 pp.
- Hist. Encyclo. of Ill. & Hist. of Edgar Co., ed. by N. Bateman & H. Van Sellar, 1905. Munsell, 781 pp.
- Port. & Biog. Album of Vermilion and Edgar Counties. Chapman. 1889. 1113 pp.
- Hist. of Edgar Co., Ill. Dir. War Records. Port. Stat. Map. Chi. LeBaron. 1879. 798 pp.
- Standard Atlas of Edgar Co., Ill. Plat. Dir. Comp. & Pub. by G. A. Ogle & Co., Chi. 1910. 129 pp.
- Atlas of Edgar Co. & State of Ill. and U.S. Maps. Phila. Warner & Higgins. 1870. 133 pp.
- D.A.R. Geneal. Rec. of Edgar, Peioria, Tazewell and Vermilion Counties, 136 pp. Evanston. 1943. Typed.

Edwards
- Flower, George. Hist. of The English Settlements in Edwards Co., Ill. Chi. Fergus. 1882. 402 pp. Chi. Hist. Socy.
- Combined Hist. of Edwards, Lawrence, and Wabash Co., Ill. Illus. Des. Biog. Phila. McDonough. 1883. 377 pp.
- Standard Atlas of Edwards Co., Ill. Comp. & Pub. by George A. Ogle & Co., Chicago. 1907.

Effingham
- Illinois Historical, ed. N. Bateman, Paul Selby. Effingham Co. Biog. Chi. Munsell. 1910. 893 pp.
- Hist. of Effingham Co., Ill. ed. by W. H. Perrin. Chi. Baskin, 1883. 286 pp.

Fayette
- Plat Book of Fayette Co., Ill. Comp. & Pub. by Alden, Ogle & Co., Chi., 1891. 88 pp.
- Bateman, Paul Selby. Hist. of Fayette Co., Editors, R. W. Ross, J. J. Bullington, Chi. Munsell. 1910. 2 Vol.
- Hist. of Fayette Co., Ill. Illus. Des. Biog. Phila. Brink. 1878, 109 pp.

Ford
- Hist. Atlas of Ford Co,, Ill, Plats, Ports. Biog. Maps, Stat. Chi. Beers. 1884. 83 pp.
- Hist. of Ford Co., Ill. From Earliest Settlement by E. A. Gardner. Illus. Part. Biog. Chi. Clarke. 1908. 2 Vol.

<u>ILLINOIS</u> (continued

Ford (cont'd)	– Portrait & Biog. Record of Ford Co., Ill. Biog. Chi. Lake City Pub. Co. 1892. 812 pp.
	– Standard Atlas of Ford Co., Ill. Comp. & Pub. by Geo. A. Ogle & Co., Chi. 1901.
	– Ford County Centennial Com. Centurama. Celebrating First 100 Years of Ford Co., 1959.
Franklin	– Aiken, H. M. – Franklin Co. Hist. Cent. ed. N.P. N.D. Frier, H.L. ed. Franklin Co., Ill. War Hist. 1832-1919 Benton (etc.) Trovillon, 1920.
	– Hist. of Gallatin, Saline, Hamilton, Franklin and Williamson Co., Ill. From Earliest Time. Biog. Chi. Goodspeed. 1887. 961 pp.
Fulton	– This Is Fulton Co., Ill. by John Drury. Chi. Loree Co. 1954.
	– Hist. Encyclopedia of Ill. ed. by N. Bateman, P. Selby and Hist. of Fulton Co., ed. by Jesse Heylin.
	– Port. & Biog. Album of Fulton Co., Port. Biog. Chi. Biog. Pub. Co. 1890. 898 pp.
	– Hist. of Fulton Co., Ill. Sketches of Cities, etc. Port from Pre-Historic Days. Polit. & Mil. Hist. Laws. Peoria. Chapman. 1879. 1090 pp.
	– Hist. of Fulton Co. and Its Townships. Biog. Lewiston Republican, VIII, No. 36, Oct. 1, 1897.
	– Plat Book of Fulton Co., Ill. Comp. & Pub. by Amer. Atlas Co., G. A. Ogle & Co. Chi. 1895. 94 pp.
	– Standard Atlas of Fulton Co., Ill. Plats, Dir. Comp. by G. A. Ogle & Co., Chi. Asst. by C. R. Beam, Chi. Ogle, 1912. 133 pp.
Gallatin	– Bender, L. R. Early Gallatin Co. 5 vols. 1936.
	– Hist. of Gallatin, Saline, Hamilton, Franklin and Williamson Counties, Chi. Goodspeed. 1887. 961 pp.
Greene	– Atlas Map of Greene Co., Ill. By Andreas, Lyter & Co. Davenport, Iowa. 1873.
	– Hist. of Greene Co., Ill. Past & Present. Biog. Dir. War Records. Port. Stat. Map. Chi. Donnelly, etc. 1879. 771 pp.
	– Past & Present of Greene Co., Ill. by Hon. Ed. Miner. Chi. Clarke. 1905. 645 pp.
	– Plat Book of Greene and Jersey Counties, Ill. by G. A. Ogle & Co. Chi. Hammond. 1893. 96 pp.
	– Hist. of Greene & Jersey Co., Ill. Towns, Townships, etc., Port. Biog. From Pre-historic Times. Springfield. Continental Hist. Co. 1885. 1156 pp.

<u>ILLINOIS</u> (continued)

Grundy
- Hist. Oration by P. A. Armstrong at Morris July 4, 1876. before Old Settlers Assn. Reformer. 1876. 15 pp.
- Hist. of Grundy Co., Ill. From Earliest Settlement. Geol. Agri. Aboriginal. Biog. Port. Chi. Baskin. 1882. 156 pp.
- Bateman, N. and Selby, Paul, editors. Hist. Encyclo. of Ill. and Hist. of Grundy Co. By Special Authors and Contributors. Chi. Munsell. 1914. 2 Vol.
- Biog. and Geneal. Record of LaSalle and Grundy Co., Ill. Chi. Lewis. 1900. 2 Vol.
- Standard Atlas of Grundy Co., Ill. Comp. & Pub. by G. A. Ogle & Co. Chi. 1909.
- Atlas of Grundy Co. and Ill. and Atlas of U.S. Maps. Chi. Warner & Beers, 1874. 93 pp.

Hamilton
- Hist. of Gallatin, Saline, Hamilton, Franklin, and Williamson Co., Chi. Goodspeed. 1887. 961 pp.
- Standard Atlas of Hamilton Co., Ill. Comp. & Pub. by Geo. A. Ogle & Co., Chi. 1906.

Hancock
- Biog. Rev. of Hancock Co. 751 pp. 1907.
- This Is Hancock Co., Ill. by John Drury. Chi. Loree Co. 1955.
- Plat Book of Hancock Co., Ill. Comp. & Pub. by Alden, Ogle & Co. Chi. 1891. 121 pp.
- Bateman, N. & Selby, P. eds. Hist. Excyclo. of Ill. & Hist. of Hancock Co., ed. by Chas. J. Scofield, Chi. Munsell. 1921 2 Vol.
- An Illus. Hist. Atlas of Hancock Co., Ill. Maps. Plats by Gen. Chas. A. Gilchrist, Chi. Andress. 1874. 137 pp.
- Hist. of Hancock Co., Ill. with Hist. of Ill. and Digest of State Laws by W. Gregg. Chi. Chapman. 1880. 1036 pp.
- Plat Book of Hancock Co., by Townships, Carthage, Helms. 1908 48 pp.
- Port. & Biog. Record of Hancock, McDonough and Henderson Co., Ill. Biog. Chi. Lake City Pub. Co. 1894. 598 pp.

Hardin
- Biog. Rev. of Johnson, Massoc, Pope and Hardin Co., Ill. Biog. Chi. Biog. Pub. Co. 1893. 622 pp.
- Centennial Record Hist. Sketch of Hardin Co., Ill. From Earliest Settlement to July 4, 1876. Elizabethtown 1876. 6 pp.

Henderson
- Hist. Encyclo. of Ill. ed. by N. Bateman & P. Selby. Hist. of Henderson Co., J. W. Gordon, ed. Chi. Munsell, 1911. 2 Vol.
- Hist. of Mercer Co. with short Hist. of Henderson Co. Biog. Stat. Old Letters Records. Chi. Hill. 1882. 912 pp.

<u>ILLINOIS</u> (continued)

Henderson
(cont'd)
- Port. & Biog. Record of Hancock, McDonough and Henderson Co., Chi. Lake City Pub. Co. 1894. 598 pp.
- Standard Atlas of Henderson Co., Ill. Comp. & pub. by G. A. Ogle & Co. Chi. 1900.

Henry
- Port. & Biog. Album of Henry Co., Ill. From Earliest Settlement. Chi. Biog. Pub. Co. 1895. 834 pp.
- Port. & Biog. Album of Henry Co., Chapman.
- Biog. Record of Henry Co., Ill. Chi. Clarke. 1901. 725 pp.
- The Hist. of Henry Co., Ill. Biog. Dir. Maps. Laws, Records, Chi. Kett. 1877. 590 pp.
- Hist. of Henry Co., Ill. by Henry L. Kiner. Biog. Chi. Pioneer Pub. Co. 1910. 2 Vol.
- Standard Atlas of Henry Co., Ill. Plats. Directory. Comp. & Pub. by Geo. A. Ogle & Co., Chi. 1911. 137 pp.
- Swank, George. Historic Henry Co.
- Atlas of Henry Co. and Ill. with Atlas of U.S. Maps, Chi. Warner & Beers. 1875. 93 pp.

Iroquois
- Beckwith, H.W. Hist. of Iroquois Co. From Early Authors, Old Maps and Mss. Chi. Hill. 1880. 1139 pp.
- This Is Iroquois Co., Ill. by John Drury. Chi. Toree Co. 1955.
- Illus. Atlas Map of Iroquois Co., Ill. From official and Personal Records. Edwardsville. Brink. 1884. 103 pp.
- Kern, J. W. Past & Present of Iroquois Co., Ill. Biog. Chi. Ill. Clark. 1907. 741 pp.
- Port. & Biog. Record of Iroquois Co., Ill. Biog. Chi. Lake City Pub. Co. 1893. 852 pp.
- Standard Atlas of Iroquois Co., Ill. Comp. & Pub. by Geo. A. Ogle & Co. Chi. 1904.

Jackson
- Port. & Biog. Rec. of Randolph, Jackson, Perry & Monroe Co's. 882 pp. Chi. 1894.
- Hist. of Jackson Co., Ill. Illus. Des. Biog. Phila. Brink. 1878. 137 pp.
- Hist. Sketches of Jackson Co., Ill., also Towns & Cities. Carbondale, Newsome. 1882. 138 pp.
- Standard Atlas of Jackson Co., Ill. Comp. & Pub. by G. A. Ogle & Co. Chi. 1907.

Jasper
- Counties of Cumberland, Jasper and Richland, Ill. Hist. Biog. Chi. Battey. 1884. 839 pp.

ILLINOIS (continued)

Jefferson
- Port. & Biog. Rec. of Clinton, Washington, Marion, and Jefferson Counties. Chi. Chapman. 1894. 285 pp.
- Hist. of Jefferson Co., Ill. ed. by W. H. Perrin. Chi. Globe. 1883. 149 pp.
- Wall's Hist. of Jefferson Co., Ill. by J. A. Wall. Indianapolis. Bowen. 1909. 618 pp.

Jersey
- Hist. Sketch of Jersey Co., Ill. Delivered at Jerseyville, July 4, 1876. By B. B. Hamilton, Jacksonville. Courier, 1876. 36 pp.
- Hamilton, O. B. ed. Hist. of Jersey Co., Ill. Chi. Munsell 1919.
- Hist. of Greene and Jersey Counties, Ill. Springfield. Continental Hist. Co. 1885. 1156 pp.
- Plat Book of Greene & Jersey Counties, Ill. By Geo. A. Ogle & Co. Chi. Hammond. 1893. 96 pp.

Jo Daviess
- Hist. Encyclo. of Ill., ed. by N. Bateman & P. Selby. and Hist. of Jo Daviess Co., ed. by Hon. W. Spensley Chi. Munsell. 1904. 705 pp.
- Port. and Biog. Album of Jo Daviess and Carroll Counties. Chi. Chapman. 1889. 1018 pp.
- Business Dir. of Jo Daviess Co., Ill. 1868. Galenn. Scott. 1868.
- The Hist. of Jo Daviess Co., Ill. Biog. War Records. Stat. Port. Map. Chi. Kett. 1878. 845 pp.
- Plat Book of Jo Daviess Co., Ill. From Actual Surveys and Records. By N. W. Pub. Co., Chi. 1893. 63 pp.

Johnson
- Chapman, L.M.C. A Hist. of John Co., Ill. Herrin News Press. 1925
- The Biog. Rev. of Johnson, Massac, Pope, and Hardin Counties. Chi. Biog. Pub. Co. 1893. 622 pp.

Kane
- Kane Co. Dir. For 1859-60 For Cities, Towns, Villages, Townships Comp. & Pub. by J.C.W. Bailey. Chi. Press & Trib. 1859. 195 pp.
- Bailey, John C. W. Kane Co., Gazettier, With City and Business Directories, Chi. Pub. by author. 347 pp.
- Hist. Encyclo. of Ill. ed. by N. Bateman, P. Selby and Hist. of Kane Co., ed. by Gen. J. S. Wilcox, Chi. Munsell. 1904. 950 pp.
- Commemorative Biog. & Hist. Record of Kane Co., Ill. Port. From Earliest Settlement. Chi. Beers. 1888. 1115 pp.
- The Biog. Record of Kane Co., Ill. Chi. Clarke. 1898. 769 pp.
- Atlas of Kane Co., Ill. Surveys & Co., Rec. By D. W. Ensign & Co. Chi. 1892. 86 pp.
- Hist. of Kane Co., Ill. By Waite Joslyn & F. W. Joslyn. Chi. Pioneer Pub. Co. 1908. 2 V.

ILLINOIS (continued)

Kane
(cont'd)

- (No author). The Past & Present of Kane Co., Ill. Illus. Chi. Wm. LeBaron & Co. 1878. Roy. 8 Vol. 821 pp.

- 20th Century Atlas of Kane Co., Ill. Maps. Chi. Mid-West Pub. Co. 1904. 125 pp.

- Past & Present of Kane Co., Ill. It's Cities & Towns, etc. Dir. War Records. Port. Stat. Map. By H. B. Peirce, A. Merril & W. H. Perrin. Chi. LeBaron, 1878. 826 pp.

- Atlas Map of Kane Co., Ill. From Surveys by Thompson & Everts, Geneva. 1872. 88 pp.

Kankakee

- Bateman, N. & Selby P. eds. Hist. Encyclo. of Ill. and Hist. of Kankakee Co., ed. by W. F. Kenaga & G. R. Letourneau. Chi. Mid-West Pub. Co. 1907. 2 Vol.

- Atlas of Kankakee Co., Ill. Maps. Stat. Illus. Chi. Beers, 1883, 170 pp.

- Port. & Biog. Records of Kankakee Co., Ill. Chi. Lake City Pub. Co. 1893. 736 pp.

Kendall

- Bateman, N. & Selby P. eds. Hist. Encyclo. of Ill. and Hist. of Kendall Co. Special authors and contributors. Chi. Munsell. 1914. 2 Vol.

- Genealogical & Biog. Record of Kendall & Will Co., Ill. Biog. Chi. Biog. Pub. Co. 1901 - 670 pp.

- Biog. Dir. of Kendall Co., Ill. Map. Dir. Laws. Societies. Chi. Fisher, 1876. 114 pp.

- Hist. of Kendall Co., Ill. From Earliest Discoveries by Rev. E. W. Hicks, Aurora. Knickerbocker & Hodder, 1877. 438 pp.

Knox

- This Is Knox Co., Ill. By John Drury. Chi. Loree Co. 1955.

- Atlas Map of Knox Co., Ill. By Andreas, Lyter & Co., Davenport, Iowa. 1870. 91 pp.

- Hist. of Knox Co., Ill. Sketches of Cities, Villages, etc., War Records, Port. Biog. by Chas. C. Chapman & Co. Chi. Blakeley. 1878. 718 pp.

- Port. & Biog. Album of Knox Co., Ill. From Earliest Settlements. Chi. Chapman. 1887. 1108 pp.

- Hist. of Knox Co., Ill. by Albert J. Perry. Chi. Clarke, 1912. 2 vol.

- Hist. Encyclo. of Ill. ed. by N. Bateman, P. Selby & Knox Co. ed. by W. S. and G. C. Gale, Chi. Munsell. 1899. 2 Vol.

- Lawrence, E. P. Centennial Annals of Knox Co., Ill. 1818-1918; by Rebecca Parke Chap., D.A.R. Galesburg. 1918.

- Standard Atlas of Knox Co., Ill. Plats. Dir. Comp. & Pub. by Geo. A. Ogle & Co., Chi. 1903. 107 pp.

- Annals of Knox Co., Com. Cent. of Ill. Statehood 1918. Galesburg Republican Reg. Press, 1918.

ILLINOIS (continued)

Lake
- Hist. Encyclo. of Ill., ed. by N. Bateman & P. Selby, and Hist. of Lake Co., ed. by Hon. Chas. A. Partridge, Chi. Munsell. 1902. 747 pp.
- Hist. & Stat. Sketches of Lake Co., Ill. by E. M. Haines, Waukegan. Howe. 1852. 112 pp.
- Halsey, J. J. ed. Hist. of Lake Co. Bates, Chi. 1912, 872 pp.
- Biog. Album of Lake Co., Chi. Lake City Pub. Co. 1891. 79 pp.
- Stat. & Biog. Hist. of Lake Co., Chi. LeBaron. 1877. 501 pp.
- Lake Co., Chi. Munsell. 1902.
- Atlas of Lake Co., Ogle. Chi. 1907.

La Salle
- Plat Book of La Salle Co. Alden & Ogle. Chi. 1892. 110 pp.
- La Salle Co. Dir. 1858-9 by J.C.W. Bailey. Rand. Chi. 1858,193 pp
- Hist. of La Salle Co. by E. Baldwin, Chi. Rand. 1877. 552 pp.
- Foster, W. R. Pioneer Days In La Salle Co. Ottawa. 1932.
- Hoffman, W. J. Hist. of La Salle Co. Clarke, Chi. 1906. 1177 pp.
- Hist. of La Salle Co. & Cities. Biog. Interstate. Chi. 1886, 2 V.
- Biog. & Geneal. Rec. of La Salle Co. Lewis. Chi. 1900. 2 Vol.
- Atlas of La Salle Co. Ogle. Chi. 1906.
- Atlas of La Salle Co. Warner & Beers. Chi. 1876. 93 pp.
- Past & Present of La Salle Co. Biog. Stat. Dir. War Records.
- Sapp, R. B. Geneal. of La Salle Co. 167 pp. 1926. Typed.

Lawrence
- Ill. Hist. Lawrence Co. J. W. McCleave, ed. Munsell, Chi. 1910 760 pp.
- Atlas of Lawrence Co., Brink. Phila. 1875. 45 pp.
- Hist. of Edwards, Lawrence & Wabash Co. McDonough, Phila. 1883 377 pp.

Lee
- Barge, W. D. Early Lee Co. Barnard & Miller. Chi. 1918.
- Hist. Encyclo. of Ill. Hist. of Lee Co. Bateman, Selby, Bardwell, Munsell. Chi. 1904. 831 pp.
- Hist. of Dixon & Lee Co. Dixon. Telegraph. 1870. 30 pp.
- Hist. of Dixon & Lee Co., Dixon. Telegraph. 1880. 66 pp.
- Atlas of Lee Co. Ogle. Chi. 1900;
- Pioneers of Lee Co. S. G. Smith, ed. Dixon, Kennedy, 1893. 583 pp.
- Hist. of Lee Co. 873 pp. Chi. 1881.
- Stevens, F. E. Lee Co. 2 V. Chi. 1914.

Livingston
- Biog. Album of Livingston Co. Chapman. Chi. 1888.
- Biog. Rec. of Livingston Co. Clarke. Chi. 1900. 584 pp.

ILLINOIS (continued)

Livingston
(cont'd)
- Hist. of Livingston Co. Cities. Mil. Rec. Le Baron. Chi. 1878. 896 pp.
- Atlas of Livingston Co. Cities. Dir. Ogle. Chi. 1911. 153 pp.
- Hist. of Livingston Co. Ill. Hist. Encyclo. Strawn. Johnson & Franzen. Chi. Munsell. 1909. 2 Vol.
- Sparks, W. Livingston Co. In World War. 656 pp.

Logan
- This Is Logan Co., Ill. by John Drury. Chi. Loree Co. 1955.
- Biog. Rec. of Logan Co., Clarke. Chi. 1901. 654 pp.
- Hist. of Logan Co. Biog. Donnelly. Chi. 1878. 560 pp.
- Hyde, J. F. Logan Co. Dir. Cities. State. Biog. Dwight. Palmer. 1880. 381 pp.
- Hyde, J. F. Logan Co. Dir. Cities, Stat. Lincoln. Herald. 1887.
- Hist. of Logan Co. Cities. Biog. Interstate. Chi. 1886. 909 pp.
- Plat & Books of Logan Co., Ogle. Chi. 1893. 87 pp.
- Atlas of Logan Co. Cities. Plats. Dir. Ogle. Chi. 1910. 107 pp.
- Hist. of Logan Co. by L. B. Stringer. Pioneer. Chi. 1911. 2 vols.

Macon
- Plat Book of Macon Co. Alden & Ogle. Chi. 1891. 91 pp.
- Atlas of Macon Co. Chi. Warner & Beers. 1874. 93 pp.
- Hist. of Macon Co. Biog. Phila. Brink. 1880. 242 pp.
- Decatur & Macon Co. Chi. Clarke. 1903. 885 pp.
- This Is Macon Co., Ill. by John Drury. Chi. Loree Co. 1955.
- Nelson, W. E. Decatur & Macon Co. Chi. Pioneer. 1910. 2 Vol.
- Smith, J. W. Hist. of Macon Co. Springfield. Rokher. 1876. 304 pp.
- Port. Rec. of Macon Co. Lake City Pub. Co. Chi. 1893. 736 pp.
- Richmond, Mabel E. Cent. Hist. of Decatur & Macon Co. Review. Decatur. 1930. 470 pp.
- Hist. of Decatur Mnfg. Biog., Decatur. 1871. 551 pp.

Macoupin
- Atlas of Macoupin Co. Warner & Beers. Chi. 1875. 93 pp.
- Biog. Rec. of Macoupin Co. Chi. Biog. Pub. Co. 1891. 902 pp.
- Hist. of Macoupin Co. Phila. Brink. 1879. 288 pp.
- Record of Macoupin Co. 1828-69 by J. Moran, Springfield, 1897. 201 pp.
- Pl. Book of Macoupin Co. Amer. Atlas Co. Chi. Ogle. 1893. 79 pp.
- Biog. Rec. of Macoupin Co. Chi. Richmond & Arnold. 1904. 558 pp.
- Walker, C. A. ed. Hist. of Macoupin Co. Biog. Chi. Clarke. 1911. 2 V.

Madison
- Biog. Rec. of Madison Co. Chi. Biog. Pub. Co. 1894. 548 pp.
- Encyclo. & Atlas of Madison Co. St. Louis. Brink. 1873. 195 pp.
- Hist. of Madison Co. Biog. Edwardville. Brink. 1882. 603 pp.

ILLINOIS (continued)

Madison — Gaz. of Madison Co. & Alton. Dir. Alton. Hair. 1866. 292 pp.
(cont'd) — Atlas of Madison Co. Ogle. Chi. 1906.

— New Atlas of Madison Co. Riniker, Hagnauer & Dickson. St. Louis.
Barnard. 1892. 84 pp.

— Cent. Hist. of Madison Co. 1812-1912 by Norton, Alton & Flagg
& Hoerner. Chi. & N. Y. Lewis. 1912. 2 V.

Marion — Brinkerhoff's Hist. of Marion Co. Bowen, Indianapolis. 1901.

— Biog. Hist. of Richland, Clay & Marion Co. Bowen, Indpls. 1909.
608 pp.

— Hist. of Marion & Clinton Co. Brink. McDonough, Phila. 1881. 316pp.

— Brinkerhoff's Hist. of Marion Co. Indpls. Bowen. 1909. 862 pp.

— Biog. Rec. of Clinton, Washington, Marion & Jefferson Co. Chi.
Chapman 1894. 285 pp.

— Pl. Book of Marion Co. Occidental. Ogle. Chi. 1892. 83 pp.

Marshall — Pl. Book of Marshall & Putnam Co. Alden. Ogle. Chi. 1890. 82 pp.

— Biog. Rec. of Bureau, Marshall & Putnam Co. Chi. Clarke.
1896. 737 pp.

— Ellsworth, S. Olden Time of Putnam & Marshall Co. Lacon Journal.
1880. 772 pp.

— Ford, H. A. Early Hist. of Putnam, Marshall, Bureau & Stark
Co. Lacon. 1860. 160 pp.

— Atlas of Marshall Co., Ill. & U.S. Chi. Warner & Beers, 1873.
95 pp.

— Atlas of Marshall & Putnam Co. Dir. Ogle. Chi. 1901. 98 pp.

Mason — This Is Mason Co., Ill. by John Drury. Chi. Loree Co. 1955.

— Hist. of Menard & Mason Co. Baskin. 1879. 872 pp.

— Biog. Rec. of Tazewell & Mason Co. Chi. Biog. Pub. 1894. 711 pp.

— Atlas Map of Mason Co. Phila. Brink. 1874. 100 pp.

— Cent. Hist. of Mason Co. by J. Cochrane. Springfield, Rokker
1876 352 pp.

— Onstot, T. G. Pioneers of Menard & Mason Co. 1830-50. Forest
City. Onstot. 1902. 400 pp.

Massac — Biog. Rev. of Johnson, Massac, Pope & Hardin Co. Chi. Biog.
Pub. Co. 1893. 622 pp.

— Page, O. J. Hist. of Massac Co. Port. Metropolis. 1900. 383 pp.

— Geo. W. May. Hist. of Massac Co. Ill. Galesburg, Wagoner, 1955.

McDonough — Atlas of McDonough Co. Andreas. Davenport. 1871. 75 pp.

— Hist. of McDonough Co. Cities. Dir. Clarke. Springfield Lusk. 1878. 692 pp.

— This Is McDonough Co., Ill. by John Drury. Chi. Loree Co. 1955.

— Hist. of McDonough Co. Pre-Hist. Mil. Springfield. Cont. Hist. Co. 1885. 1158 pp.

— Port. & Biog. Rec. of Hancock, McDonough & Henderson Counties. Chi. Lake City Pub. 1894. 598 pp.

— Hist. of McDonough Co. Hist. Encyclo. of Ill. ed. by Bateman, Selby & McLean. Chi. Munsell. 1907. 1055 pp.

— McDonough Co. Hist. Add. at 100th Anniv. Macomb. Ill. 1926.

McHenry — McHenry Co. 2 Vol. Chi. 1922.

— Atlas of McHenry Co. Everts, Bakin & Stewart. Chi. 1872. 66 pp.

— Hist. of McHenry Co. Biog. Pre-Hist. Mil. Chi. Interstate Pub. 1885. 941 pp.

— Plat Book of McHenry Co. Ogle. Chi. 1892. 104 pp.

— Biog. Dir. of McHenry Co. Walker. Chi. 1877. 852 pp.

McLean — William B. Brigham. The Story of McLean Co. & Its Schools. Bloomington, Ill. 1951.

— Gazette of McLean Co. & Cities. Dir. Mil. Bailey. Chi. 1866. 276 pp.

— Port. Biog. Chi. Chapman. 1887. 1210 pp.

— Duis, Dr. E. Old Times In McLean Co. Biog. Mil. Bloomington Leader. 1874. 865 pp.

— Hasbrouck, J. L. Hist. of McLean Co. Topeka. Hist. Pub. 1924. 2 V.

— Hist. of McLean Co. Port. Stat. Chi. LeBaron. 1879. 1078 pp.

— Port & Biog. Album of McLean Co., Ill.

— Pl. Book of McLean Co. Surveys & Rec. H. W. Pub. Co. Chi. Ogle, 1895. 85 pp.

— Atlas of McLean Co. & Atlas of U. S. Chi. Warner. 1874. 89 pp.

— Biog. Rec. of McLean Co. Chi. Clarke. 1899. 830 pp.

— Hist. Record of McLean Co. Hist. Encyclo. of Ill. Bateman, Selby, Prince & Burnham. Chi. Munsell. 1908. 2 V.

Menard — This is Menard Co., Ill. by John W. Drury. Chi. Loree 1955.

— Hist. of Menard & Mason Co. Chi. Baskin. 1879. 872 pp.

— Illus. Atlas of Menard Co. Phila. Brink. 1874. 117 pp.

— Menard & Salem - Lincoln Souvenir Album. Pub. by Women's Club. Petersburg 1893. 30 pp.

— Miller, Rev. R. D. Menard Co. Chi. Clarke. 1905. 552 pp.

— Onstot, T. G. Pioneers of Menard & Mason Co. Forest City, Onstot. 1902. 400 pp.

ILLINOIS (continued)

Mercer
- Bassett, I. N. Hist. of Mercer Co. 2 V. Chi. 1914.
- This Is Mercer Co. by John W. Drury. Chi. Loree. 1955.
- Plat Book of Mercer Co. Alden. Ogle. Chi. 1892. 85 pp.
- Hist. of Mercer Co. Hist. Encyclo. of Ill. Bateman, Selby, Lorimer, Chi. Munsell. 1903. 798 pp.
- Hist. of Mercer & Henderson Co. Chi. Hill. 1882. 912 pp.

Monroe
- Port. & Biog. Rec. of Randolph, Jackson, Perry & Monroe Co. Chi. Biog. Pub. 1894. 882 pp.
- Hist. of Randolph, Monroe & Perry Co. Phila. McDonough. 1883 510 pp.
- Atlas of Monroe Co. Ogle. Chi. 1901.

Montgomery
- Hist. of Montgomery Co. Hist. Encyclo. of Ill. Bateman, Selby & Strange. ed. Chi. Munsell. 1918. 2 V. 572 pp.
- Illus. Atlas of Montgomery Co. Phila. Brink. 1874. 109 pp.
- Port. & Biog. Rec. of Montgomery & Bond Co. Chi. Chapman, 1892. 518 pp.
- Traylor, J. L, Montgomery Co. Chi. Clarke. 1904. 770 pp.
- Atlas, Montgomery Co. Dir. Ogle. Chi. 1912. 125 pp.
- Perrin, W. H. ed. Hist. of Bond & Montgomery Co. Chi. Baskin. 1882. 333 pp.
- Montgomery & Bond Co. Port & Biog. Chi. 1892. 520 pp.

Morgan
- Pl. Bank of Morgan Co. Amer. Atlas Co. Chi. Ogle, 1894. 87 pp.
- Atlas of Morgan Co. Andress, Lyter. Davenport, 1872. 127 pp.
- Hist. of Morgan Co. Hist. Encyclo. of Ill. Bateman, Selby & Short. Chi. Munsell. 1906. 984 pp.
- Port. & Biog. Album of Morgan & Scott Co. Chapman, 1889. 620 pp.
- Hist. of Morgan Co. Biog. Stat. Dir. Mil. Chi. Donelly. 1878. 768 pp.
- Earnes, C. M. Hist of Morgan & Classic Jacksonville. 1884. Journal 1885. 336 pp.
- English, S.J. Morgan Co. 156 pp. 1927.
- Henderson, J. G. Hist. of "Sangamon Country". Early Morgan, Scott & Cass Co. Davenport. Day. 1873. 33pp.
- Wheeler, G. S. Morgan Co. Geneal. 90 pp. 1945. Type.

Moultrie
- Port. & Biog. Rec. of Shelby & Moultrie Co. Chi. Biog. Pub. 1891. 726 pp.
- Hist. of Shelby & Moultrie Co. Phila. Brink. 1881. 344 pp.
- Atlas of Moultrie Co. Cities. Dir. Ogle. Chi. 1896, 54 pp.
- Atlas of Moultrie Co. & U. S. Chi. Warner & Beers, 1875. 93 pp.

ILLINOIS (continued)

Ogle
- Hist. of Ogle Co. Hist. Encyclo. of Ill. Bateman, Selby, Horace & R. Kauffman. Chi. Munsell. 1909. 2 V.
- Hist. of Ogle Co. & Early N. W. Polo Advertiser. Boss. 1859. 76 pp.
- Port. & Biog. Album of Ogle Co. Chi. Chapman, 1886. 905 pp.
- Biog. Rec. of Ogle Co. Chi. Clarke. 1899. 492 pp.
- Atlas of Ogle Co. Everts, Baskin & Stewart. Chi. 1872. 99 pp.
- Hist. of Ogle Co. Cities. Biog. Dir. Mil. Stat. Chi. Kett. 1878. 858 pp.
- Atlas of Ogle Co. Cities. Dir. Ogle. Chi. 1912. 129 pp.
- Pl. Bk. of Ogle Co., Ogle, Chi. 1893. 112 pp.

Peoria
- Atlas of Peoria Co. Andreas. Chi. 1873. 196 pp.
- Hist. of Peoria Co., Ill. Hist. Encyclo. Bateman, Selby, McCulloh ed. Chi. & Peoria. Munsell. 1902.
- Port. & Biog. Album of Peoria Co., Chi. Biog. Pub. 1890. 984 pp.
- Daily, J. Peoria Co's Centennial Address, Aug. 26, 1925.
- Atlas of Peoria City & Co. Dir. Henbinger. Chi. Ogle. 1896. 148 pp.
- Hist. of Peoria Co. & N.W. Mil. Stat. Biog. Chi. Johnson 1880 851 pp.
- McCulloch, D. Early Peoria & Chi. Address. Chi. Hist. Socy. 1904.
- Peoria City & Co. by Col. J. M. Rice, Chi. Clarke. 1912. 2 V.

Perry
- Perry Co. Agri. Assn. Cent. Com. 1956. Pinckneyville, Ill.
- Port. & Biog. Rec. of Randolph, Jackson, Perry & Munroe Co., Chi. Biog. Pub. 1894. 882 pp.
- Hist. of Randolph, Monroe, Perry Co. Phila. McDonough 1883. 510 pp.

Piatt
- Bateman, N. & Selby, eds. Hist. Encyclo. of Hist of Piatt Co. Chi. Munsell. 1917. 2 V.
- Bateman, Hist. Encyclo. of Ill. & Hist. of Piatt Co. 1937. Munsell.
- McIntosh. Past & Present of Piatt Co. Clarke. 1903.
- Hist. of Piatt Co. (no date) Shepard & Johnson.
- This Is Piatt Co., Ill. by John Drury. Chi. Loree. 1955.
- Port. & Biog. Album of DeWitt & Piatt Co. Chi. Chapman, 1891. 992 pp.
- Piatt, E. C. Hist. of Piatt Co. & Ill. Illus. Chi. Shepard & Johnston, 1883. 643 pp.
- Atlas of Piatt Co. Cities, Dir. Ogle. Chi. 1910. 73 pp.
- Atlas of Piatt Co., Ill. & U.S. Chi. Warner & Beers. 1875. 93 pp.

Pike
- Atlas of Pike Co. Andreas, Lyter. Davenport. 1872. 138 pp.
- Port. & Biog. Album of Pike & Calhoun Co. Chi. Biog. Pub. Co. 1891 808 pp.
- Hist. of Pike Co. Cities. Port. Biog. Chi. Chapman. 1880. 966 pp.

ILLINOIS (continued)

Pike
(cont'd)
- This Is Pike Co., Ill. John Drury. Chi. Loree. 1955.
- Hist. of Pike Co. Cent. Address by W.A. Grimshaw at Pittsfield. July 4, 1876. Pittsfield, Democrat. 1877. 46pp.
- Massie, M. D. Pike Co. Past & Present. Biog. Chi. Clarke. 1906 751 pp.
- Atlas of Pike Co. Cities. Dir. Ogle. Chi. 1912. 121 pp.

Pope
- Biog. Rev. of Johnson, Massac, Pope & Hardin Co., Chi. Biog. Pub. 1893. 622 pp.

Pulaski
- Perrin, W. H. Hist. of Alexander, Union & Pulaski Co. Chi. Baskin. 1883. 338 pp.
- Moyers, W. N. Hist. of Pulaski Co. 1843-1943. Enterprise-Mound City. 1943. 100 pp.

Putnam
- Pl. Bk. of Marshall & Putnam Co., Alden. Ogle. Chi. 1890. 82 pp.
- Biog. Rec. of Bureau, Marshall & Putnam Co. Chi. Clarke. 1896. 737 pp.
- Ellsworth, S. Rec. of Co. of Putnam & Marshall, Lacon. Journal. 1880. 772 pp.
- Ford, H. A. Hist. of Putnam & Marshall Co. Early Bureau and Stark Co. Lacon. 1860. 160 pp.
- Atlas of Marshall & Putnam Co. Ogle. Chi. 1911. 98 pp.

Randolph
- Port. & Biog. Rec. of Randolph, Jackson, Perry & Monroe Co. Chi. Biog. Pub. 1894. 882 pp.
- Hist. Atlas of Randolph Co. Phila. Brink. 1875. 102 pp.
- Hist. of Randolph, Monroe & Perry Co. Phila. McDonough 1883 510pp.
- Meese, W. A., Ill. & Randolph Co., Ill. Hist. Socy Journal, V 2. 1918.
- Montague, E. J. Randolph Co. and Kaskockia Is. 1859. Leighty 158 pp. Sparta. 1948.
- Dir. & Hist. of Randolph Co., E. J. Montague, Alton, Courier 1859. 246 pp.

Richland
- Co. of Cumberland, Jasper & Richland. Chi. Battey. 1884, 839 pp.
- Biog. Hist. of Richland, Clay & Marion Co. Indpls. Bowen 1909 608 pp.
- Atlas of Richland Co., Dir. Ogle. Chi. 1901. 33pp.

Rock Island
- Hist. of Rock Island Co., Ill. Hist. Encyclo., Bateman, N. & Selby. Chi. Munsell. 1914. 2 Vol.
- Port. & Biog. Album & Rock Is. Co., Chi. Biog. Pub. 1885, 812 pp.
- Biog. Rec. of Rock Island Co. Chi. Clarke 1897. 466 pp.

ILLINOIS (continued)

Rock Island
(continued)
- Atlas of Rock Is. Co., Dir. Davenport, Iowa Pub. 1905. 184 pp.
- Past & Present of Rock Is. Co. Biog. Mil. Chi. Kett. 1877. 474pp.
- Hist. Rock Is. Co. From Earliest Period. Rock Is. Kramer. 1908.
- Meese, W. A. Early Rock Is. Moline Hist. Socy. 1905.
- Pl. Bk. of Rock Is. Co. Rec. of W.W. Pub. Ogle. Chi. 1894. 74 pp.
- Illus. Souvenir of Rock Is. Co. Mil. Rock Is. Quayle. 1895. 76 pp.
- Past & Present of Rock Is. Co. Biog. Dir. Mil. Chi. 1877. 474 pp.
- Port. & Biog. Album of Rock Is. Co. Illus. Chi. 1885.

St. Clair
- Hist. of St. Clair Co. Hist. Encyclo. Ill. Bateman, Selby & Wilderman. Chi. Munsell. 1907. 2 V.
- Hist. of St. Clair Co. Biog. Brink. McDonough. Phila. 1881, 400pp.
- Port. & Biog. Record of St. Clair Co., Chi. Chapman. 1892. 672 pp.
- Kern, J. F. Early Hist. of Oldest Co. In Ill. Springfield, 5-12-16 n.p.-n.d.
- Illus. Hist. Atlas of St. Clair Co. Warner & Beers, Chi. 1874, 115 pp.
- Hist. of St. Clair Co. Cent. Cel. July 4, 1876. West. Belleville 41 pp.
- Hist. of St. Clair Co. Port. Biog. Edwardsville, Phila. 1881. 371pp.

Saline
- Hist. of Gallatin, Saline, Hamilton, Franklin & Williamson Co. Chi. Goodspeed. 1887. 961 pp.
- Atlas of Saline Co. Ogle. Chi. 1909;

Sangamon
- Sangamon Co. Hist. Gazetteer. Bailey. Chi. 1866. 426 pp.
- Hist. of Sangamon. Hist. Encyclo. of Ill. Bateman & Selby, ed. Chi. Munsell. 1912. 2 V.
- Blankmeyer, Mrs. C. H. The Sangamon Co., Bd. of Educ. 1935. 60 pp.
- Atlas of Sangamon Co. Phila. Brink. 1874. 108 pp.
- Port. & Biog. Album of Sangamon Co. Chi. Chapman 1891. 856 pp.
- Hist. of Sangamon Co. Port. Biog. Chi. Interstate. 1881. 1067 pp.
- Pl. Bk. of Sangamon Co. Field. Chi. Ogle. 1894. 88 pp.
- Power, J. C. Hist. of Early Sangamon Co. Springfield, Wilson 1876. 797 pp.
- Power, J. C. Hist. of Sangamon Co. Port. Illus. 1067 pp.
- Springfield, Dir. & Sangamon Co. Rec. Biog. Springfield. Tousley. 1877. 276 pp.
- Wallace, J. Past & Present of Springfield & Sangamon Co. Chi. Clarke. 1904. 2569 pp.

ILLINOIS (continued)

Schuyler
- Atlas of Schuyler Co. Andreas, Lyter. Davenport. 1872. 65pp.
- Hist. of Schuyler Co. Hist. Encyclo. of Ill. Bateman, Selby & Dyson. Chi. Munsell. 1908. 975 pp.
- Hist. of Schuyler & Brown Co. Phila. Brink. 1882. 412 pp.
- This Is Schuyler Co., Ill. John W. Drury. Chi. Loree. 1955.
- Metz, H. S. Hist. of Schuyler Co. Cent. Address. July 4, 1876. Rushville. 14 pp.

Scott
- Atlas of Scott Co. Andreas, Lyter. Davenport. 1873. 51 pp.
- Port. & Biog. Album of Morgan & Scott Co. Chi. Chapman. 1889 620pp.
- Henderson, J. G. Early Hist. of "Sangamon Country" & Early Morgan, Scott & Cass Co. Davenport. 1873. 33pp.
- Knapp, N. M. Hist. of Scott Co. Speech at Winchester,

Shelby
- Hist. of Shelby Co. Hist. Encyclo. Ill. Bateman, Selby, Chafee. Chi. Munsell. 1910. 1103 pp.
- Port. & Biog. Rec. of Shelby & Moultrie Co., Chi. Biog. Pub. 1891. 726 pp.
- Hist. of Shelby & Moultrie Co. Phila. Brink. 1881. 344pp.
- Pl. Bk. of Shelby Co. Ogle. Chi. 1895. 56 pp.
- Atlas of Shelby Co. & Ill. & N.S. Chi. Warmer & Beers, 1875 93 pp.
- Hist. & Biog. Album of Shelby Co. Port. Shelbyville, Wilder. 1900. 313 pp.

Stark
- This Is Stark Co. By John W. Drury. Chi. Loree. 1955.
- Ford, H. A. Hist. of Putnam & Marshall Co. & Early Bureau & Stark Co. Lacon. 1860. 160 pp.
- Hall, J. K. Stark Co. People & Settlements. Chi. Pioneer. 1916. 2 V.
- Leeson, M. A. Stark Co. Biog. War Rec. Chi. Leeson. 1887. 708 pp.
- Atlas of Stark Co. Ogle. Chi. 1907.
- Shallenberger, Mrs. E. H. Stark Co. Pioneers. Cambridge. Seaton. 1876. 328 pp.
- Atlas of Stark Co. & Ill. & U.S. Chi. Warner & Beers. 1873. 95pp.
- Atlas of Stark Co. Biog. 1873. 39 pp.

Stephenson
- Atkins, S. D. Hist. of Stephenson Co. Freeport Journal, July 4, 1876.
- Port. & Biog. Album of Stephenson Co. Chapman. 1888. 776 pp.
- Lucille McGray, "A Story of Stephenson Co. & Freeport". Freeport. 1950. mimeo.
- Fulwider, A. Hist. of Stephenson Co. Clark. 1910.

ILLINOIS (continued)

Stephenson - Johnston, W. J. Hist. of Stephenson Co. & Early N.W. Freeport.
(cont'd)   Burnside 1854. 102 pp.

           - Johnston, Wm. Hist. of Stephenson Co. Pub. By Ill. 1923. 217-320pp.

           - Philip L. Keister, Stephenson Co. Roads. Freeport. 1955.

           - Pl. Bk. of Stephenson Co., N.W. Pub. Co. Chi. 1894. 67 pp.

           - Atlas of Stephenson Co. Thompson & Everts. Geneva. 1871. 66 pp.

           - Tilden, M. H. Hist. of Stephenson Co. Western Hist. 1880, 786 pp.

           - Pioneers of Stephenson Co. Pioneer Pub. 1900.

           - Pease, T. C. Co. Archives of Ill. Pub. By State. 1915. 619-32pp.

           - Stephenson Co. W.P.A. Proj. Hist. Rec. Survey. 1938.

Tazewell   - Allensworth, Ben C. Hist. of Tazewell Co. Chi. Munsell. 1905.
             1103 pp.

           - This Is Tazewell Co. By John W. Drury. Chi. Loree. 1955.

           - Atlas of Tazewell Co. Andreas, Lyter. Davenport. 1873. 133pp.

           - Hist. of Tazewell Co., Ill. Hist. Encyclo. Bateman, Selby, Allens-
             worth, ed. Chi. Munsell. 1905. 2 V.

           - Port. & Biog. Rec. of Tazewell & Mason Co. Chi. Biog. Pub. 1894,
             711 pp.

           - Hist. of Tazewell Co. Port. Biog. Chi. Chapman. 1879. 794 pp.

           - Atlas of Tazewell Co. Dir. Ogle. Chi. 1910. 127 pp.

Union   - Atlas of Union Co. Griffing, Phila. Lake. 1881. 49 pp.
           - Atlas of Union Co. Ogle. Chi. 1908.

           - Hist. of Alexander, Union & Pulaski Co., ed. by W. H. Pervin.
             Chi. Baskin. 1883. 338 pp.

Vermillion - Beckwith, W. H. Hist. of Vermillion Co. Hill. 1879. 1041 pp.

           - Atlas of Vermillion Co. Cities. Danville. Boudinot. 1907. 57 maps.

           - This Is Vermillion Co., Ill. by John W. Drury. Chi. Loree. 1954.

           - Hixon, W. W. & Co. Atlas of Vermillion Co. Hixon. Rockford, 275 pp.

           - Hixon, W. W. & Co. Hist. Atlas Map. Brink. 1875. 121 pp.

           - Port. & Biog. Album of Vermillion Co. Chapman. Chi. 1889. 772 pp.

           - Coffeen, H. A. Hist. of Vermillion Co. Danville. 1870. 116 pp.

           - Pearson, G. Past & Present Vermillion Co. Chi. Clarke. 1903. 1158pp.

           - Jones, Lottie. Hist. of Vermillion Co. Pioneer Pub. 1911.
             Chi. 892 pp.

           - Pearson, G. Past & Present. Vermillion Co. Clarke. Chi. 1903,
             1158 pp.

           - Atlas of Vermillion Co. Dir. Ogle. Chi. 1895. 84 pp.

           - Tilton, C. C. ed. Cent. of Vermillion Co. 1826-1926. Danville, 1926.

           - Tuggle, L. A. Hist. Days In Vermillion Co. 1934-40. Pamphlet 102pp.

ILLINOIS (continued)

Vermillion — Williams, J. M. Vermillion Co. Hist. Pub. Indpls. 1930. 1070 pp.
(cont'd) — W.P.A. Inventory of Co. Archives #92 Vermillion Co. 1940. 200 pp.
— Atlas of Vermillion Co. Ogle. Chi. 1915. 200 pp;

Wabash — Wabash Co., Ill. Hist. Encyclo. Bateman, Selby, Risley, Chi.
Munsell. 1911. 828 pp.
— Hist. of Edward, Lawrence & Wabash Co. Phila. McDonough 1883 377pp

Warren — Hist. of Warren Co. Hist. Encyclo. of Ill. Bateman, Selby,
Moffett & Rogers. Chi. Munsell. 1903. 2 V.
— Port. & Biog. Album of Warren Co. Chi. Chapman, 1886. 779 pp.
— Past & Pres. of Warren Co. Biog. Dir. Mil. Stat. Chi. Kett.
1877. 352 pp.
— Pl. Bk. of Warren Co. Ogle. Chi. 1893. 79 pp.
— Atlas of Warren Co. Dir. Ogle. Chi. 1912. 83 pp.
— Robinson, L. E. ed. Hist. & Biog. Rec. of Monmouth & Warren
Co. Chi. Munsell. 1927. 2 V.
— Atlas of Warren Co. & Ill. & U. S. Chi. Warner. 1872. 95 pp.

Washington — Blue Book of Wash. Co., Ill. Sept. 1, 1959. Prep. by Wm. F.
Boeschen, County Clerk. (n. p. n. d.)
— Hist. of Wash. Co. Biog. Phila. Brink. 1879. 97 pp.
— Port. & Biog. Rec. of Clinton, Wash., Marion & Jefferson Co.
Chi. Chapman. 1894. 285 pp.
— Atlas of Wash. Co. Ogle. Chi. 1906.

Wayne — Hist. of Wayne & Clay Co. Chi. Globe. 1884. 242 pp.
— Atlas of Wayne Co. Griffing. Phila. Lake. 1881. 63 pp.
— Atlas of Wayne Co. Dir. Ogle. Chi. 1910. 85 pp.

White — Hist. of White Co. Port. Biog. Chi. Interstate, 1883. 972 pp.
— Atlas of White Co. Evansville. Keller & Fuller. 1901. 45 pp.
— Robert M. Smith. The Salt Creek Colony of Egypt (White Co.,
Ill. Carmi, Ill. Times. 1955.

Whiteside — Whiteside Co. Educ. Assn. Centennial Anniversary. 1856-1956
(Sterling, Ill. 1956).
— Bent, C. ed. Hist. of Whiteside Co., Ill. Biog. 1877. 536 pp.
— Port. & Biog. Album of Whiteside Co. Chi. Chapman 1885 942 pp.
— Biog. Rec. of Whiteside Co. Chi. Clarke. 1900. 522 pp.
— Davis, W.H. Hist. of Whiteside Co. Biog. Chi. Pioneer Pub. 1908
1908, 2 V.
— Pl. Bk. of Whiteside Co. Ogle. Chi. 1893. 118 pp.
— Atlas of Whiteside Co. Dir. Ogle Chi. 1912.
— Atlas of Whiteside Co. Ill. & U.S. Chi. Warner & Beers 1872 95pp

Will — Biog. Rec. of Kendall & Will Co. Chi. Biog. 1901 670 pp.
— Port. & Biog. Album of Will Co. Biog. Chi. Chapman 1890 771 pp.
— Pioneer Settlement of Will Co. Chi. Hist. Dir. Pub. Co. Mill.
1884. 485 pp.
— Knight, R. & Zench, L. Mt. Joliet In Ill. Hist. Springfield 1930
Journal of Ill. Hist. V. 23 #1 Apr. 1930.

ILLINOIS (continued)

Will
(cont'd)
- Mane, A. Hist. of Will Co. Topeka Hist. Pub. Co. 1928. 2 V.
- Pl. Bk. of Will Co. Ogle. Chi. 1893. 81 pp.
- Atlas of Will Co. Dir. Ogle. Chi. 1909. 163 pp.
- Stevens, W. W. Elwood, J. J. Ferriss, Grinton, Henderson & Clement. Past & Present of Will Co. Chi. Clarke. 1907 2 V.
- Atlas Map of Will Co. Thompson's & Burr. Elgin. 1873. 135 pp.
- Early Hist. of Joliet & Will Co. Lectures by G. H. Woodruff at Hist. Socy of Joliet Dec. 1873 and Mar. 1874. Joliet, Goodspeed 1874. 108 pp.
- Woodruff, G. H. Patriotism of Will Co. War Records. Joliet Goodspeed. 1876. 82 pp.
- Hist. of Will Co. Cities, Port. by Woodruff, Perrin & Hill, Chi. LeBaron. 1878. 995 pp.

Williamson
- Paul M. Angle. Bloody Williamson. (N.Y. Knopf 1952).
- Erwin, Milo. Hist. of Williamson Co. Mil. Hist. Marion 1876. Herrin News 1914. 286 pp.
- Hubbs, B. B. Williamson Co. 246 pp. Herrin 1939.
- Hist. of Gallatine, Saline, Hamilton, Franklin & Williamson Co. Chi. Goodspeed. 1887. 961 pp.
- Atlas of Williamson Co. Ogle. Chi. 1908.
- Wilcox, J. F. Hist. Souvernir of Williamson Co. Le Cross Pr. Effingham. 1905. 223 pp.
- Wilcox, J. F. Hist. Souvenir of Williamson Co. From Founding Effingham. Le Crosse. 1905. 47 pp.

Winnebago
- Hist. of Winnebago Co., C. A. Church, ed. Hist. Encyclo. of 1916, Munsell. 347 pp. 2 V.
- Port. & Biog. Rec. of Winnebago Co. & Boone Co. Biog. Pub. Chi. 1892. 1325 pp.
- Church, C. A. Hist. of Rockford & Winnebago Co. 1834. 1861 N. Eng. Lacy. Rockford. 100 387 pp.
- Church, C. A. Rockford & Winnebago Co. Biog. Clarke Chi. 1905 840 pp.
- Hist. of Winnebago Co. Cities. Biog. Mil. Chi. Kett. 1877 672 pp.
- Atlas of Winnebago Co. Ogle. Chi. 1905.
- Atlas of Winnebago Co. & Boone Co. Chi. Page 1886 120 pp.

Woodford
- Port. & Biog. Album of Woodford Co. Chi. Chapman 1889 597 pp.
- This Is Woodford Co. by John Drury. Chi. Loree. 1955.
- Biog. Rec. of Livingston & Woodford Co. Chi. Clarke. 1900. 682 pp.
- Past & Present of Woodford Co. Dir. Mil. Chi. La Baron 1878. 660 pp.
- Moore, R. L. Hist. of Woodford Co. Eureka Co., Republican 1910 248pp
- Moore, R. L. ed. Geog. Hist. & Civics of Woodford Co. Eureka, Woodford Co. Teachers Assn. n. d.
- Atlas of Woodford Co. Pl. Dir. Ogle. Chi. 1912 101 pp
- Radford, B. J. Hist. of Woodford Co. Peoria. Dowdall. 1877.
- Atlas of Woodford Co. & Ill. & U.S. Chi. Warner & Beers 1873. 95 pp.
- Alvord, C. W. The Counties of Ill. State Hist. Lib. 1907.
- W.P.A. Inventory of County Archives of Ill.

INDIANA

W.P.A. **Inventory of County Archives of Indiana.**
County Histories in some form have been written of every County.

Adams
- Adams & Wells Co., Lewis, 1887. 1025 pp.
- Lynch, M.C.M., Adams, Jay, Randolph Co. 1896. 396 pp.
- Quinn, F., Adams Co. 1945. 141 pp.
- Snow, J. F. Hist. of Adams Co. Bowen, 1907. 477 pp.
- Zyndall, J. W. & Leah, O.E.Adams & Wells Co., Lewis. 1918 985 pp.

Allen
- Helm, T.B. ed. Allen Co. Hist. Biog. Kingman, Chi. 1880. 188 pp.
- Taylor, Mrs. I. H., Township of Allen Co.

Bartholomew
- Atlas with Maps. Hist. 1879.
- Hist. of Bartholomew Co. Brant & Fuller. Chi. 1888. 892 pp.
- Biog. Rec. Bartholomew & Jackson Cos. 1904. 752 pp.

Benton
- Birch, J. S., Hist. of Benton Co. & Oxford.
- Brace, E. & Swan, R. Hist. of Benton Co. Fowler, 1930. 4 vol.
- Brace, Elmore. Annals of Benton Co.
- Brace, Elmore. Land of Potawatoni. Benton Co.
- Mitten, George. Union Township. Benton Co.
- Biog. Hist. of Tippecanoe, White, Jasper, Newton, Benton, Warren and Pulaski Cos. 1899. 2 v.

Blackford
- Biog. & Hist. Rec. of Jay and Blackford Cos. 901 pp. Chi. 1887.
- Shinn, B. G., Blackford & Grant Cos. 1914. 2 v.
- Shinn, B. G. Blackford Co. Memoirs. Bowen. Chi. 1900. 750 pp.

Boone
- Crist, L. M. Boone Co. 2 v. Indpls. 1914.
- Harden, S. Early Boone Co., Indpls. 1887. 498 pp. Boone & Clinton Co. Biog. 1895.

Brown
- Blanchard, C., Counties of Morgan, Monroe & Brown. Hist. & Biog. 800 pp. Chi. 1884.

Carroll
- Helm, T.B. Carroll County. Illus & Biog. 352 pp. Chi. 1882.
- Stewart, J. H., Early Carroll Co. 372 pp. Cin. 1872.
- Odell, J. C., Hist. of Carroll Co. Bowen. Indpls. 1916. 107 pp.
- Atlas. Hist. Illus. 1874.

Cass
- Atlas. Kingman. 1878.
- Blanchard, Chas. Hist. of Cass, Miami, Howard & Tipton Co, Chi. Lewis. 1898. Biog.
- Helm, T. B., Cass Co. 1878. 63 pp.

Cass
(cont'd)
- Helm, Thos. B., Hist. of Cass Co. Chi. Brand & Fuller,
  1886. 976 pp.
- Powell, John Z., Hist. of Cass Co. Lewis. Chi. & N.Y., 1913.
  1207 pp.
- Tabor, G., Logansport & Cass Co. 1947. 142 pp.
- Biog. & General Hist. of Cass, Miami, Howard & Tipton Cos.
  1898. 2 v.

Clark
- Baird, Lewis C., Hist. of Clark Co. 1909.
- Counties of Clark, Crawford, Harrison, Floyd, Jefferson,
  Jennings, Scott & Washington. Biog. Hist. John M. Gresham,
  1889. 300 pp.

Clay
- Blanchard, Chas. ed. Co. of Clay & Owen, Biog. Chi. 1884,
  966 pp.
- Travis, W. ed. Clay Co. 1909. 2 v.

Clinton
- Boone & Clinton Co., Biog. Bowen. Chi. 1885. 908 pp.
- Claybaugh, Jos., Hist. of Clinton Co., Biog. Indpls. Bowen, 1913.
  982 pp.
- Clinton Co. Cent. By Frankfort Morn.Times. 1930. 103 pp.
- Hist. of Clinton Co. Inter-State Pub. 1886. Chi. 924 pp.
- Kingman Bros. Illus. Atlas of Clinton Co. Chi. 1878. 105 pp.
- Map & Hist. of Clinton Co. Frankfort. 1927.

Daviess
- Fulkerson, A. O. ed. Daviess Co. 1915.

Dearborn
- Shaw, Archibald, ed. Hist. Dearborn Co. Bowen, 1915. 171 pp.
- Griffing, B. N. & Lake, D. J., Atlas of Dearborn Co. 1875.
- Hist. of Dearborn & Ohio Co. Weakley. 1885. 987 pp.

Decatur
- General & Biog. Rec. Decatur Co. 1900.
- Harding, L. A., Decatur Co. 1915.
- Stat. Atlas, Decatur Co. 1882.

De Kalb
- Hist. of De Kalb Co., Biog. Chi. Interstate Pub. 1885.
- De Kalb Co. 1914.

Delaware
- Del. Co. Illus. Biog. 303 pp. Chi. 1881
- Ellis, J. S., Our County Hist. 1898.
- Delaware Co. Biog. Illus. Chi. 1894. 807 pp.
- Port. & Biog. Rec. of Del. & Randolph Co. 1445 pp. Chi. 1894.
- Haimbaugh, F. D. ed. Del. Co. 1924. 2 v.
- Hill, L. L., Del. Co. Marriage Rec. Wills. 1934. Typed.
- Delaware Co., Kingman. 1881.
- Kemper, G. W. H., 20th C. Hist. of Del. Co. 2 v. Chi. 1908.

INDIANA (continued)

Dubois
- Pike & Dubois Cos. 784 pp. Chi. 1885.
- Wilson, G. R., Dubois Co. 1910. 412 pp.
- Wilson, Geo. R., Hist. of Dubois Co. Biog. Ratti. Indpls. 412 pp.
- Wilson, Geo. R., Hist. Souvenir of Dubois Co. Illus. 1896. 79 pp.

Elkhard
- Bartholomew, H.S.K. Hist. of Elkhard Co.Goshen.1930.337 pp.
- Bartholomew,H.S.K.Stories Elkhard Co.E.V.Pub.Nappance.1936.336 pp.
- Chapman,C.C. Elkhard Co. 1181 pp. Chi. 1881.
- D.A.R. Cemetery Records. 161 pp. Attica. 1933.
- Beckwith, H. W., Fountain Co. 224 pp. Chi. 1881.
- Clifton, T. A., Fountain and Warren Cos. 939 pp. Chi. 1913.
- Deahl, Anthony. Biog. Memoirs of Elkhart & St. Joseph Co. Goodspeed Bros. 1893. 777 pp.
- Deahl, Anthony. Twentieth Century Hist. of Elkhart Co. Lewis. 1905. 793 pp.
- Weaver, Abraham. Hist. of Elkhart Co. Amer. Hist. Society, 2 vol. 1916. 944 pp.

Fayette
- Barrows, F., Hist. of Fayette Co. Bowen. 1917. 1159 pp.
- Higgins, Belden & Co. Hist. Atlas. Illus. 1875. 53 pp.
- Warner, Beers & Co. Hist. of Fayette Co. 1885. 331 pp.
- Hist. of Wayne, Fayette, Union & Franklin Co., Biog. Chi. 1899 2 vol.

Franklin
- Atlas. 1882.
- Reifel, A. J., Hist. of Franklin Co. Bowen. 1915. 1475 pp.

Fulton
- Barnhart, H. A., ed. Fulton Co. Dayton. 1923. 3 vol. 305 pp.
- Kingman, A. L. Atlas. Kingman. 1883 and 1896. 121 pp.
- Plattie, E. W. Hist. of Ind. & Fulton Co. National. 1896. 153 pp.

Gibson
- Dragoo, Don W., An Archaeological Survey of Gibson Co., Ind. Ind. Hist. Bur. 1955.
- Stormont, Gil R., Hist. of Gibson Co. Biog. Bowen. 1914. 1076 pp.
- Hist. of Gibson Co. Biog. Tartt, Edwardsville. 1884. 244 pp.

Grant
- Brant & Fuller. Hist. of Grant Co. Chi. 1886. 269 pp.
- Whitson, R., Cent. Hist. of Grant Co. 2 v. 1429 pp.
- Biog. Memoirs of Grant Co. 894 pp.
- Hist. of Ind. & Grant Co. 944 pp.

Greene
- Baber, J., Greene Co. 1875. 96 pp. Biog. Memoirs. 3 v. 1908.
- Black, G. A. Archaeology of Greene Co., Ind. Bull #X, No. 5, Feb. 1933. 165 pp.
- Biog. Memoirs of Greene Co. Bowen. Indpls. 1908.
- Earliest Hist. of Greene & Sullivan Co. Biog. Goodspeed, 1884. 824 pp.

INDIANA (continued)

Hamilton
- Cline & McHaffie. Hist. of Hamilton Co. & Township. Indpls. 1874. 413 pp.
- Haines, J. F., Hist. of Hamilton Co. Bowen. Indpls. 1915. 254 pp.
- Port. & Biog. Rec. Madison & Hamilton Cos. 852 pp. Chi. 1893. Hamilton Co. 1880.
- Shuts, G. F., Hist. of Hamilton Co. 1818-1866. 1901. 370 pp.
- Hamilton & Darroch Cos. Lewis. 1916. 2 v.

Hancock
- Binford, J. H., Hist. of Hancock Co. 1818-1882.
- Biog. Memoirs of Hancock Co. Bowen. Logansport. 1902.
- Hist. of Hancock Co., Ind. Illus. Greenfield. 1882. 536 pp.
- Richman, Geo. J., Hist. of Hancock Co. Mitchell. Greenfield. 1916.

Harrison
- Bulleit, F. A. Illus. Atlas & Hist. 1906.
- Roose, W., Hist. of Harrison Co. Tribune. New Albany. 1911. 78 pp.

Hendricks
- Hadley, J. V., Hendricks Co. 845 pp. Indpls. 1914.
- Hendricks Co., Ind. Stat. Atlas. Maps. 1878.
- Hist. of Hendricks Co., Ind. Illus. Chi. 1885. 755 pp.

Henry
- Hazzard, G., Henry Co. 1822 - 1906. 2 v. New Castle. 1906.
- Hist. of Henry Co. Ind. Inter-State. 1884. 248 pp.
- Pleas, Elwood. Henry Co. 1821-71. 1871

Howard
- Blanchard, Charles, Co. of Howard & Tipton. Battey. Chi. 445 pp.
- Jackson, Morrow. Hist. of Howard Co. Bowen. 1908. 2 v. 1078 pp.
- Howard Co. Atlas. Map. 1877.
- Hist. of Howard & Tipton Co. Ind. Chi. 1883. 948 pp.

Huntington
- Bash, F.S. ed. Huntington Co. 1914. 2 v.
- Biog. Mem. Huntington Co. 1901. 743 pp.
- Hist. Sketch of Huntington Co., Ind. 1877.
- Hist. of Huntington Co., Ind. 1887.

Jackson
- Chadwick, H. W., Jackson Co. 1943. 73 pp.
- DAR Ft. Vallovia Chap. Hist. General Records to Jackson Co. Ind. 1952. Seymour.
- Hist. of Jackson Co. Ind. 1886.

Jasper
- Warren, Benton, Jasper & Newton Cos. Hist. & Biog. 810 pp. Chi. 1883.

INDIANA (continued)

Jay
- Jay & Blackford Cos. Biog. 901 pp. Chi. 1887.
- Jay, Milton T., ed. Hist. of Jay Co. Hist. Pub. Indpls. 1922. 262 pp.
- Biog. Mem. Jay Co. 1901. Atlas. 1881.
- Kelley, J. W. Atlas of Jay Co. 1901
- Montgomery, M. W., Hist. of Jay Co., Ind. 1864.

Jefferson
- Muncie, Emery O., Hist. of Jefferson Co. 179 pp.
- Vawter, John. Pioneers of Jefferson Co. 1850.

Jennings
- Jennings Co., Ind. Atlas. 1884.

Johnson
- Banta, David D., Hist. of Johnson Co. Chi. 1881. 170 pp.
- Branigin, E. L. Johnson Co. 1913. 863 pp.
- Johnson Co. 1888. 918 pp.

Knox
- Atlas 1880.
- Greene, Geo. E., Hist. of Old Vincennes & Knox Co. Clarke. Chi. 2 v. 1911. 893 pp.
- Hist. of Knox & Daviess Co. Goodspeed. Chi. 1886. 914 pp.
- Hardacre, F. C. Atlas. 1903.

Koscinsko
- Atlas. Kingman. 1879.
- DAR Cemetery Records. 2 v. 1942. Typed.
- Koscinsko Co. Logansport. Bowen. Illus. 1902. 641 pp.
- Biog. & Hist. Record of Kosciusko Co. Lewis. 1887. 734 pp.
- Royse, Hon. L. W., Hist. of Kosciusko Co. Lewis. 1919. 2 v. 709 pp.

La Grange
- Ford, I., La Grange, Steuben, Noble & De Kalb Cos. Lewis 1920 2 v.
- Hanan, J. W., La Grange Co. Cent. Hist. La Grange Pub. 1928.
- La Grange Co. Ind. Illus. Atlas.
- Co. of La Grange & Noble. Battey. 1882. 502 pp.
- Waddell, Marjorie. Hist. of La Grange Co. Log. 1936.

Lake
- Ball, Rev. T. H., Lake Co. Ind. 1834-1872. Chi. 1873. 364 pp.
- Ball, T. H. ed. General & Biog. of Lake Co. Lewis. 1904. 674 pp.
- Cannon, T. H. ed. Hist. of Lake & Calumet. Porter & LaPorte 2 v. 160 pp.
- Goodspeed, W. A. ed. Co. of Porter & Lake. Biog. Battery 1882. 771 pp.
- Howat, W. F. ed. Lake Co. Lewis. 1915. 2 v.
- Wood, Sam B., First 100 yrs. of Lake Co. Crown Point. 1938. 418 pp.

58

La Porte
- Daniels, E. E. 20th C. Hist. & Biog. Rec. La Porte Co. 1904.
- Biog. Rec. La Porte, Porter, Lake & Starke Cos. 1894. 569 pp.
- Atlas. 874.
- Packard, J., Hist. of La Porte Co. 1876. 467 pp.
- Hist. of La Porte Co. Ind. Chi. 1880. 914 pp.

Lawrence
- Atlas. 1879.
- Hist. of Lawrence & Monroe Co. Bowen. 1914.
- Lawrence, Orange & Wash. Co. Goodspeed. Chi. 1884. 937 pp.

Madison
- Harden, S., Hist. of Madison Co. 1820-74. Markleville 1874. 411 pp.
- Harden, S., Pioneer, Madison & Hancock Co. Mitchell. Greenfield. 1895. 457 pp.
- Madison Co. Hist. of Townships. Anderson. 1897. 1038 pp.
- Forkner, John L., Hist. of Madison Co. Lewis. Chi. 1914. 2 v. 791 pp.
- Hist. of Madison Co. Biog. Kingman Bros. Chi. 1880.
- Netterville, J. J. ed. Cent. Hist. of Madison Co. 1823-1923. Hist. Assn. Anderson. 1925.
- Madison & Hamilton Co., Biog. O. Pub. Co. 1893. 852 pp.

Marion
- Cline & McHoffie Peoples Guide. Dir. Ind. Print. & Pub. 1874. 600 pp.
- Robinson, Perry. Hist of Indpls. & Marion Co. Everts. 1884. 666 pp.
- Robb & Herschell. Indpls. & Marion Co. Dayton. 1924. v. 3-4 Esarey's Ind. Hist.
- Indpls. & Marion Co., Ind. Atlas 1889.
- Biog. Memoirs of Indpls. & Marion Co. Chi. 1893. 466 pp.

Marshall
- Hist. of Marshall Co. Biog. 1890. 2 v. 458 pp.
- Holland, T. A., Cent. Hist. & Marshall Co. Western. 1876. 168 pp.
- McDonald, D., Hist. of Marshall Co. 1836-1880. Kingman. Chi. 1881. 154 pp.
- McDonald, D. 20th Cent. Hist. of Marshall Co. Lewis. Chi. 1908. 648 pp.
- Swindell, Minnie H., Story of Marshall Co., Swindell. Plymouth. 1923. 87 pp.
- Atlas Marshall Co. Ogle. Chi. 1908. 77 pp. 1922. 55 pp.

Martin
- Hist. of Martin Co. Ind. H.G. Holt. 1953. 366 pp. Stout's. Paoli.

INDIANA (continued)

Miami
- Atlas 1877.
- Bodurtha, A. L. ed. Miami Co. Lewis. 1914. 2 v.
- Hist. of Miami Co., Ind. 1887.
- Stephens, J. H., Miami Co. 1896. 383 pp.

Monroe
- Bowen, B. F. & Co., Lawrence & Monroe Cos. 764 pp.
  Indpls. 1914.

Montgomery
- Beckwith, H. W., Montgomery Co. Chi. 1881.
- Montgomery Co. Bowen. n.d. 2 v.
- Chapman Bros. Port. & Biog. Rec. Montgomery, Parke & Fountain
  Cos. 718 pp. Chi. 1893.
- Gronert, Theodore G., Sugar Creek Saga. Hist. & Dev. of
  Montgomery Co. Illus. by H. McDonald. Wabash Coll. Crawfords-
  ville, Ind. 1958. 496 pp.
- Stat. Atlas Montgomery Co. 1878.

Morgan
- Blanchard, C. Morgan, Monroe & Brown Co., Ind. 1884.
- Major, N. J. Morgan Co. v. 5. 1915.

Newton
- Ade, John. Newton Co. 1853-1911. Bobbs-Merrill. 1911.
- Ade, John. Warren, Benton, Jasper & Newton Co. Biog. Battey.
  Chi. 1883.
- Hamilton, L. F. & Darrock, W. ed. Hist. of Jasper & Newton Co.
  Chi. & N.Y. Lewis. 1916.

Noble
- Alvord, S. E., Hist. of Noble Co. Bowen. Logansport. 1902
  602 pp.
- Durant, S. W. & P. A. Hist. Atlas & Noble Co. Andress &
  Baskin. Chi. 1874. 83 pp.
- D.A.R. Noble Co. Tombstone Records. 324 pp. 1934. Kendallsvilles.

Ohio
- Dearborn & Ohio Cos. 978 pp. Chi. 1885.

Orange
- Lawrence, Orange & Wash. Cos. 937 pp. 1884.
- Hist. of Orange Co. Ind. v. 1. Paoli Bus. & Prof. Women's Club.
  1950. 320 pp. Reprint of Parts III & IV. Hist. of Lawrence,
  Orange & Wash. Cos. Goodspeed. 1884.

Owen
- Helmen, Vernon R., Archaeological Survey of Owen Co., Ind.
  Indpls. Ind. Hist. Bur. 1950.

Parke
- Hist.of Parke & Vermillion Co. Bowen. 1913.
- Strouse, I. R., Parke Co. Cent. Mem. 1916. 128 pp.

Perry
- Warrick, Spencer & Perry Cos. 837 pp. Chi. 1885.
- De La Hunt, T. J., Perry Co. 359 pp. Indpls. 1916.

INDIANA (continued)

Pike — Hist of Pike & Dubois Co. Goodspeed. Chi. 1885. 776 pp.

Porter &
Lake
— Goodspeed W. A. ed. Cos. of Porter & Lake. Biog. Battery
1882. 771 pp.
— McAllister, J. G., Archaeology of Porter Co., Ind. Hist. Bull
X. 96 pp. Oct. 1932.
— Hist of Porter Co. Lewis. 1912. 2 v. 881 pp.
— Moore, Powell A. The Calumet Region. Ind. Last Frontier.
Ind. Hist. Bur. 1959. 654 pp.

Posey — Hist. of Posey Co. Goodspeed. Chi. 1886. 714. pp.
— Posey Co. Atlas, Biog. Keller & Fuller. Evansville, 1900.
— Leffel, J. C., Hist. of Posey Co. Chi. 1913. 401 pp
— Leonard, W. P., Hist. & Dir. of Posey Co. Isaacs, 1882.
Evansville. 260 pp.

Putnam — Weiks, J., Hist. of Putnam Co. Bowen, 1910.
— Biog. & Hist. Record of Putnam Co. Lewis. 1887.
— DAR & Putnam Co., Hist. Washburn Chapter, Greenweather.

Randolph — Smith, J. L. & Driver, T. L., Randolph Co. Bowen, 1914.
1603 pp.
— Tucker, E. Hist. of Randolph Co. Biog. 1882. 512 pp.

Ripley — Jerman, E. C., Ripley Co. 1888. 88 pp.

Rush — Atlas. 1879
— Rush Co. 1888
— Alexander & Dill. Rush Co. 1915. 97 pp.
— Gary, A. L. & Thomas, E. B. Cent. Hist. Rush Co. 2 v.
Indpls. 1921.
— DAR Rush Co. Cemetery Rec. Before 1886. 446 pp. 1936. typed.

St. Joseph — Hist. of St. Joseph Co. Chapman. Chi. 1880. 971 pp.
— South Bend & St Joseph Co. by Schuyler, Colfax Chap.
DAR. South Bend. 1927. 71 pp.
— Baker, G. A., St. Joseph-Kankekee Portage. N. Ind. Hist.
Soc'y. South Bend. 1899. 48 pp.
— Biog. Memories of Elkhart & St. Joseph Co. Goodspeed. Chi.
1893. 777 pp.
— Hist. Atlas of St. Joseph Co. Higgins Belden. Chi. 1875.
105 pp.
— Howard, T. E., Hist. of St. Joseph Co. 1907. 2 v. 1158 pp.
— Montgomery, H. T., Geol. Hist. of St. Joseph Co. N. Ind.
Hist. Soc'y. South Bend. 1929. 19 pp.
— Ogle, G. A. & Co. Atlas of St. Joseph Co. 1911. Chi. 113 pp.

INDIANA (continued)

St. Joseph   - Stoll, J. B., St. Joseph Co. Fron Its Org. Esarcy. 1923.
(Cont'd.)   3 v. 565 pp.
           - Hist of St. Joseph Co. Chi. 1180. 971 pp.

Scott   - Bogardus, Carl P., Pioneer Life In Scott Co., Ind.
           Austin. Muscatatuck. 1957.

Shelby   - Atlas 1880.
           - Brant & Fuller. Hist. of Shelby Co. 1887. 794 pp.
           - Chadwick, E. H. Hist. of Shelby Co. Bowen. Indpls. 1909
           - Hist. of Shelby Co. Illus. Chi. 1887 794 pp.
           - Hist. of Shelby Co. 1822-1876. Com. of Citizens. Shelbyville.
            Spicer. 1876. 40 pp.
           - Gragoo, Don W., Archaeological Survey of Shelby Co., Indpls.
            Hist. Bur. 1951.

Spencer   - Keller, James H., Archaeological Survey of Spencer Co., Indpls.
            Hist. But. 1951.
           - Ehrmann, B. V., Lincoln and His Neighbors. 1948. 42 pp.
           - Ehrmann, B. V., Missing Gap In Life of A.Lincoln . 1938. 150 pp.
           - Warrick, Spencer & Perry Cos. 837 pp. Chi. 1885.

Starke   - McCormick, J. N. Starke Co. Lewis. 1915. 1 v.
           - McCormick, C. A. Guide 20. Starke Co.

Steuben   - Hist. of Steuben Co., Ind. 1885.
           - Steuben Co., Ind. Atlas, 1898.

Sullivan   - Atlas 1899.
           - Hist. of Green & Sullivan Co. Goodspeed 1884. 824 pp.
           - Wolf, T. J., ed. Hist. of Sullivan Co. Lewis. Chi. 1909
            2 v. 809 pp.

Switzerland - Brown, E. S., Hist. of Switzerland Co., In War. 1919. 142 pp.
           - Dufour, P. Swiss Settlement of Switzerland Co., Hist. Com. 1925
            446 pp.
           - Hist. of Dearborn, Ohio & Switzerland Co. Chi. Weakley 1885.
            1282 pp.
           - Switzerland & Ohio Co. Atlas. 1883.

Tippicanoe - DeHart, R. P. ed. Tippicanoe Co. Bowen. 1909. 135 pp.
           - Biog. Hist. of Tippicanoe Co. Chi. 1883. 826 pp.
           - Biog. Hist. of Tippicanoe, White, Jasper, Newton, Benton, Warren
            and Pulaski Cos. Lewis. 1899. 2 v.
           - v. 3 Esarey's, Ind. Hist. Tippicanoe Co. & Wabash Valley.
            Dayton. 1928.

Tipton   - Pershing, M. W., Hist. of Tipton Co. Bowen. 1914. 636 pp.

INDIANA (continued)

Union — Atlas 1884. Biog. & Geneal. Hist. of Wayne, Fayette, Union and Franklin Cos. 2 V. Chi. 1899.

Vanderburgh — Biog. Cycle of Vanderburgh Co. 1897.
— Elliott, J. P. Hist. of Evansville & of Vanderburgh Co. Ind. 1897.
— Hist. of Vanderburgh Co. Ind. 1889.
— Gilbert, F. M. Evansville & Vanderburgh Cos. 1910-2 V.
— Atlas 1880.
— Iglehart, J. E. Vanderburgh Co. Dayton, 1923 V. 3 Esarey's.
— Hist. of Ind.

Vermillion — Coffeen. Handbook of Vermillion Co. 1870-71. Danville n.d.
— Biog. & Hist. Record of Vermillion Co. 1888.
— Parke & Vermillion Cos. 816 pp. Indpls. 1913.

Vigo — Andreas, A. T. Vigo Co., Ind. Atlas. Map. 1874.
— Beckwith, H. W. Hist. of Vigo & Parke Co. Chi. 1880. 1293 pp.
— Cronin, W. F. Hist. of Vigo Co. Dayton. 1922. 496 pp.
— Hist. of Vigo Co. Biog. Chi. Nelson. 1891. 1080 pp.
— Oakey, C. C. Terre Haute & Vigo Co. 1808-1908. Chi. Lewis 1908.
— Hist. of Vigo & Parke Co. 1880.
— Helmer, Vernon R. Archaeological Survey of Vigo Co., Ind. Hist. Bur. 1952.
— Markle, A. R. Vigo Co. Hist. & Geneal. Cem. Rec. 2 V. 1929 Typed.

Wabash — Biog. Mem. of Wabash Co. Bowen. 1901. 705 pp.
— Wabash Co. 492 pp. Chi. 1884.
— Beckwith, H. W. Vigo & Parke Cos. and Wabash Valley Chi. 1880.
— Helm, T. B. Hist. of Wabash Co. 1884. 492 pp.
— Hosea, P. and Wabash Co. Atlas. Ind. 1875.
— Weesner, Clarkson W. Hist. of Wabash Co. 1914. 970 pp.

Warren — Clifton, T. A. Fountain & Warren Cos. 989 pp. Chi. 1913.
— Warren, Benton, Jasper & Newton Cos. 1883. 810 pp.

Warrick — Adams, E. Hist. of Warrick Co. Crescent City. 1868. 80 pp.
— Curry, Hilda Jane - Archaeological Notes on Warrick Co. Ind. Indpls. Hist. Bur. 1954.
— Brandstand, S. A. Hist. of Warrick, Spencer & Perry Co. Goodspeed. Chi. 1885. 837 pp.
— Fortune, Will. Warrick & Its People. Courier, Evansville 1881 172 pp.
— Katterjohn, M. M. Hist. of Warrick & Its People. Crescent, Boonville. 1909. 106 pp.

INDIANA (continued)

Washington - Stevens, W. W. Cent. Hist. of Wash. Co. Bowen. 1917. 1060 pp.

Wayne
- Biog. & Geneal. Hist. of Wayne, Fayette, Union & Franklin Cos. Chi. 1899. 2 V.
- Feeger, Luther M. The Hist. of Transportation In Wayne Co. Ind. Reprint From Palladium-Item Richmond. 3-18-53 nd 7-8-54 Index
- Fox, H. C. Wayne Co. 1912. 2 V.
- Young, A. W. Hist. of Wayne Co. Clarke. Ciuti. 1872. 459 pp.
- Hist. of Wayne Co. Biog. Chi. 1884. 2 V. 736 pp.

Wells
- Atlas 1881. Biog. Mem. of Wells Co. 597 pp. Logansport 1903.
- Biog. & Hist. Rec. of Adams & Wells Cos. 1025 pp. Chi. 1887.

White
- White Co. 2 V. Lewis. 1915.
- Cos. of White & Pulaski, Ind. Battey, Chi. 1883. 772 pp.

Whitley
- Carver, Edna B. Whitley Co. Hist. Ind. U. 1937. 93 pp.
- D.A.R. Cemetery Records Whitley Co. 23 pp. 1948.
- Goodspeed, W. A. & Blanchard, C. Cos. of Whitley & Noble. Battey, 1882. 502 pp.
- Kaler, S. P., Morning, R. H. Hist. of Whitley Co. Bowen 1907. 861 pp.
- Ogle, Geo. A. Atlas of Whitley Co. Ogle. 1916. 95 pp.
- Hist. of Ohio Falls Cities & Their Counties, Williams, Cleveland. 1882.
- Rev. of W.P.A. Inventory of Co. Archives in Ind. Hist. Bull. #3 Vol. 21. Mar. 1944.
- Pub. of Ind. Hist. Bur. & Ind. Hist. Socy. Ind. 1940

IOWA

- Glass, Remley, Jr. Iowa Counties of Iowa and Something of Their Origin & Histories. Mason City, Ia. Lipto-Loose-Leaf Co. 1940.

Adair
- Kilburn, Lucian M. ed. Hist. of Adair Co. Iowa & Its People. 2 Vol. 1915. Pioneer. Chi.
- Hist. of Guthrie & Adair Co. 1884. Cont. Hist. Pub. Co. Springfield, Ill.

Adams
- Biog. Hist. of Montgomery & Adams Cos. Ia. 1892. Lewis. Chi.

Allamakee
- Hancock, Ellery M. Past & Present of Allamakee Co. Inc., 2 Vol. 1913. Clarke. Chi.
- Hist. of Winneshiek & Allamakee Co., Ia. 1882. Western. Western. Sioux City.

IOWA (continued)

Appanoose
- Taylor, L. L. Ed. Past & Present of Appanoose Co. Ia., 2 Vo. 1913. Clarke. Chi.
- Hist. of Appanoose Co., Ida. 1878. Western. Chi.
- Biog. & Geneal. Hist. of Appanoose & Monroe Co. Comp. & Ed. by Lewis. Chi. 1903. Lewis.
- Biog. & Hist. Rec. of Wayne & Appanoose Co., Ia. 1886. Inter-State. Chi.

Audubon
- Andrews, H. F. ed. Hist. of Audubon Co., Ia. 1915. Brown, Indpls.
- Biog. Hist. of Shelby & Andubon Cos., Ia. 1889. Dunbar, Chi.

Benton
- Hist. of Benton Co., Ia. 1878. Western. Chi.
- Port. & Biog. Album of Benton Co., Ia. 1887. Benton. Chi.
- Hill, Luther B. Comp. Hist. of Benton Co., Ia. 2 V. n.d.
- Rice, U. T. S. Hist. of Benton Co. Waterloo. 1868.

Black Hawk
- Black Hawk Co. Biog. Chi. 619 pp. 1886.
- Hist. of Black Hawk Co., Ia. 1878. Western. Chi.
- Hartman, J. C. ed. Hist. of Black Hawk Co. Ia. 2 Vol. 1915, Clarke, Chi.
- Ven Metre, Isaiah ed. Hist. of Black Hawk Co., Ia. Biog. 1904. Biog. Pub. Co. Chi.

Boone
- Goldthwait, N. E. ed. Hist. of Boone Co., Ia. 2 V. 1914 Pioneer, Chi.
- Hist. of Foone Co., Ia. 1880. Union. Des Moines.
- Biog. Rec. of Boone Co., Ia. 1902. Clarke. Chi.

Bremer
- Hist. of Butler & Bremer Co., Ia. 1883. Union. Springfield.

Buchanon
- Church, H. & Chappell, K. J. Buchanon Co., 2 V. Chi. 1914.
- C.S. & Eliz. Percival eds. 1881. Williams. Cleveland.

Buena Vista
- Wegerslev, C.H. & Walpole, Thomas, eds. Past & Present of Buena Vista, Ia. 1909. Clarke. Chi.

Butler
- Hist. of Butler & Bremer Co., Ia. 1883. Union. Springfield.
- Hart, Irving H. Hist. of Butler Co., Ia. 2 V. 1914. Clarke, Chi.

Calhoun
- Biog. Rec. of Calhoun Co., Ia. 1902. Clarke. Chi.
- Stonebraker, Beaumont E. ed. Past & Present of Calhoun Co. Ia. 2 V. 1915. Pioneer. Chi.

Carroll
- MacLean, Paul. Hist. of Carroll Co. 1912. Clarke. Chi.
- Biog. & Hist. Rec. of Greene & Carroll Co. Ia. 1887. Lewis. Chi.

IOWA (continued)

Cass — Hist. of Cass Co., Ia. 1884. Cont. Hist. Co. Springfield.
— Young, Tape. Hist. of Cass Co. Biog. Atlantic. 1877.

Cedar —Hist. of Cedar Co., Ia. 1878. Western. Chi.
— Awner, C. R. Topical Hist. of Cedar Co., 2 V. 1910. Clarke. Chi.

Cerro Gordo — Wheeler, J. H. ed. & Comp. Hist. of Cerro Gordo Co., Ia. 2 V.
1910. Lewis. Chi.
— Hist. of Franklin & Cerro Gordo Co., Ia. 1883. Union. Springfield.

Cherokee — Biog. Hist. of Cherokee Co., Ia. 1889. Dunbar. Chi.
— McMulla, T. Cherokee Co. 2 V. Chi. 1914.

Chickasaw — Alexander, W. E. Hist. of Chickasaw & Howard Cos., Ia. 1883.
Western. Decorah, Ia.
— Powers, J. H. Hist & Rem. of Chickasaw Co., Ia. 1894. Printing.
Des Moines.

Clarke — Biog. & Hist. Rec. of Clarke Co., Ia. 1886. Lewis. Chi.

Clay — Gillespie, Sam & Steele, J. E. Hist. of Clay Co. Ia. Chi. 1909
Clarke.
— Gilbreath, W. C. Hist. of Clay Co., Ia. 1889.

Clayton — Hist. of Clayton Co., Ia. 1882. Interstate Pub. Co. Chi.
— Price, Realto E. ed. Hist. of Clayton Co. 2 V. 1916. Law. Chi.
— Port. & Biog. Rec. of Dubuque, Jones & Clayton Co., Ia. Chapman.
Chi. 1894.

Clinton — Port. & Biog. Album of Clinton Co., Ia. 1886. Chapman. Chi.
— Biog. Rec. of Clinton Co., Ia. 1901. Clarke. Chi.
— Hist. of Clinton Co., Ia. with Hist. of N.W. 1879. Western. Chi.
— LePrevost, Mrs. E. Hist. of Clinton Co., Allen. 1930. 128 pp.
— Wolfe, P. B. ed. Hist. of Clinton Co., Ia. 2 V. 1911. Bowen,
Indpls.
— Youle, Estelle Goodwin Le Provost. Hist. of Clinton Co. Ia. 1948.

Crawford — Biog. Hist. of Crawford, Ida & Soc Co., Ia. 1893. Lewis. Chi.
— Meyers, F. W. Hist of Crawford Co., Ia. 2 V. 1911. Clarke. Chi.

Dallas — Wood, R. F. Past & Present of Dallas Co. 1907. Clarke. Chi.
— Hist. of Dallas Co. Ia. 1879. Union. Des Moines.

Davis — Hist. of Davis Co. 1882. State Historical. Des Moines.
— Davis Co. Fed. of Women's Clubs, Pioneer Hist. of Davis Co.,
Ia. 1907. Bloomfield Democrat. Ia.

IOWA (continued)

Decatur
- Howell, J. M. & Smith, H. E. eds. Hist. of Decatur Co., Ia. and Its People. 2 V. 1915. Clarke. Chi.
- Biog. & Hist. Rec. of Ringgold & Decatur Co., Ia. 1887. Lewis. Chi.

Delaware
- Hist. of Del. Co., Ia. 1878. Western. Chi.
- Bailey, Bell. Hist. of Del. Co. 1850-70. Manchester, author. 1935.
- Merry, John J. ed. Hist. of Del. Co., Ia. 2 V. 1914. Clarke. Chi.

Des Moines
- Antrobus, Augustine M. Hist. of Des Moines Co. & Its People 2 Vol. 1915. Clarke. Chi.
- Biog. Rev. of Des Moines Co. 1905. Hobart. Chi.
- Hist. of Des Moines Co. 1879. Western. Chi.
- Pl. Bk. of Des Moines Co. N. W. Pub. Chi. 1897.
- Pl. Bk. of Des Moines Co. N. W. Pub. Hickson. Rockford, n.d.
- Port. & Biog. Album of Des Moines Co. 1888. Acme. Chi.

Dickinson
- Smith, R. A. A Hist. of Dickinson Co. with an Account of The Spirit Lake Massacre & Indian Troubles on the N.W. Frontier. 1902. Kenyon. Des Moines, Ia.
- Hist. of Emmet Co. & Dickinson Co. 2 V. 1917. Pioneer. Chi.

Dubuque
- Port. & Biog. Rec. of Dubuque, Jones & Clayton Co. 1894. Chi. Chapman.
- Hist. of Dubuque Co., 1880. Western. Chi.
- Goodspeed, W. A. & K. C. Hist. of Dubuque Co., Ia. 1911. Goodspeed Chi.
- W.P.A. Dubuque Co., Hist. Ia. Dubuque, 1942.

Emmet
- Hist. of Emmet and Dickinson Co., Ia. 2 V. 1917. Pioneer. Chi.

Fayette
- Port. & Biog. Album of Fayette Co. Ia. 1891. Lake City. Chi.
- Hist. of Fayette Co. 1878. Western. Chi.

Floyd
- Hist. of Floyd Co. Ia., 1882. Inter-State Pub. Chi.
- Webster, C. L. Hist. of Floyd Co. 1897. Intelligencer. Charles City, Ia.

Franklin
- Stuart, I. L. ed. Hist. of Franklin Co. 2 V. 1914. Clark. Chi.
- Hist. of Franklin & Cerro Gordo Co's. 1883. Union. Springfield.

Fremont
- Hist. of Fremont Co. 1881. Ia. Hist. Co. Des Moines, Ia.
- Biog. Hist. of Fremont & Mills Co., Ia. 1901. Lewis. Chi.
- Lingenfelter, L. Fremont Co. 63 pp. St. Jo. Mo. 1877.

IOWA (continued)

Greene
- Biog. & Hist. Rec. of Greene & Carroll Cos. 1887. Lewis. Chi.
- Stillman, E. B. Greene Co. 664 pp. Chi. 1907.

Grundy
- Port. & Biog. Rec. of Jasper Marshall & Grundy Co. Ia. 1894. Chi. Biog. Pub. Co.

Guthrie
- Hist. of Guthrie & Adair Co., Ia. 1884. Continental, Springfield.
- Maxwell, Mrs. S. B. 1876. Cent. Hist. of Guthrie Co. Carter & Hussey. Des Moines.
- Past & Present of Guthrie Co., Ia. 1907. Clarke. Chi.

Hamilton
- Hist. of Hamilton Co., Ia. 2 V. 1912. Clarke. Chi.
- Biog. Rec. & Port. Album of Hamilton & Wright Co. Ia. 1889. Lewis, Chi.
- Biog. Rec. of Hamilton Co., Ia. 1902. Clarke. Chi.

Hancock
- Hist. of Hancock & Kossuth Co., Ia. 2 V. 1917.
- Hist. of Kossuth, Hancock & Winnebago Co's. 1884. Union. Springfield.

Hardin.
- Hist. of Hardin Co., Ia. 1883. Union. Springfield.

Harrison
- Hist. of Harrison Co., Ia. 1891. Natl. Pub. Co. Chi.
- Smith, Jos. H. Hist. of Harrison Co., Ia. 1888. Printing. Des Moines.
- Clark, Will, Leach & Others. Hist. of Harrison Co., Ia. 1915.

Henry
- Port. & Biog. Album of Henry Co., Ia. 1888. Acme. Chi.
- Hist. of Henry Co., Ia. 1879. Western. Chi.
- Biog. Rev. of Henry Co. 1906. Hobart. Chi.

Howard
- Alexander, W. E. Hist. of Chickasaw & Howard Cos. 1883. West.

Humboldt
- Hist. of Humboldt Co. 1901. Historical Pub. Cedar Rapids.
- Hist. of Kossuth & Humboldt Co. 1884. Union. Springfield.

Ida
- Biog. Hist. of Crawford, Ida & Soc Co's., Ia. 1893. Lewis. Chi.

Iowa
- Dinwiddie, James C. Hist. of Iowa Co. and Its People, 2 V. 1915. Clarke. Chi.
- Hist. of Iowa Co. 1881. Union. Des Moines.
- Portrait & Biog. Rec. of Johnson Poweshick & Iowa Co., 1893. Chapman, Chi.
- Iowa Co. Geneal. Rec. 189 pp. 1935. Typed.
- Iowa Co. Union Hist. Co. 774 pp. Des Moines. 1881

IOWA (continued)

Jackson
- Hist. of Jackson Co., Ia. 1879. West. Chi.
- Annals of Jackson Co., 1905-9. Jackson Co. Hist. Socy.
- Ellis, James W. Hist. of Jackson Co. 2 V. 1910. Clarke. Chi.

Jasper
- Hist. of Jasper Co. 1878. Western. Chi.
- Port. & Biog. Rec. of Jasper, Marshall & Grundy Co., Ia. 1894. Biog. Chi.
- Weaver, James B. ed. Past & Present of Jasper Co., Ia. 2 V. 1912. Bowen, Indianapolis.

Jefferson
- Fulton, Chas. J. Hist. of Jefferson Co. 2 V. 1914. Clarke. Chi.
- Geneal. Rec. Jefferson Co. Marriages 255 pp. Atlantic. 1938.
- Hist. of Jefferson Co., 1879. Western. Chi.
- Port. & Biog. Album of Jefferson & Van Buren Co., 1890. Lake City. Chi.
- Fletcher, Chas. H. Cent. Hist. of Jefferson Co., Ia. 1876. Ledger. Fairfield

Johnson
- Hist. of John Co., Ia. its townships, cities, 1833. Iowa City.
- Aurner, Clarence R. Leading Events In Johnson Co. Hist. 2 V. 1912. Torch Press. Cedar Rapids, Ia.
- Port. & Biog. Rec. of Johnson. Poweshiek & Ia. Co., Ia. 1893. Chapman, Chi.
- Hist. of Johnson Co. 1836-1882. Iowa City.

Jones
- Corbit, R. M. ed. Hist. of Jones Co. 2 V. 1910, Clarke. Chi.
- Genealog. Rec., Marriage & Grave Rec. Jones Co. 172 pp. 1934.Typed.
- History of Jones County, 1879, Wextern, Chi.
- Port & Biog. Rec. of Dubuque, Jones & Clayton Counties, 1894. Chapman, Chi.

Keokuk
- Hist. of Keokuk Co., 1880. Union Hist. Co. Des Moines.

Kossuth
- Hist. of Kossuth & Humboldt Cos. Ia. 1885. Union. Springfield.
- Hist. of Kossuth, Hancock & Winnebago Co. 1884. Union. Springfield.
- Marriages 1870-80, Ia. Geneal. Rec. V. 23, pp. 172-86. Typed.
- Reed, Benj. F. Hist. of Kossuth Co., Ia. 2 V. 1913. Clarke. Chi.
- Tjoden, M. K. Kossuth Co. 2 V. Montezuma. 1948. Typed.
- Hist. of Hancock & Kossuth, 2 V. 1919.

Lee
- Biog. Rev. of Lee Co., Ia. 1905. Hobart. Chi.
- Port. & Biog. Album of Lee Co. Ia. 1887. Chapman. Chi.
- Coffman, J. F. & Co. Lee Co., 343 pp. Keokuk. 1868.
- D.A.R. Lee Co. Marriage & Grave Rec. 132 pp. 1943. Typed

IOWA (continued)

Lee
(cont'd)
- Hist. of Lee Co., Ia. 1879. Western. Chi.
- W.P.A. Lee Co. Hist. Ia. Keokuk. 1942.
- Roberts, Nelson C. & Moorhead, S. W. eds. Story of Lee Co.
  2 V. 1914. Chi. Clarke.

Linn
- Art Work of Linn Co. Oshkosh, Wis. Art Photo Co., 1899.
- Linn Co. Biog. 993 pp. Chi. 1901.
- Brewer, L. A. & Wick, B. L. Hist. of Linn Co. 2 V. 1911.
  Clarke, Chi.
- Dotson, A. F. Honor Roll of Linn Co. Cedar Rapids, Aorch. 1919.
- Hanson, Evans. Linn Co. Dir. Rockford. 1935.
- Linn Co. Cent. Marion Sentinel 1837-1937. Marion 1937.
- Mitchell, W. A. Linn Co. 1928-40. Chase Co. Hist. Socy.
- Port. & Biog. Album of Linn Co. 1887. Chapman. Chi.
- Hist. of Linn Co. 1878. Western. Chi.

Louisa
- A Port. & Biog. Album of Louisa Co. 1889. Acme Pub. Co. Chi.
- Springer, A. Hist. of Louisa Co. From Earliest Settlement
  to 1912. 2 V. 1912. Clarke. Chi.

Lucas
- Dix, M. N. Marriage Rec. Butler & Lucas Co. 1941. V 60 Ia.
  Gen. Rec.
- Hist. of Lucas Co. 1881. State Hist. Co. Des Moines.
- Stuart, Theod. M. Past & Pres. of Lucas & Wayne Co. 2 V.
  1913. Clarke. Chi.

Lyon
- Hyde, S. C. Hist. of Lyon Co., Sentinel Pr. Lemars.
  Plymouth. 1872. 40 pp.
- Monlux, Geo. Early Hist. of Lyon Co. 1909. Rock Rapids, Ia.
- Pioneer Assoc. of Lyon Co., Compendium of Hist. Rem. &
  Biog. of Lyon Co. 1904-5. Ogle. Chi.

Madison
- Davies, J. J. Madison Co. 254 pp. Des Moines. 1869.
- Hist. of Madison Co., Ia. 1879. Union Hist. Co. Des Moines.
- Mueller, Herman A. Hist. of Madison Co. 2 V. 1915. Clarke, Chi.

Mahaska
- History of Mahaska Co. 1878. Union Hist. Co. Des Moines.
- Port. & Biog. Album of Mahaska Co. 1887. Chapman. Chi.
- Hedge, Manoak. Past & Pres. of Mahaska Co. Ia. Chi.
  1906. Clarke.
- Maddy, O. Wills of Mahaska Co. 1851-1900. 34 pp. Oskaloosa.
  1949. Typed.
- Miller, M. H. Geneal. Rec. Mahaska Co. 2 V. 1938. Rec.
  43 and 34.
- Phillips Semira A. Proud Mahaska, 1843-1900. 1900 Herald Print.
  Oskaloosa.

IOWA (continued)

Marion
- Donnel, W. M. Marion Co. 346 pp. 1872. Des Moines.
- Hist. of Marion Co. 1881. Union. Des Moines.
- Wright, John W. & Young, W. A. eds. Hist. of Marion Co. Ia. 2 V. 1915. Clarke. Chi.

Marshall
- Schultz, Gerard. Hist. of Marshall Co., Ia. Marshall Print. Marshalltown.
- Battin, Wm. & Moscrip. F. A. eds. Past & Pres. of Marshall Co. 1955. 2 V. 1912. Bowen, Indpls.
- Hist. of Marshall Co. 1878. Western. Chi.
- Port. & Biog. Rec. of Jasper, Marshall & Grundy Co. 1894. Biog. Chi.
- Sanford, Mrs. N. Hist. of Marshall Co. Leslie. McAllaster Prs. 1867. 158 pp.

Mills
- D.A.R. Marriages of Mills Co. Rec. 1937. V. 42. Typed.
- Hist. of Mills Co. 1881. State Hist. Co. Des Moines.
- Biog. Hist. of Fremont & Mills Co. Ia. 1901. Lewis. Chi.

Mitchell
- Anderson Pub. Co. Mitchell Co. Chi. 1911.
- Hist. & Mitchell & Worth Co., Ia. 1884. Union. Springfield.
- Hist. & Mitchell & Worth Co., Ia. 2 V. 1918.

Monona
- Hist. of Monona Co., Ia. 1890. Nat'l. Pub. Co. Chi.

Monroe
- Hist. of Monroe Co., Ia. 1878. Western. Chi.
- Biog. & Gen. Hist. of Appanoose & Monroe Co. Ia. Comp. by. S. T. Lewis, 1903. Chi. Lewis.
- Hickenlooper, Frank. Illus. Hist. of Monroe Co. 1896. Albia. Ia.
- W.P.A. Monroe Co. Hist. , Ia. Des Moines. 1940.

Montgomery
- Biog. Hist. of Montgomery & Adams Co. 1892. Lewis. Chi.
- Merritt, W. W. Hist. of Montgomery Co. From Earliest Days 2 V. 1906
- Hist. of Montgomery Co. 1881. Ia. Hist. & Biog. Co. Des Moines

Muscatine
- Hist. of Muscatine Co., 1879. Western. Chi.
- Muscatine Co. Port. & Biog. 666 pp. Chi. 1889.
- Richman, Irving B. ed. Hist. of Muscatine Co. 2 V. 1911. Clarke. Chi.
- Elston, Hattie Phinette. White Men Follow After a Collection of Stories About the Okoboji-Spirit Lake Region, Iowa City, Athens. 1946.

O'Brien
- Peck, J. L. E. Monthzeimer, O. H. & Miller, Wm. J. Past & Present of Osceola Co., Ia. 2 V. 1914. Bowen. Indianapolis.
- Perkins, D.A.W. Hist. of O'Brien Co., Ia. 1879 Sioux Falls.
- Past & Present of O'Brien & Osceola Co. 2 v. 1914. Bowen, Indpls.

IOWA (continued)

Osceola — Perkins, D. A. W. Hist. of Osceola Co. 1892. Lewis. Chi.

Page — Hist. of Page Co. 1880. Ia. Hist. Co. Des Moines.
— Biog. Hist. of Page Co. 1890. Lewis & Dunbar. Chi.
— Kershaw, W. L. & Others. Hist. of Page Co., 2 V. Chi. 1909. Clarke. Chi.
— Miller, E. Hist. of Page Co., 1876. Clarinda Herald, Ia.
— Page Co. Hist., Ia. Clarinda Herald, Ia.

Palo Alto — McCarty, D. C. Hist. of Palo Alto Co. 1910. Torch Press. Cedar Rapids, Ia.
— Martin, P. M. Hist. of Palo Alto Co. 1877. Emmetsburg, Ia.

Plymouth — Freeman, W. S. Plymouth Co., 2 V. Indpls. 1917.
— Hist. of Cos. of Woodbury & Plymouth, Ia. & Sketch of Sioux City. 1890-91. Aramer. Chi.

Pocahontas — Flickinger, R.E. Pioneer Hist. of Pocahontas Co. 1904. Robt. E. Flickenger. Fonda, Iowa.

Polk — Andrews, L. F. Polk Co. 2 V. Des Moines. 1908.
— Brigham, Johnson. Hist. of Des Moines & Polk Co. 2 V. 1911 Clarke. Chi.
— D.A.R. Burial Rec. Polk Co. 102 pp. 1943 Typed.
— Dixon, J.M. Cent. Hist. of Polk Co. 1876. State Register, Des Moines.
— Laird, A. Polk Co. Marriage Rec. 1856-61. 1871-81. 151pp. Des Moines. 1944.
— Polk Co. 1037 pp. Des Moines. 1880.
— Porter, Will. Polk Co. & Des Moines. 1898. 1064 pp.
— W.P.A. Polk Co. Hist., Ia.
— Sanford, Mrs. N. Early Polk Co., Newton, 1874. Clark. Newton, Ia.
— Port. & Biog. Album of Polk Co. 1890. Lake City. Chi.
— Union Hist. Co. Hist. of Polk Co. with Cities, Towns, etc. 1880. Union. Des Moines.

Pottawattamie — Hist. of Pottawattamie Co. 1883. Baskin, Chi.
— Biog. Hist. of Pottawattamie Co. 1891. Lewis. Chi.
— Field, H.H. and Reed, J.P. eds. Hist. of Pottawattamie Co. 2 V. 1907. Clarke. Chi.

Poweshiek — Parker, L.F. Hist. of Poweshiek Co. 2 V. 1911. Clarke, Chi.
— Hist. of Poweshiek Co. 1880. Union. Des Moines.
— Port. & Biog. Rec. of Johnson Poweshiek & Iowa Co. 1893, Chapman. Chi.
— Poweshiek Co. Des. Montezuma. 1865. Map. 36 pp.

IOWA (continued)

Ringgold
- Biog. & Hist. Rec. of Ringgold & Decatur Co. 1887. Lewis. Chi.
- Leson, Mary M. Hist. of Ringgold Co. 1844-1937. Mount Ayr. 1937. 259 pp.
- W.P.A. Ringgold Co.. Hist. Mount Ayr, Ia. 1942.

Sac
- Hart, Wm. H. Hist. of Sac Co., Ia. 1914. Bowen, Indpls.
- Biog. Hist. of Crawford, Ida & Soc. Cos. 1893. Lewis. Chi.

Scott
- Biog. Hist. & Port. Gallery of Scott Co. 1895. Amer. Biog. Chi.
- Douner, H.E. Hist. of Davenport & Scott Co. Chi. 1910. 2 V. Clarke. Chi.
- Miller, M.H. Scott Co. Marriages. 2 V. Gen. Rec. V 51-2. 1939.
- Hist. of Scott Co. with Hist. of Ia. Inter-State Pub. Co. Chi.
- W.P.A. Scott Co. Hist. Ia. Davenport. 1942

Shelby
- Biog. Hist. of Shelby & Aubudon Co. 1889. Dundar. Chi.
- White, Edw. S. Past & Present of Shelby Co. 1915. Bowen, Indpls.

Sioux
- Dyke, Charles L. The Story of Sioux Co. & Sioux City. Verstegen. 1942.
- Miller, M. H. Sioux Co. 1934. V. 54. Typed.

Story
- Allen, Wm. G. Hist. of Story Co., 1887. Ia. Print. Des Moines.
- Payne, W. O. Hist. of Story Co. 1911. Clarke. Chi.
- Biog. & Hist. Mem. of Story Co. 1890. Goodspeed Pub. Co. Chi.

Tama
- Chapman, Sam D. Hist. of Tama Co., Toledo Times.
- Census of 56 Cemeteries. 1931. Typed.
- Hist. of Tama Co. 1883. Union. Springfield.

Taylor
- Hist. of Taylor Co. 1881. State Hist. Des Moines.

Union
- Colby, E.J. Illus. Map. Dir. Union Co. 145 pp. Creston. 1876.
- Ide, Geo. A. Hist. of Union Co., 1908. Clarke. Chi.

Van Buren
- Hist. of Van Buren Co. 1878. Western. Chi.
- Porter, O.K. Marriages & Grave Rec. of Van Buren Co. 307 pp. 1936. Typed.
- Port. & Biog. Album of Jefferson & Van Buren Co. 1890. Lake City,Chi.
- W.P.A. Van Buren Co. Hist., Ia. Amer. Leg. Farmington. Keith 1940.

Wapello
- D.A.R. Marriage Rec. 146 pp. 1945-6. Typed.
- Evans, S.B. ed. & Comp. Hist. of Wapello Co. & Citizens 1902. Biog. Pub. Chi.
- Hist. of Wapello Co. 1878. Western. Chi.
- Port. & Biog. Album of Wapello Co., 1887. Chapman. Chi.
- Waterman, Harrison J.E. ed. Hist. of Wapello Co. 2 V. 1914 Clarke. Chi.

IOWA (continued)

Warren   - Schultz, Gerard. Hist. of Warren Co. Ia. Indianola Rec. &
          Trib. 1953.
          - Hist. of Warren Co., 1879. Union Hist. Co. Des Moines.

Washington - Hist. of Washington Co. 1880. Union Hist. Des Moines.
          - Port. & Biog. Album of Wash. Co., 1887. Acme Pub. Chi.
          - Speer, M.E. Geneal. Rec. Wash. Co. Journ. & Ind. 2 Vo.
          Wash. 1934. Typed.

Wayne   - Biog. & Hist. Rec. of Wayne & Appanoose Co. 1886. Inter-
          state. Chi.
          - D.A.R. Wayne Co. Marriages. Geneal. Rec. 1937. V. 47.

Webster   - Biog. Rec. Webster Co. 732 pp. Chi. 1902.
          - Biog. Rec. of Webster Co. 1910. Clarke. Chi.
          - D.A.R. Cemeteries In Webster Co. Geneal. Rec. 1937. V. 46. Typed.
          - Morgan, E.G. Cent. Hist. Webster Co. 1876. Ft. Dodge Times
          Press, Ia.
          - Pratt, H.M. & Others. Hist. of Ft. Dodge & Webster Co., Ia.
          1913. Pioneer. Chi.

Winnebago - D.A.R. Cemeteries In Winnebago. Gen. Rec. 1937. V. 46.
          - Hist. of Kossuth, Hancock & Winnebago Co. 1884. Allamekee Co.
          1882. Western. Sioux City, Ia.

Winneshiek - Alexander, W.E. Hist. of Winneshiek & Allamekee Co. 1882
          Western. Sioux City, Ia.
          - Bailey, Edwin C. Past & Present of Winneshiek Co. 2 Vo. 1913
          Clark. Chi.
          - Sparks, Chas. H. Hist. of Winneshiek Co., Biog. Sketches. 1877
          Leonard. Decorah. Ia.

Woodbury   - Hist. of Cos. of Woodbury & Plymouth, Ia. Sketch of Sioux City
          1890-1. Aramer. Chi.

Worth   - Hist. of Mitchell & Worth Co., 1884 Union. Springfield.
          - Hist. of Mitchell & Worth Co., 1884 2 V. 1918.

Wright   - Birdsall, B.P. ed. Hist. of Wright Co., Ia. People,Industries
          & Institutions. 1915. Bowen. Indpls.
          - Biog. Record & Port. Album of Hamilton & Wright Co. 1889.
          Lewis. Chi.
          - D.A.R. Cemeteries In Wright Co. Gem. Rec. 1937. V. 46.
          - Wright, Clyde Franklin. Buckeye-Prairie and Three River Country
          Falls, Ia. Omoha. Aroka. 1945.

Iowa State - Edgar R. Harlan. A Narrative Hist. of The People of Iowa.
          5 V. 1931. Amer. Hist. Socy. Inc. Chi. & N. Y.

IOWA (continued)

W.P.A. Projects- Sponsored by County Supts. of Schools. Co. Hist. Pub.

- Buena Vista   1942   Lee   1942
- Cherokee   1940   Monroe   1940
- Crawford   1941   Osceola   1942
- Dubuque   1942   Page   1942
- Franklin   1941   Polk   1940 (Polk Co. Hist. Socy).
- Jackson   1942   Ringgold   1942
- Johnson   1941   Scott   1942
- Dyke, Chas. L. The Story of Sioux Co., Pub. by Author. Orange City, Iowa. 1942.
- Van Buren, 1940. By Local Amer. Leg., Woodbury, 1942.

KANSAS

Allen
- Hist. of Allen & Woodson Cos. Duncan, Wallace & Scott, eds. Iola Reg. 1901 894 pp.

Anderson
- Johnson, H. Hist. of Anderson Co., Garnett, 1936. 383 pp.
- Johnson, W.A. Hist. of Anderson Co., Garnett, Kauffman, 1877. 289pp.

Atchison
- Ingalls, S. Hist. of Atchison Co., Lawrence. 1916. 887 pp.
- Tombstone Records of Atchison Co., 252 pp. 1940. Typed.

Barton
- Biog. Hist. of Barton Co. Great Bend Trib. 1912. 318pp.
- Stoke, W.E. Early Cent. & West Kan. Great Bend. author. 1926.

Bourbon
- Barlow, Mary L. Ft. Scott. 1921. 117pp.
- Marriage Rec. of Bourbon Co. 1857-75. Pittsburg, Typed.
- Robbey, T.F. Hist. of Bourbon Co. To 1865. 210pp.

Brown
- Harrington, C.W. Annals of Brown Co. To 1900. Hiawatha 1903. 564pp.
- Ruley, A.N. Hist. of Brown Co. 401pp. Hiawatha. 1930.

Butler
- Butler Co. Cemetery Rec. El Dorado. 1941.
- Chesney, E. Butler Co. Marriage Records. 17pp. Eldorado. Typed.1935
- Mooney, Vol. P. Hist. of Butler Co., Lawrence. Standard 1916 89pp.
- Stratford, Jessie P. Butter Co. 1855-1935. Eldorado News. 1934. 418pp.

Cherokee
- Allison, N.T. Hist. of Cherokee Co. Chi. Biog. Pub. 1904 630pp.

Clay
- Chapman, Bros. Port & Biog. Wash. Clay & Riley Cos. 1231pp. Chi. 1890.

KANSAS (continued)

Cloud — Hollinbaugh, Mrs. E.F. Biog. Hist. of Cloud Co. 1903 919pp.

Cowley — Biog. Rec. of Cowley Co. Chi. Biog. 1910. 510pp.

Crawford — 20C. Hist. & Biog. Rec. of Crawford Co. Home authors. Chi.
Lewis. 1905. 856pp.

Doniphan — Gray, P.L. Doniphan Co. Hist. for 50 years. Bendena. Roycroft.
1905. 166 ft.
— Montgomery, W.B. Illus. Doniphan Co. Troy. Chief. 1915. 384pp.
— Symms, A.B., Brenner, G. Masonic Cemetery Rec. Old Doniphan
Sta. 15pp. Atchison. 1946. Typed.

Douglas — D.A.R. Tombstone descriptions 1854. 1940. Douglas Co. 2 V.
1941-6. Typed.
— Port. & Biog. Rec. of Leavenworth, Douglas & Franklin Cos.
845 pp. Chi. 1899.

Ellsworth — D.A.R. Cemetery Records of Ellsworth Co. 3 V. Ellsworth. 1939-41.
— Rollins, Alice W. Story of a Ranch. N.Y. Cassell. 1885 469pp.

Finney — Hist. of Finney Co., Kan. Co. Hist. Socy. Garden City. 1950-54.

Geary — D.A.R. Tombstone descriptions, Geary Co. To 1911. 139pp. 1940
Typed.

Grant — Hist. of Grant Co. Kan. Wilson R.R. and Sears, Ethel M.
Witchita, Eagle Press. 1950 278pp.

Jackson — Port. & Biog. Jackson, Jefferson and Pottawatomie Cos. 782pp.
Chi. 1890.

Jefferson — Census of 1870. Jewell & Jefferson Co. 30pp. Typed.

Johnson — Blair, E. Hist. of Johnson Co. Lawrence. Standard. 1915. 469pp.
— Atlas of Johnson Co., Heisler, Smith, Coffin, Lott.
— Gregg, O.H. Hist. of Johnson Co. Heisler, Wyandotte, 1874.101pp.

Labette — Case, Nelson, ed. Hist. of Labette Co. Topeka. Crane 1893 372pp.
— Case, Nelson, ed. Hist. of Labette Co. Chi. Biog. 1901 822pp.
— D.A.R. Birth Records Labette Co. 1885-92. Pittsburg 1940. Typed.

Leavenworth — Andreas, A.T. Comp. Leavenworth Co. 1883. Leavenworth.
Dodsworth. 1906. 339pp.
— Baum, J.E. Leavenworth Co. Cemeteries. 175pp. Leavenworth
1947. Typed.
— Biog. Rec. of Leavenworth, Douglas & Franklin Co. Chapman Chi.1899
— Hall, J.E. & Hand, L.T. Hist. of Leavenworth Co., Topeka.
Hist. 1921. 680pp.
— Moore, H.M. Early Hist. of City & Co. of Leavenworth.
Dodsworth. 1906. 339pp.

KANSAS (continued)

Lincoln
- Barr, Elizabeth N. Hist. of Lincoln Co. Topeka 1908 123pp.
- Bernhardt, C. Indians In Lincoln Co. 1864-9. Lincoln Sentinel. 1910. 62pp.

Linn
- Mitchell, W. A. Linn Co., 1928. 404pp.

Lyon
- Blue Book of Lyon Co. Emporia Gazette. 1908. 48pp.
- D.A.R. Tombstone Inscriptions Lyon Co. 7 vols. Emporia. 1938-48. Type.
- French, Laura M. Hist. of Emporia & Lyon Co. Gazette Pr. 1929. 292pp.
- Jones, Carolyn. The First 100 yrs. Hist. of The City of Manhattan, Kansas. 1855-1955. Manhattan Tribune-News 1955. 96pp.

Marshall
- Porter, Emma E. Hist. of Marshall Co. Biog. Indpls. Bower. 1917 1041pp.

McPherson
- Nyquist, Edna. Pioneer McPherson Co. 1932. McPherson. 184pp.

Meade
- Pioneer Stories of Meade Co. Council of Women's Clubs. Marceline, Mo. Wadsworth Bros. 1950. 109pp.
- Sullivan, F.S. Hist. of Meade Co., Topeka. Crane. 1916. 184pp.

Montgomery
- Duncan, L.W. Hist of Montgomery Co. Iola. Duncan. 1903. 852pp.

Nemaha
- Crevecoeur, F.F. Old Settlers Tales To 1877. Onaga. Repub. 1902. 162pp.
- Tennal, R. Nemaha Co. 816pp. Lawrence. 1916.

Neosho
- Duncan, L.W. Hist. of Neosho & Wilson Cos. Ft. Scot Monitor. 1902. 922pp.
- Graves, William W. Neosho Co. St. Paul Journ. Press. 1949-51 544pp.

Norton
- Bowers, D.N. Norton Co. 1872-1942. 238pp. Norton 1942.

Pawnee
- Progress In Pawnee Co. Tiller & Toiler 80th Anniv. Ed. Larned 1952. 142pp.

Phillips
- Phillips Co. Review, Comp. Progress & Hist. Edition. Phillipsburg 1952. 40pp.

Pottawatomie
- Crevecoeur, F.F. Old Settlers Tales To 1877. Onaga Repub. 1902. 162pp.
- Early Hist. of Pottawatomie Co. Cent. Ed. 1854-1954 n.p.1954 40pp

Reno
- Ploughe, S. Hist. of Reno Co. Biog. Indpls. Bowen. 1917. 2V.

Republic
- Tolbert, Agnes Margaret (Hodgins) Log Cabin Days along Salt Creek Republic Co., Kans. Chi. Adams. 1959.
- Savage, I.O. Hist. of Republic Co. To 1883. Topeka Capital Pr. 1883. 106pp.
- Hist. of Republic Co. To June 1, 1901. Beloit. Jones & Chubbic Pr. 1901.

KANSAS (continued)

Rice   - Jones, H. Early Rice Co. Wichita Eagle Pr. 1928. 135pp.

Saline   - Chapman, Port & Biog. Dickinson, Saline, McPherson & Marion Cos. 614pp. Chi. 1893.

Sedgwick   - Bentley, O.H. ed. Hist. of Wichita & Sedgwick Co. Cities Chi. Cooper. 1910.
    - Port. & Biog. Sedgwick Co. 1123pp. Chi. 1888.

Shawnee   - Giles, F.W. Shawnee Co. 68pp. Topeka 1876.
    - King, J.M. Comp. Hist. of Shawnee Co. Biog. Chi. Richmond 1905. 628pp.

Sumner   - Freeman, G.D. 20 Yrs. Hist. S. Kan. & Ind. Ter. Caldwell, Freeman. 1892. 406pp.
    - Port. & Biog. Sumner Co. 461pp. Chi. 1890.

Thomas   - Kinkel, G.H. & Jones, C.A. Comp. Golden Jubilee of Thomas Co. 1885-1895. Rexford News. 1935. 188pp.

Wabaunsee   - Thomson, Matt. Early Hist. of Wabaunsee Co. Biog. author. 1901. 368pp.
    - Thomson, Matt. Early Hist. of Wabaunsee Co., Alma. Thompson. 1902. 368pp.

Western   - Millbrook, Minnie (Dubbs) Ness. Detroit, Mich. Western Co. Kan. Millbrook. 1955. 319pp.

Wilson   - Duncan, L.W. Hist. of Neosho & Wilson Co. Ft. Scott Monitor 1902. 922pp.

Woodson   - Duncan, L.W. & Scott, C.F. eds. Hist. of Allen & Woodson Co., Iola, Reg. 1901. 894 pp.

Wyandotte   - Harrington, Grant W. Historic Spots & Mile Stones In The Progress of Wyandotte Co. Kan. Merian. 1935. 360pp.
    - Morgan, Pearl Wilbur. A Hist. of Wyandotte Co. Kans. Chi. Lewis. 360 pp. 1911.
    - Wyandotte Co. & Kansas City. Hist. Biog. Chi. Goodspeed. 1890. 895 pp.

   The Bibliography of Town & County Histories of Kansas compiled by Lorene Anderson and Alan W. Farley, reprinted from the Kan. Hist. quart. Topeka, Kan. 1955 is one of the best Bibliographies of this kind found in all the fifty states. Three Hundred and twenty-two known town and county histories have been published of ninety-one of all the one hundred and five counties in Kansas. No town or county histories are found for the following fourteen Kansas Counties: Cheyene, Greeley, Harper, Kearney, Kiowa Lane, Morton, Rawlins, Rooks, Russell, Stafford, Stanton, Stevens and Wichita.

KANSAS (continued)

One Hundred and Ninety-Two County Atlases have been prepared for ninety-two Kansas Counties: Finney, Grant, Gray, Greeley, Hamilton, Haskell, Jearney, Logan, Morton, Scott, Seward, Stanton and Stevens.

The Kansas State Hist. Socy. has County Directories of the following Kansas Counties: Allen, Crawford, Davis, Dickinson, Doniphan, Douglas, Elk, Finney, Ford, Fort, Franklin, Douglas, Geary, Gray, Labette, McPherson, Mitchell, Osage, Riley, Russell, Saline, Seward, Shawnee, and Wabaunsee. This Socy. has City Directories of the following cities: Abilene, Atchison, Caldwell, Chanute, Cheney, Cherryvale Chetopa, Clay Center, Coffeyville, Colby, Columbus, Concordia, El Dorado, Ellis, Elwood, Emporia, Fredonia, Galena, Garden City, Goodland, Great Bend, Harper, Hiawatha, Hutchinson, Independence, Junction City, Kansas City, Kingman, Lawrence, Leavenworth, Liberal, McPherson, Manhattan, Medicine Lodge, Newton, North Topeka, Olathe, Osage City, Ottawa, Parsons, Pittsburg, Pratt, Salina, Topeka, Wellington, Wichita and Winfield.

KENTUCKY

- Hallenberg, Leone W. Anchorage: A Casual Gathering of Facts & Stories pf XVII.
- From The Past & Present of a Unique Ky. Town Anchorage Press, Ky. 223-1959.

Adair
- Hist. of Adair Co.

Anderson
- McKee, L.W. & Bond, Mrs. L.K. Hist. of Anderson Co. 1780. 1936. Frankfort, Roberts 219pp.

Barren
- Hist. of Barren Co.
- Gorin, F. Barren Co. 131pp. 1929. Louisville.
- McGhee, L.K. Barren Co., Ky. and Its People. 1956.

Boone
- Bell, A.W.V. Census 1810. Boone Co. 17pp. 1935. Wash. D.C.
- Rea, R. R. Boone Co., Ky. and Its People. 1955.

Bourbon
- Bell, A.W.B. Census 1810. Bourbon Co. 92pp. 1934.
- Perrin, W.H. Peter. R. Hist. of Bourbon, Scott, Harrison & Nicholas Co. Baskin 1882. 815pp.

Boyle
- Hist. of Boyle Co.
- Davies, M.T. Mercer & Boyle Cos. V. 1. Harrodsburg, 1924.

Bracken
- Burns, A.W. Census 1810. Bracken Co. 13pp. Wash. 1936.
- Jillson, Willard House. A glimpse of Old Bridgeport and Its Environs In the Bluegrass of Ky. 1774-1899. Frankfort, Ky. Ky. Hist. Socy. 1956. pp. 108.

KENTUCKY (continued)

Breckinridge - Hist. of Breckinridge Co.

Bullitt - Bell, Burns, A.W. Census 1810. Bullitt Co. 24pp. Wash. 1935.

Butler - Bell, Burns, A.W. Census 1810. Butler Co. 15pp. Wash. 1935.

Caldwell - Baker, Clausine R. Hist. of Caldwell Co. Madisonville. Conn.
Pr. 218pp.

Campbell - Jones, M. K. Hist. of Campbell Co. Cent. Cel. July 4, 1876.
Newport. 1876. 16 pp.
- Bell. Burns, A.W. Census 1810. Campbell. 30pp. Wash. 1935.

Casey - Watkins, W. M. Casey Co. Lore 223. Louisville. 1939.

Christian - Meacham, C. M. Christian Co. 695 pp. Nashville. Marshall 1930.
- Perrin, W.H. Co. of Christian. Battery. Chi. & Louisville 1884.

Clark - Bell, A.W.B. Marriages of Clark Co. 1792-1851. 125 pp.
- Bell, A.W.B. Census 1810 Clark Co. 50 pp. Wash. D.C. 1934 Typed

Daviess - Daviess Co. Hist. Interstate Pub. Chi. 1883.

Fayette - Land Records Fayette Co. 130pp. 1949. Typed.
- Maccabe, J.B. Dir. of Lexington & Fayette Co. 1838. 136 pp.
- Panek, G.W. Lexington & Fayette Co.
- Perrin, W. E. Hist. of Fayette Co.
- Peter, R. ed. By Perrin, H.W. Hist. of Fayette Co. Baskin. Chi.
1882. 905 pp.

Fleming - Hist. of Fleming Co. Fischer. Flemingsburg. 1908. 24 pp.

Floyd - Scalf, Henry P. Historic Floyd. 1800-1950. Prestonburg 1950.
132 pp.

Franklin - James, C. E. Hist. of Franklin Co. For Cent. July 4, 1876.
Lewis. 1881. Frankfort. 11 pp.
- Jillson, W. R. Frankfort & Franklin Co. 1950-1850. Louisville.
Standard. 182 pp.
- Johnson, Frank. Hist. of Franklin Co.

Garrard - Bell, A.W.B. U.S. Census 1810. Garrard Co. 49pp Wash. 1935
- Calico, F. Hist. of Garrard Co., Ky. & Its Churches, 1947.
- Kinnard, Dr. J. B. Hist. of Lancaster & Garrard Co. Record.
1924. 55 pp.

Grant - Hist. of Grant Co., Ky. Comp. By Robt. H. Elliston, Speech On
July 4, 1876. Reprint. Williamstown, Ky. 1951 23pp.

KENTUCKY (continued)

Greenup
- Biggs, Nina Mitchell & Mabel Lee Mackay. Hist. of Greenup Co., Ky. Louisville 1951.

Hardin
- Briggs, Richard A. The Early Hist. of West Point (Hardin Co.) Ky. Print. Western Recorder. Louisville. 1955. pp 168.
- Co. Hist. Socy. Who Was Who In Hardin Co. 2 V. Elizabethtown 1946. Typed.

Harlan
- Middleton, E. Harlan Co. 544 pp. Big Laurel, Va. 1934.
- Hist. of Harlan Co.

Harrison
- Perrin, W. H. Bourbon, Scott, Harrison & Nicholas Co. 815 pp. Chi. 1882.
- Hist. of Harrison Co.

Hart
- Gardiner, F. E. Cyrus Edward's Stories of Early Barren, Hart, and Metcalfe Cos. 364 pp. Louisville 1940.
- Hist. of Hart Co.

Henderson
- Bell, A.W.B. Census 1810. Henderson Co. 32 pp. Wash. D. C.
- Starling, E. L. Hist. of Henderson Co. Biog. Henderson 1887, 840 pp.

Henry
- Drane, M. J. Henry Co. 274 pp. 1948. 288pp. Louisville 1898.

Hickman
- The Hickman Co. Gazette. 100th Anniv. Ed. Apr. 3, 1953. Clinton, Ky.
- Hist. of Hickman Co.

Jefferson
- Johnson, S. Louisville & Jefferson Co. 1896.

Jessamine
- Johnston, S. Jessamine & Jefferson Co. by Jonny, B.H.

Johnson
- Hall, M. Johnson Co. Standard. Louisville. 1928. 1260pp.

Kenton
- Christopher, Gist H.S. Kenton Co., Ky. Cemeteries 1958. Sentinel-Echo. Laurel Co., Ky. 1954.

Litcher
- Hist. of Litcher Co.
- Bowles, I. A. Litcher Co. Hazard 1949 75 pp. Illus.

Lewis
Ragan, Rev. O. G. Hist. of Lewis Co. Cinn. 1912 504 pp.

Livingston - Hist. of Livingston Co.

Logan
- Finley, A.C. Russellville & Logan Co. 63 pp. Russellville 1890.
- Stratton, Margaret Barnes. Place Names of Logan Co. Russellville. New-Dem. 1950
- Finley, Alex C. - Logan Co. (pamphlet) Russellville.

KENTUCKY (continued)

Madison
- Burnam, R.R. Masonry in Madison Co. 1812-1913. 124 pp. 1914
- Darris Jonathan Truman and Maud Weaver. Glimpses of Historic Madison Co., Ky. Nashville. Williams 1955 pp 334.
- Hist. of Madison Co.

Marshall
- Freeman, L.L. Olds, E.C. Shenowell, O. Hist. of Marshall Co. Tribune, Benton. 1933.

Mason
- Clift, G.G. Hist. of Maysville & Mason Co. Lexington. Trans. Pr. 461 pp.
- Lee, L. C. Mason Co. 46 pp. Louisville.

Mercer
- Hist. of Mercer Co.
- Daviess, M. T. Mercer & Boyle Cos. V. 1 1924 Harrodsburg.
- McGhee, Lucy Kate. Mercer Co., Ky. Marriages 1785-1852. Stamford, Wash. 1959.
- Mercer Co., Mercer Co., Ky.

Metcalfe
- Hist. of Metcalfe Co., Ky. 1950. 26 pp Mimeo. Wolf Creek Dam. Homemakers Club.

Montgomery
- O'Rear, E.C. Montgomery Co. Bar 121 pp. 1945.
- Reid R. Montgomery Co. 69 pp. 1926. Lexington.

Muhlenberg
- Rothert, O. Hist. of Muhlenberg Co.

Nelson
- Pack, E. C. Hist. of Irvine & Nelson Co.

Nicholas
- Perrin, W.E. Hist. of Bourbon, Scott, Harrison & Nicholas Co.

Ohio
- Taylor, H. D. Hist. of Ohio Co.

Pendleton
- Rev. War Soldiers From Order Book #1 Pendleton Co. Circuit Court Records, 3 pp. Falmouth. 1946. Typed.
- Hist. of Pendleton Co.

Perry
- Hist. of Perry Co., Ky. Johnson, Mrs. E. T. Hazard 1953 286 pp.

Pulaski
- D.A.R. Pulaski Co. Graveyard Records. 28 pp. 1944. Typed.
- Tibbals, Alma Owens. A Hist. of Pulaski Co., Bagdad, Ky. 1952 Moore.
- Ramey, Clarice P. Hist. of Pulaski Co. M.A. Thesis, Univ. of Ky. 1935.

Scott
- Gaines, B. O. Hist. of Scott Co. author 1904 764 pp.

Shelby
- Willis, G. L. Hist. of Shelby Co. Hist. Socy. Com. on Pr.

Taylor
- Nesbitt, R. L. Early Taylor Co., Ky. Hist.

KENTUCKY (continued)

Todd
— Kennedy, U. E. Early Todd Co. 73 pp.

Union
— Union Co. 892 pp. Evansville, 1886.
— W.P.A. Inventory of The County Archives of Ky.

Warren
— Hist. of Warren Co.

Washington
— Baylor, O.W. Early Washington Co. 1942.

Wayne
— Hist. of Wayne Co.

Wolfe
— Wolfe Co. Woman's Club. Early & Modern Hist. of Wolfe Co., Ky.
n.p.,n.d., 1958 pp. 340.
— Hallenberg, Leone W. Anchorage: A Casual gathering of Facts &
Stories From Past & Present of a Unique Ky. Town. Anchorage Press.
Ky. pp. XVI, 223 - 1959.

Woodford
— Railey, W.E. Woodford Co. Robert. Frankfort. 1938. 449 pp.

LOUISIANA

The W.P.A. made Historical Record Surveys of 20 Parishes.

Ascension
— Marchand, Sidney Albert. A Century (1800-1900) In Ascension
Parish, La. Donaldsonville, La. 1936. 237 pp.
— Marchand, Sidney Albert. The Story of Ascension Parish, La.
Baton Rouge, La. Artlieb Print. 1931. 194 pp.

Assumption
— Alleman, Elise A. Place names of Assumption Parish. 1936.
104 pp. Thesis L.S.U. (M.A.) 1936.

Attakapas
— Griffen, H.L. The Attakapas (Lafayette Parish). New Orleans.
Pelican. 1959.

Avoyelles
— Saucier, Corinne L. Hist. of Avoyelles Parish, La. New Orleans.
Pelican 1943. 543 pp.

Beauregard
— Frasar, Mrs. Lily (Hopper) Early Annals of Beauregard Parish.
70 pp. Thesis (M.A.) L.S.U. 1933.

Calcasieu
— Ulmer, Grace. Econ. & Soc. Dev. of Calcasieu Parish, La. 1840-
1912. 148 pp. Thesis (M.A.) L.S.U. 1935.

Claiborne
— Harris, D. W. Hist. of Claiborne Parish, La. 1828-85. Comp. by
D. W. Harris & B. M. Hulse. New Orleans Press of Stanbury Co.
1886. 263 pp.

East
Baton Rouge
— Booth, Fannie D. Annal of The Parish of East Baton Rouge. 61 pp.
Thesis. (M.A.) L.S.U. 1933.

LOUISIANA (continued)

East
Feliciana   - Robinson, Early. Early Feliciana Politics. St. Francisville
      Democrat. 1936. 109 pp.

      - Skipwith, Henry. East Feliciana, La. Past & Present.
      New Orleans. Hopkins. 1892. 61 pp.

Evangeline   - Gahn, Robert. Hist. of Evangeline Parish. 141 pp. Thesis
      (M.A.) L.S.U. 1941.

Iberville   - Grace, Albert L. Iberville (Parish) Plaquemine, La. Author
      1946. 246 pp.

Lafayette   - Buchanan, Ann S. Early Days of Lafayette Parish. 70 pp.
      Thesis (M.A.) L.S.U. 1931 (unpublished)

      - Lafayette Parish, La. Community Service. Cent. Celebration.
      Apr. 6, 1933. Morgan City. King-Hannaford. 1923. 48 pp.

LaSalle   - Taylor, L.H. & Plummer, W.E. Hist. of La Salle Parish, La.
      The Jena La. Times, 11-19-1959 to 2-4-1960

Lincoln   - Lincoln Parish, La. Dev. Bd. Lincoln Parish La. Baton Rouge 1953

      - Graham, Kathleen, Notes on a Hist. of Lincoln Parish,
      Ruston, La. Polytechnic Inst. Bulletin 33 #4, 1935

      - Mondy, Robert W. Hist. of Lincoln Parish. Thesis (M.A.) Univ.
      of Tex. 1934.

Morehouse   - Davenport, Chris. C. Memoirs of Early Settlement of Morehouse
      Parish. Mer Rouge, La. Mer Rouge Democrat 1911. 50 pp.

Natchitoches- Berry, Nora. Place Names of Natchitoches Parish. 133 pp.
      Thesis (M.S.) L.S.U. 1935.

Sabine   - Armstrong, Amos Lee. Sabine Parish Story. Shreveport 1958.
      Jones-Stringfellow.

      - Belisle, John G. Hist. of Sabine Parish, La. Sabine Banner.
      1912. 319 pp.

St. James   -Bourgeois, Lillian C. Cabanocey: The Hist. Customs & Folk Lore
      of The Parish of St. James. New Orleans. Pelican 1957.

      - Peichardiere, A.L. Un Proisse La. St. Michel du Comte d'acadie.
      by R. deSenney, N. Orleans 1877. 144 pp.

St. Martin   - St. Martin's Parish, La. Dev. Bd. St. Martin Parish Survey.
      Baton Rouge. 1950.

      - Willis, Edwin Edward. Notes on Hist. of St. Martin Parish.
      Ann Arbor, Mich. Univ. Microfilm, Inc. 1957.

St. Landry   - Dupre, Gilbert L. Imperial St. Landry, mother of Parishes.
      La. Hist. Quart. 8: 420-427, July 1925.

LOUISIANA (continued)

St. Tammany - Burns, Phillip & Swarts, A. (Comp.) Hist. of St. Tammany
Parish. Covington, La. St. Tammany Hist. Socy. 1955.

Tangipahoa - Lanier, Lee. Bloody Tangipahoa. Hist. of Tangipahoa Parish.
News Digest. Amite. 2-13-50.
- Merry, J. F. Comp. Twenty-Five Years' Growth of Tangipahoa Parish,
La. 1885-1910. Passenger Dept. Ill. Central RR. 1910. 23 pp.

Terrebonne - Watkins, Marguerite Emma. Hist. of Terrebonne Parish to 1861.
238 pp. Thesis (M.A.) L.S.U. 1939.

Union - Union Parish, La. Dev. Bd. Union Parish. Survey. Baton Rouge.
D.P.W. 1953.

Washington - Carter, Prentiss B. Hist. of Wash. Parish, La. Hist. Quart.
14:36-59 Jan. 1931.

Webster - Turner, Sarah Anne. Place Names of Webster Parish. 93 pp.
Thesis (M.S.) L.S.U. 1935 (unpublished).

West
Feliciana - Butler, Louise. W. Feliciana, Glimpse of Its Hist. La. Hist.
Quart. 7: 90-120. Jan 1924.
- Robinson, Elrie. Early Feliciana Politics. St. Francisville
Democrat. 1936. 109 pp.

MAINE - 16 Counties

- Howard, R. H. A Hist. of New England. 2 Vols. Boston. 1880.
gives Histories of N. Eng. Counties & Towns.

Androscoggin - Hist. of Androscoggin Co. Me. Georgia Drew Merrill. Editor. Boston.
W.A. Ferguson. 1891. 879 pp.
- Atlas & Hist. of Androscoggin Co., Sanford, Evert & Rol. Phila.
1873 120 pp.

Aroostock - Roe, F. B. & Colby, N. G. Atlas of Aroostock Co. Phil. 1877.
- Wiggins, Hist. of Aroostock Co., Pub. in Presque Isle 1922.

Cumberland - Biog. Leading Citizens of Cumberland Co. 706 pp. Boston 1896.
- Clayton, Woodford, W. Hist. of Cumberland Co. Biog. Mil. Phila.
Lippincott 1880 456 pp.

Franklin - Biog. Rev. of Franklin & Oxford Cos. Biog. Rev. Pub. Co. 1897.
Boston 639 pp.

Hancock - Halfpenny, H.E. & Stewart, J.H. Atlas of Hancock Co. Colby
1881 96 pp.
-Old Hancock Co. Me. Families. Pierce MacBeth Hancock Co. Pub. 1933.
- Wasson, S. Survey of Hancock Co. Pub. In American, Augusta
1878. 91 pp.

MAINE (continued)

Kennebec
- Kingsbury, H.D. Deyo, S. L. Hist. of Kennebec Co., N.Y. 1892 2 V.
- Kennebec, Me. Yesterdays. Marriner Ernest Cummings, Colby Coll. Pres. 1954.

Knox
- Gould, E.K. Rev. War Pensioners Knox Co. 45 pp. Rockland. 1935. Courier Gazette.

Lincoln
- Hist. of Lincoln Co.

Mt. Desert
- Morison, S.E. Story of Mt. Desert Is., Me. 1960.

Oxford
- Stone, T.T. Oxford Co. 111 pp. Port. 1830.
- Hist. of Oxford Co.

Penobscot
- Ford, H.A. Hist. of Penobscot Co. Biog. Cleveland 1882 922 pp.
- Godfrey, J.E. Duren, E.F. Hist. of Penobscot Co., Biog. Cleveland 1882 922 pp.

Piscataquis
- Colby. Piscataquis Co. Atlas.
- Loring, Amasa. Hist. of Piscataquis Co. to 1880. Hoyt. Portland. 1880. 304 pp.
- Sprague, Piscataquis Biog. & Fragments.

Sagadahoc
- Hist. of Sagadahoc Co.

Somerset
- Colby, G.N. Atlas of Somerset Co. Houlton. 1883 76 pp.

Waldo
- Lang, J.W. Survey of Waldo Co. Augusta. Sprague, Owen & Nash. 1873. 131 pp.

York
- Clayton, Woodford W. Hist. of York Co. 1880. Biog. Phila. 442 pp. Evarts & Peck.
- Sanford, E.F. Everts, W.P., Roe, F.B. Atlas of York Co. Phila. 1872 127 pp.
- Thirty-Four Cemeteries In York Co. 53 pp. Biddleford, 1940. Typed. D.A.R. Cemeteries In York Co. 70 pp. 1946 Biddleford.
- Dr. Ava Chadbourne - Maine Place Names. Pamphlet.

MARYLAND - 23 Counties

Alleghany
- Thomas & Williams. Hist. of Alleghany Co.
- 1800 Census Alleghany Co. 52 pp. Balt. 1936. Typed.
- Alleghany Co. Geological Survey. Hopkins Press. 1900-1903.
- Thomas James Walter. Alleghany Co. Cumberland. Titsworth. 1923.

MARYLAND (continued)

Anne Arundel — Bell, Mrs. Anne (Walker) Burns. Anne Arundel Co. Index. Executors Accts. Annapolis. 1939.

- 1800 Census Anne Arundel Co. 109 pp. Balt. 1936. Type.

- Inscriptions From Graves In Anne Arundel Co.

- Hodges, Mrs. Margaret Roberts. General Index of Wills, Anne Arundel Co., Md. 1777-1917.

- Newman, Harry Wright. Anne Arundel Md. Gentry. Lord Baltimore Press. Balto. 1933.

- Riley, E.S. Hist. of Anne Arundel Co. Feldmeyer, Annapolis 1905.

- Warfield, Joshua Dorsey. Founders of Anne Arundel & Howard Cos. Md. Kohn & Pollock. 1905.

Baltimore — Geneal. & Biog. of Leading Families of Balto. City & Co. 1061 pp. N. Y. 1897.

- Balto. Co. Md. Pub. Schools. Here Is Balto. Co. Towson Bd. of Educ. Balto. Co. 1956.

- Burns, Annie (Walker). Balto. Co., Md. A Registry of Administrations. Annapolis. 1939.

- Davidson, Isobel. Real Stories From Balto. Co. Hist. Balto. Warwick & York 1917.

- Offutt, Thieman Scott. Balto. Co., Towson, Md. Jeffersonian Pub. 1916.

- Scharf, Thos. Hist. of Baltimore Co.

- Ida Charles Wilkins Foundation. Balto., Md. Genealogical Notes. Balto. Co. 1954.

Calvert — Berkley, H.J. First Cent. of Co. of Calvert. 1934-1734.

- Burns Annie (Walker). Index Rent Roll Calvert Co., Md. 1651-1723. Balto. 1940.

- Census, Calvert Co. 1800 46 pp. Balt. 1936. Type.

- Md. Geological Survey. Calvert Co., Md. Hopkins 1907.

Caroline — Cochrane, Crouse, Gibson, Thompson & Noble. Hist. of Caroline Co. Stowell, Federalsburg. 1920.

- Cramor, Henry Downes. Marriage Licenses of Caroline Co., Md. 1774-1815. Phila. 1904.

- Noble, E. M. Caroline Co. 348 pp. 1920.

Carroll — Elderdice, Dorothy. The Carroll Co. Md. Caravan. Westminster Times. 1937.

- Lynch. B. J. Hundred Years of Carroll Co. 1837-1937. Advocate. Westminster 1939.

Cecil — Ash, Mollie Howard. Cecil Co., Md. Signers of Oath of Allegiance.

- Mar. 2, 1778. Elkton, Cecil Whig Print. 1940.

MARYLAND (continued)

Cecil   - Burns, Annie (Walker) Index Cecil Co., Md. Rent Roll 1658-1724.
(cont'd)
             - D.A.R. Capt. J. Baker Chap Cecil Co., Md. Marriage Licenses
               1777-1840.
             - Johnston, George. Hist. of Cecil Co., Md. Elkton, Md. 1881.
             - Md. Geol. Survey. Cecil Co., Md. Hopkins Press. 1902.
             - Johnson, Geo. Hist. of Cecil Co.
             - Miller, Alice Etta. Cecil Co., Md. Study In Local Hist.
               Elkton, Md. C. & L. Print 1949.
             - Port. & Biog. Harford & Cecil Cos. 596 pp. N. Y. 1897.

Charles   - Burns, Annie (Walker) - Index To Court Records. Charles Co.,
               Md. Annapolis. 1939.
             - Burns, Annie (Walker) Index Rent Rolls, Charles Co. Md.
               Baltimore 1940
             - D.A.R. Charles Co. Tombstones & Bible Records 235 pp.
               Wash, D.C. 1940 V. 64.

Dorchester -- Burns, Mrs. Annie (Walker) Dorchester Co., Md. Rents.
               Balto. 1940.
             - Burns, Mrs. Annie (Walker) Dorchester Co. Marriage Licenses
               Annapolis 1939.
             - Dorchester Co., Md. Marriage Records 1780-1865 Cambridge 1930.
             - Jones, Elias. Hist. of Dorchester Co., Md. Williams &
               Wilkins Co. Press. Balto. 1902.
             - Jones, Elias. Revised Hist. of Dorchester Co. Balto. Read-
               Taylor Press. 1925.

Frederick   - Delaplaine, Edward Schley. The Origin of Frederick Co., Md.
               Wash. Judd, 1949.
             - Hinks, William H. Cent. Celebration In Frederick Co., Md.
               6-28-1876. Frederick, Baughman. 1879.
             - Williams, Thomas John Chew. Hist. of Frederick Co., Md.
               Frederick, 1910. Titsworth.

Garrett   - Hoye, Charles Edward. Garrett Co. Hist. of Pioneer Families.
               Oakland, Md.
             - Md. Geological Survey. Garrett Co., Md. Balto. Hopkins
               Press. 1902.

Harford   - Preston, W. W. Hist. of Harford Co. 1608-1814. Sun. Balto.
               1901.
             - Holland, Charles D. Some Landmarks of Colonial Hist. In
               Harford Co., Md. Balto. Fosnot. 1933.
             - Mason, Samuel. Harford Co., 119 pp. 1940 Lancaster, Pa.
               Intelligence.
             - Port. & Biog. Record of Harford & Cecil Co., Md. N.Y. & Chi.
               Chapman, 1897.

MARYLAND (continued)

Howard
- Founders of Anne Arundel & Howard Cos., Geneal. & Biog. Wills, Deeds, and Church Rec. 543 pp. Balto. 1905.

Kent
- Burns, Annie Walker. Index To Rent Roll of Kent Co., Md. 1940 Balto.
- Hanson, G. A. Hist. of Kent Co.
- Usilton, F. G. Hist. of Kent Co. 1630-1916.

Montgomery
- Boyd, Thomas Hulings Stockton. Hist. of Montgomery Co., Md. 1650-1879. Balto. Boyle. 1879.
- Centennial of Montgomery Co., Sept. 6, 1876. Sappell Balto.
- Farquhar, Roger Brooke - Historic Montgomery Co., Md. Silver Spring 1952.
- Greater Montgomery Co., Md. Cent. 9-6-1876. Balto. Saffell. 1877.
- Greater Montgomery Co., Md. Wash. D.C. Judd Detweiler 1932.

Prince George's-Bowie E.G. Across The Years In Prince George's Md. Co. 1954.
- Bowie, Effie Augusta, Across The Years In Prince George's Co. Md. Richmond, Garrett. 1947.
- D.A.R. Prince George's Co., Md. Tombstone Records. Dietrich.1955.

Queen Anne's- Burns, Annie Walker. Index To Rent Roll. Queen Anne's Co., Md. Balto. 1940.
- Emory, Frederic. Queen Anne's Co., Md. Balto. Md. Hist. Socy.
- Emory, F. Hist. of Queen Anne. Centreville Observer, 1886.
- Burns, Annie Walker - Index St. George's Parish, Md.

St. Mary's
- Burns, Annie Walker - Index To Rent Roll of St. Mary's Co. Md.
- Md. Geol. Survey. St. Mary's Co. Md. Balto. Hopkins 1907.

Somerset
- Bell, Mrs. Annie Walker Burns. Index Rent Roll Somerset Co. Md. Balto. 1940.
- Bell, Mrs. Annie Walker Burns. Births, Marriages, etc. Before 1720 Somerset Co., Md. Annapolis. 1939.
- Torrence, Clayton. Old Somerset On Eastern Shore of Md. Richmond. Whittet. 1935.

Talbot
- Tilghman, Oswald. Hist. of Talbot Co., Md. 1661-1861. Balto. Williams. 1915.
- Tyler, W.M. Talbot Co. Necks, Eastern Star Dem. 1927-8.

Washington
- Hicks, E.R. Wash. Co. Hagerstown. 1947.
- Miller, L.E. Rec. of Cemeteries, Wash. C. 7V. Hagerstown 1942-46. Typed.
- Williams. Thomas John Chew. Hist. of Wash. Co., Md. Hagerstown Titsworth. 1906.

MARYLAND (continued)

Western Md. - Scharf, Thos. Hist. of Western Md., Gives Hist. of Garrett,
Alleghany, Washington, Frederick, Carroll & Montgomery.

Wicomico   - Tilghman, I.B. Wicomico Co. Rec. 129 pp. Balto. 1935 Typed

Worcester   - Hudson, Millard Fillmore. Heads of Families In Worcester Co.
Md. 1790. First Census. Wash. 1931.
- Old Burial Grounds In Worcester Co. On Eastern Shore. By P.D.and
      66 · pp. Silver Spgs. 1937. Typed.   F.P.V.Lines
- Counties of Maryland. By Mathews, E.B.
- Balto. Co., Md. In The State & Nation Public Schools, Towson
Bd. of Educ. Balto. Co. 1957.

MASSACHUSETTS - 14 Counties

Barnstable - Freeman, F. Annals of Barnstable Co. 1860.
- Deyo, S.L. Barnstable Co. 1010 pp. N.Y. 1890.

Berkshire   - Allen, T. Co. of Berkshire & Pittsfield. Boston. Belcher
1808 14 pp.
- Child, H. Gazateer of Berkshire Co. 1725-1885. Syracuse.1885.
947 pp.
- Dewey, C. Hist. of Berkshire Comp. Pittsfield. Bush. 1829 468pp.
- Palmer, C. J. Berkshire Co.
- Smith, J.E.A. Hist. of Berkshire Co. Biog. N.Y. 1885.
- Hist. of Berkshire Co. Biog. N. Y. 1885 2 Vol.
- Picturesque Berkshire Co., Springfield 1893 230 pp.

Bristol   - Bristol Co. Hist. Des. & Biog. Borden. Boston Hist. Co.
1899. 418 pp.
- Bristol Co. Hist. & Dir. 1875-6. Dudley. Boston. 1876.
- Hurd, D.H. Hist. of Bristol Co. Biog. Phila. Lewis. 1883 922pp.
- Hutt, F.W. ed. Bristol Co. Hist. Lewis. N.Y. & Chi. 1924. 1246 pp.

Dukes   - Hough, F.B. Early Papers On Present Dukes Co. Albany. 1856.

Essex   - Hurd, D.H. Hist. of Essex Co. Biog. Phila. Lewis. 1888 2V 2460pp
- Hist. & Dir. of Essex Co., Towns. Boston 1870. 670 pp.
- Hist. of Essex Co. Cities, Towns, Boston. 1878. 424 pp.

Franklin   - Josiah S. Holland. Hist. of Western Mass. 2 Vols. 1852.

Hampden   - Copeland, A.M. ed. Our County and Its People 1902.Springfield.3V.
- Johnson, C. Hampden Co. 1636-1936 N.Y. Amer. Hist. Socy. 3V

MASSACHUSETTS (continued)

Hampshire
- Gay, W.B. Gazeteer of Hampshire Co. 1654-1887. Gay. Syracuse. 482 pp.
- Johnson, C. Historic Hampshire In Conn. Valley To 1900. Springfield. Bradley. 1932. 406 pp.

Middlesex
- Drake, S.A. Hist. of Middlesex Co. Cities. Boston, Maps, Port. Estes & Lawriat. 1880 2V. 1077 pp.
- Hurd, D.H. Hist. of Middlesex. Biog. Phila. Lewis 3V. 1890.
- Gould, L.S. Ancient Middlesex. Biog. 1905.

Nantucket
- Cook, R.H. Hist. Notes of Is. of Nantucket. 1871.
- Douglas, R. A. Leithgow, Nantucket. A Hist. N.Y. 1914.
- Starbuck, A. Hist. of Nantucket Co. Island & Town Boston 1924.

Norfolk
- Cook, T. A. ed. Hist. of Norfolk Co. 1622-1918. Clarke, N.Y. 2V 817 pp.
- Hurd, D.H. Hist. of Norfolk Co. Biog. Phila. Lewis. 1884.

Plymouth
- Dudley, D. Plymouth & Barnstable Co. Hist. & Dir. Boston. 1873. 206 pp.
- Hurd, D.H. Hist. of Plymouth Co. Biog. Phila. Lewis 1884 1199 pp.
- Thompson, E.S. Hist. of Plymouth, Norfolk & Barnstable Co. 1928. Lewis. 3V.

Suffolk
- David, W.T. ed. Prof. & Ind. Hist. of Suffolk Co. Hist. 1894. 3V.

Worcester
- Crane, E. B. ed. Hist. of Worcester Co. Williams. Lewis N.Y. 1924. 3V.
- Hurd, D.H. Hist. of Worcester Co. Biog. Phila. Lewis. 1889. 2V
- Marvin A.P. & Others. Hist. of Worcester Co. To Pres. Jewett. Boston 1879. 2V.
- Nelson, J. Worcester Co. Narrative. Amer. Hist. Socy. 1934 3V.
- Whitney, P. Hist. of Co. of Worcester & Towns. Worcester 1793.
- Hist. of Worcester Co. 2 Vo. 1879. C.F. Jewett & Co.

MICHIGAN - 83 Counties

Allegan
- Chapman, Port. Biog. Kalamazoo, Allegan & Van Buren Cos. 986 pp. Chi. 1892.
- Johnson, C. Hist. of Allegan & Barry Co. Biog. Phila. Ensign 1880 521 pp.

Alpena
- Oliver, D. D. Alpena Co. Cent. 186 pp. Alpena 1903.

Barry
- Potter, W.W. Hist. of Barry Co. Zandler, 1912.

MICHIGAN (continued)

Bay
- Hist. of Bay Co., Chi. pp. 1883
- Butterfield, G.E. Bay Co. 212 pp Bay City 1918.
- Butterfield, George Ernest. Bay Co., Mich. Past & Present Bay City, Midh. Bd. of Educ. 1957.
- Gansser, A.H. Bah Co. Biog. 726 pp. Chi. 1905.

Berrien
- Port. & Biog. Berrien & Cass Cos. 922 pp. Chi. 1893.
- D.A.R. Cem. Rec. Berrien Co. 304 pp. 1943 Typed.
- Cowles, E.B. Hist. & Dir. of Berrien Co., Buchanan, 1871 384 pp.
- Ellis, F. Hist. of Berrien & Van Buren Co.
- Hist. of Berrien & Van Buren Co., Phila. Ensign. 1880.
- Ensign, D.W. Berrien & Van Buren Co. Lippincott. 1880.

Branch
- Biog. Album of Branch Co. Chapman, Chi. 1888.
- Collins, H.P. Branch Co. Hist. Lewis. 1906.
- Hist. of Branch Co. Biog. Everts. Phila. 1879.
- Johnson, C. Hist. of Branch Co. Phila. Everts. 1879 347 pp.
- Sharer, R.E. Hist. of Branch Co. 1936. M.A. Thesis U. of Mich.
- Sowers, R.D.F. Hist. Rev. of Branch Co. 1933.

Colbam
- Gardner, W. Hist. of Calbam Co. Lewis. Chi. 1913. 606 pp.
- Pierce, H. B. "   "   "   "
- Rust, E.G. Calbam Co. Dir. & Hist. Battle Creek. 1869. 425 pp.
- 1830 Hist. of Calbam Co. Everts Phila. 1877. 212 pp.

Calhoun
- Chapman. Port. & Biog. Calhoun Co. 1046 pp. Chi. 1891.
- Everts, L.H. & Co. Calhoun Co. 212 pp. Phila. 1877.
- Gardner, W. Calhoun Co. 2V Chi. 1913.

Cass
- Cass Co. 432 pp. Chi. 1882.
- Berrien & Cass Cos. 922 pp. Chi. 1893.
- Rogers, H.S. Cass Co. 1825-75, 406 pp. Cassopolis 1875.

Cheboygan
- Van Fleet, Rev. J.A. Hist. of Cheboygan & Mackinac Co. 1873.
- Story of Salt St. Marie & Chippewa Co. Sault St. Marie Pr.Co. 1923

Clinton
- Daboll, S.B. & Kelly, D.W. Past & Present of Clinton Co. Clarke, Chi. 1906. 575 pp.
- Ellis, F. Hist. of Shieawassee & Clinton Co. Ensign. Phila. 1880. 541 pp.

Eaton
- Strange, D. Pioneer Hist. of Eaton Co. 1923. Pioneer. 192 pp.
- Williams, W. Past & Pres. of Eaton Co. Pub. Assn. Lansing 633 pp.

MICHIGAN (continued)

Genesee — Ellis, F. Hist. of Genesee Co. Phila. Everts. 1879. 446 pp.
— Genesee Co. Biog. 401 pp. Indpls. 1908. Port. & Biog.
— Genesee, Lapeer & Tucola Cos. 1056 pp. Chi. 1892.

Grand Traverse—Sprague, E.L. & Smith, Mrs. G.N. Grand Traverse & Leelanow Cos. 806 pp. 1903.

Gratiot — Chapman, Port & Biog. Gratiot Co. 820 pp. Chi. 1884.
— Port. & Biog. Album Gratiot Co. Chapman. Chi. 1884 821 pp.
— Tucker, W.D. Gratiot Co. Biog. Seaman & Peters, Saginaw 1913 1353 pp.

Hillsdale — 1850 census Hillsdale Co. 3 V. 1937. Typed.
— In Hillsdale Co. 95 pp. Hillsdale. 1947.
— Johnson, C. Hist. of Hillsdale Co. Phila., Everts. 1879 334 pp.
— Moore, V.L. Early War Veterans. Rev. War. War of 1812.
— Port. & Biog. Album. of Hillsdale Co. Chapman. 1885.
— Reynolds, E.G. ed. Hist. & Biog. of Hillsdale Co. 1903 460 pp.

Huron — Gwinn, F.M. Pioneer Huron Co. 100 pp. 1922.
— Port. & Biog. Huron Co. 500 pp. Chi. 1884.

Ingham — Adams, Mrs. F. L. Pioneer Hist. of Ingham Co. Lansing, Wynkoop 1923. 856 pp.
— Cowles, A.E. Lansing & Ingham Co. Hist. Pub. Lansing 1900 583 pp.
— D.A.R. Cen. Rec. Ingham Co. 294 pp. Lansing 1943. Typed.
— Durant, S.W. Hist. of Ingham & Eaton Co. Lippincott Phila 1800. 586 oo.

Ionia — Branch, Rev. E.E. Hist. of Ionia Co. Indpls. Bowen. 1916. 1035 pp.
— Dillenback, G.D. Hist. & Dir. of Ionia Co. Grand Rapids. 1872 195 pp.
— Schenck, J.S. Hist. of Ionia & Montcalm Co. Ensign, Phila. Lippincott. 502 pp.
— Schenck, J.S. Port. & Biog. Album of Ionia & Montcalm Co. 1891.

Isabella — Faricher, I.A. Issabella Co. 1911.
— Port. & Biog. Album of Isabella Co. Chapman. Chi. 1884. 589 pp.

Jackson — Deland, Col. C.V. Hist. of Jackson Co. Bowen. 1903 1122 pp.
— D.A.R. Jackson Co. Cem. Rec. 2 V. Jackson 1942.
— Port. & Biog. Jackson Co. 878 pp. Chi. 1890.

Kalamazoo — Durant, S.W. & P.A. Hist. of Kalamazoo Co. Biog. Phila. Everts 1880 552 pp.
— Fisher, D. & L.F. eds. Hist. & Biog. of Kalamazoo Co. Bowen Chi. 1906 571 pp.
— Thomas, J.M. Early Kalamazoo Co. Dir. Kalamazoo 1869 374 pp.

MICHIGAN (continued)

Kent
- Hist. of Kent Co. Chi. Chapman 1881. 1426 pp.
- Hist. & Dir. Kent Co. Dillenbach. Grand Rapids, Eagle 1870 319pp.
- Leeson, M.A. Hist. of Kent Co. 1882. Leeson. Chi.

Lapeer
- Hist. of Lapeer Co. Chi. Page. 1884.

Lenawee
- Art Work of Lenawee & Monroe Co. Chi. Parish. 1894. 168 pp.
- Bonner, R.I. ed. Memoirs of Lenawee Co., Mich. W. Hist. Assn. Madison, 2 V. 1909. Illus.
- Bowen, Harriet Cole. Comp. Gravestone Rec. of Lenawee Co. Compiler the Editor.
- Cadwell, G. R. Atlas of Lenawee Co. 1893.
- Chapman Bros. Port & Biog. Album of Lenawee Co. Chi. Chapman 1888
- Everts & Stewart. Comb. Atlas of Lenawee Co. 1874.
- Fuller, G.M. Hist. Mich. 3V.-Vol. 3 Lenawee Co. Mich. Hist. Socy. 1924.
- Knapp, John I. Illus. Hist. & Biog. Rec. of Lenawee Co. Mich. Knapp & Bonner, R.I. Times Print. 1903.
- Millard, A.L. Early Hist. of Lenawee Co. & City of Adrian. Hist. Oration on July 4, 1876.
- Ogle, G.A. & Co. Stand. Atlas of Lenawee Co. 1916.
- Whitney, W.A. & Bonner, R.L. Hist. & Biog. Rec. of Lenawee Co. 2 V. Adrian 1879.

Livingston
- D.A.R. Rec. of 24 Cemeteries of Livingston Co. 141 pp. 1943. Typed.
- Ellis, F. Livingston Co. Evarts 462 pp.

Mackinac
- Van Fleet, Rev. J.A. Hist. of Sheboygan & Mackinac Co. 1873.

Macomb
- Leeson, M.A. Hist. of Macomb Co. Chi. Leeson. 1882.
- Macomb Co. Biog. 709 pp. Chi. 1905.

Manistee
- The Lumberman's Legacy. By Russell, C.N. & Baer, D.D. Manistee Hist. Socy. 1954. 67 pp. Illus. Manistee.

Mecosta
- Port. & Biog. Mecosta Co. Chi. Chapman. 1883.

Menominee
- Ingalls, E.S. Cent. Hist. of Menominee Co. 1876.
- Schuyler, Ethel. Menominee Co. School 1941. 400 pp.

Midland
- Port. & Biog. Midland Co. 433 pp. 1883.

Monroe
- Buckley, J.M. Hist. of Monroe Co. Lewis 1913. 1023 pp.
- Wing, T.E. Hist. of Monroe, Munsell, 1890. 659 pp.

Montcalm
- Dosef, J. Hist. of Montcalm Co. Bowen, Indpls. 1916.
- Atlas of Montcalm Co. Ogle. Chi. 1921.

MICHIGAN (continued)

Muskegon — Muskegon & Ottawa Co. Biog. Chi. 1893. 577 pp.
— Page, H.R. Muskegon Co. Chi. 1882.

Newaygo — Port. & Biog. Newaygo Co. 572 pp. Chi. 1884.

Oakland — Avery, Lillian D. ed. Oakland Co. Vol 3 of 1924. Fuller, G.N. ed.
Historic Mich. 451 pp.
— Biog. Pub. Co. Leading Citizens 1903 581 pp. Chi. Author.
— Chapman Bros. Port & Biog. Album 1891. Oakland 959 pp. Chi.
Author.
— Hist. of Oakland Co., Mich. Phil. Everts 1877. 354 pp.
— Seeley, Thaddeus, Comp. Hist. of Lakland Co. 2V 1912 Chi. Lewis.

Oceana — Hartwick, L.M. Zuller, W.H. Oceana Co. Cities. Biog.
Pentwater 1890 432 pp.

Osceola Port. & Biog. Osceola Co. 418 pp. Chi. 1884.

Ottawa — Lillie, L.C. Grand Haven & Ottawa Co. Grand Haven 1931 394 pp.
— Hist. of Ottawa & Muskegon Co., Chi. Page. 1882.
— Hist. & Bus. Comp. of Ottawa Co., Ptts. Grand Haven 1892 280 pp.

Saginaw — Beers, F.W. & Co. Atlas of Saginaw Co., N.Y. F.W. Beers & Co. 1877.
— Hist. of Saginaw Co. Cities, etc. Prehistoric Races, Early
White Settlers, Chapman, 1881.
— Emery, B. Frank. Fort Saginaw 1822-3. Forgotten Frontier Post.
Detroit. Old Fort & Hist. Mem. Assn. 1932.
— Fuller, G.N. ed. Hist. of Saginaw Co. (In His Historic Mich.)
1924. V. 3, pp. 17-65.
— Imperial Pub. Co. The Co. of Saginaw. Imperial Pub. 1896.
— Mills, J.C. Hist. of Saginaw Co. Saginaw, Seemann & Peters 1918.
— Ogle, G.A. & Comp. Stand. Atlas of Saginaw Co. Cities, etc.
Maps, Dir. Chi. Ogle 1916.
— Hist. of Saginaws and Saginaw Co. 1819-1879. East Saginaw.

St. Clair — Hist. of St. Clair Co. Chi. Andreas. 1883. 790 pp.
— Jenks, Wm. Lee. St. Clair Co. 2 Vols. Chi.&N.Y. Lewis, 1912

St. Joseph — Cutler, H.G. Hist. of St. Joseph Co. Lewis. Chi. 1911 2V 837 pp.
— Hist. of St. Joseph Co. Everts. Phila. 1827-77. 232 pp.

Shiawassee — Hist. of Shiawassee & Clinton Co. Mich. Phila. Ensign. 1880.

Tuscola — Hist. of Tuscola & Bay Cos. Biog. Illus. Chi. 1883 83 pp Folio 211.

Van Buren — Johnson, Crisfield. Hist. of Van Buren Co.
— Rowland, Capt. O.W. Hist. of Van Buren Co. 2V Lewis 1912

MICHIGAN (continued)

Washtenaw — Hist. of Washtenaw Co., Mich. Port. Biog. Chi. Chapman
1881. 1452 pp.

— Beakes, S.W. Washtenaw Co. 823 pp. Chi. 1906.

Wayne — Burton, Clarence M. Hist. of Wayne Co. & City of Detroit.
eds. C. M. and A. B. Burton. H.T.O. Blue & Gordon K. Miller.
Assoc. ed. Chi. Detroit. Clarke 1930. 5 Vols.

— Wayne Co., Mich. Hist. & Pioneer Socy. N.W.Ter. & Wayne Co.
Chronology 1531-1890. Biog. Comp. By F. Carlisle. Gulley &
Bornman Print. 1890. 484 pp.

— Catlin, G.B. ed. Detroit & Wayne Co. (Fuller, G.N. ed. Hist.
Mich. 1924 V3.) 658 pp.

— Farmer, Silas. Hist. of Detroit & Wayne Co. & Early Mich.
Detroit. 1890. 2V Illus.

—Ross, Robert Budd. Landmarks of Wayne Co. & Detroit. Eve. News
Assn. 1898. 2V.

— Comp. of Hist. & Biog. of Detroit & Wayne Co., Mich. Chi.
Taylor. 1909. 719 pp.

Wexford — Wheeler, John H. The Hist. of Wexford Co. Pub. Bowen 1903 557pp.

MINNESOTA — 87 Counties

Anoka — Goodrich, Albert M. Hist. of Anoka Co. & Towns of Champlin
& Dayton in Hennepin Co., 1905. Hennepin Pub. Minneapolis.

Becker — Wilcox, Alvin H. A Pioneer Hist. of Becker Co., 1907.
Pioneer Press. St. Paul.

Big Stone — Wulff, Lydia Sorenson. Big Stone Co. Hist. Ortonville.
Koercher. 1959.

Blue Earth — W.P.A. Minn. Blue Earth Co., 1938 Minneapolis.

— Hughes, Thomas. Hist. of Blue Earth Co. Biog. 1909. Mid-West
Pub. Co. Chi. Ill.

Brown — Carver, Centenary, One Hundredth Anniv. of the Council of Treaty
of Capt. Jonathan Carver, with the Nandowessies, at the Great
Cane (now in St. Paul). St. Paul. 1867 8 Vols. 23pp

— Fritsche, L.A., ed. Hist. of Brown Co. Minn. 2V 1916 Bower
Indpls.

Carlton — Carlton Co. Centennial 1857-1957. Cloquet. Minn. 1957. 40 pp.

Carver — Carver Co. Statehood Cent. Com. Carver Co. Today & Yesterday
Wacomia 1958 70 pp.

— Holcombe, R.I. Comp. of Hist. & Biog. of Carver & Hennepin Co.
1915. Taylor, Chi.

MINNESOTA (continued)

Chippewa
— Moyer, L.R. & Dale, O.G. eds. Hist. of Chippewa & Lac. Qui Parle Co. 2 Vols. 1916 Bowen. Indpls.

Clay
— Turner, John & Semling, C.K. eds. Hist. of Clay & Norman Cos. 2 V. 1918. Bowen. Indpls.

Cottonwood
— Brown, John A. Hist. of Cottonwood & Watonwan Co. 2 V. 1916. Bowen. Indpls.

Crow Wing
— Zapffe, Carl. It Happened Here, Especially Crow Wing Co. Brainard Journal 1948.

Dakota
— Curtiss-Wedge, Franklyn, ed. Hist. of Dakota & Goodhue Counties. 2 Vol. 1910. Cooper. Chi.
— Hist. of Dakota Co. by Rev. Edw. D. Neill & Hist. of Minn. by J. Fletcher Williams. 1881 Star Pub.
— Mitchell, W.H. Dakota Co., 1868. Trib. Print. Minneapolis, Minn.

Dodge
— Hist. of Winona, Olnstead & Dodge Cos. 1884. H.H. Hill. Chi.
— Mitchell, W.H. & Curtis, U. Hist. Sketch of Dodge Co. 1870. Fed. Union Bk. ' Job Print. of Rochester, Minn.

Douglas
— Larson, Constant, ed. Hist. of Douglas & Grant Cos. 2V. 1916 Bowen, Indpls.

Faribault
— Faribault Co. Minn. 1868. 24 pp.
— Kiester, Jacob A. Hist. of Faribault Co. To 1879. 1896. Harrison & Smith. Minneapolis.
— Memorial Record of The Counties of Faribault, Martin, Watonwan & Jackson, Minn. 1895. Lewis. Chi.

Fillmore
— Bishop, Judson Wade. Hist. of Fillmore Co. 1858. Holly & Brown Chatfield.
— Neill, Edw. D. Hist. of Fillmore Co. Minn. Hist. Co. Minneapolis.
— Curtiss-Wedge, Franklyn. Comp. Hist. of Fillmore Co. 2V 1912 Cooper. Chi.

Freeborn
— Curtiss-Wedge, Franklyn. Comp. Hist. of Freeborn Co. 1911.
— Neill, Edw. D. Hist. of Freeborn Co., 1882. Minn. Hist. Co. Minneapolis.

Goodhue
— Curtiss-Wedge, Franklyn, ed. Hist. of Goodhue Co. Minn. 1909 Cooper. Chi.
— Curtiss-Wedge, Franklyn, ed. Hist. of Dakota & Goodhue Co. Minn. 2 V. 1910 Cooper. Chi.
— Hancock, Jos. W. Goodhue Co., Minn. by An Old Settler. 1893. Red Wing Print. 349pp. Illus.
— Hist. of Goodhue Co. 1878. Wood, Alley & Co. Red Wing

MINNESOTA (continued)

Goodhue (cont'd)
- Mitchell, W.H. Past & Pres. of Goodhue Co. 1869. King's. Minn.
- Rasmussen, Christian A. Hist. of Goodhue Co. 1935. Red Wing Print.

Grant
- Larson, Constant, ed. Hist. of Douglas & Grant Cos. 2V 1916. Bowen, Indpls.

Hennepin
- Co-op with W.P.A. Hennepin Co., Minn. Hist. V. 1.
- A Hist. of Minneapolis, ed. by Judge Isaac Atwater & Hennepin Co. ed by Col. John H. Stevens 2V 1895. Munsell. N.Y. & Chi.
- Holcombe, R.I. ed. Hist. & Biog. of Carver & Hennepin Co. Minn. 1915. Taylor. Chi.
- Holcombe, R.I. ed. Hist. & Biog. of Minneapolis & Hennepin Co. 1915 Taylor. Chi.
- Mitchell, W.H. & Stevens, J.H. Hist. of The County of Hennepin, 1868. Russell & Peljoy. 149 pp. Minneapolis.
- Warner, Geo E. Hist. of Hennepin Co. & Minneapolis. Explorers & Pioneers of Minn. by Edw. D. Neill, Minn. by J. F. Williams 1881. North Star Pub. Co. Minneapolis.

Houston
- Hist. of Houston Co. 1882. Minn. Hist. Co. Minneapolis.
- Houston Co. Its Advantages & Resources. Hokah, Minn. 1858 34 pp.

Itasca
- Dobie, John - The Itasca Story. Minneapolis. Ross 1959.

Jackson
- Memorial Record of The Counties of Faribault, Martin, Watonwan & Jackson, Minn. 1895. Lewis. Chi.
- Rose, Arthur P. Illus. Hist. of Jackson Co. 1910 Northern Hist. Pub. Co. Jackson.

Kandiyohi
- Thurn, Karl. Round Robin of Kandiyohi Co. Cent. yr. 1858-1958. Thurn.
- Lawson, Victor E. & Lew, Martin E. Comp. Illus. Des. Biog. Review of Kandiyoli Co. 1905. Pioneer Press Manufacturing Depts. St. Paul.

Kitson
- WPA. Kittson Co. Co. Hist. Socy. 1940. Writers Program.

LacQuiParle
- Moyer, L.R. & Dale, O.G. eds. Hist. of Chippewa & Lac Qui Parle Cos. 2 V. 1916. Bowen. Indpls.

Le Sueur
- Gresham, W.G. Hist. of Nicollet. Le Sueur Cos. 2V 1916. Bowen, Indpls.

Lincoln
- Tasker, A.E. Comp. Early Hist. of Lincoln Co. 1936. Lake Benton News Print. Lake Benton.

Lyon
- Case, Christopher F. Hist. & Des. of Lyon Co. 1884 Messenger Print. Marshall.
- Rose, Arthur P. Illus. Hist. of Lyon Co. 1912. Northern Hist. Pub. Co. Marshall

MINNESOTA (continued)

McLeod
- Curtiss-Wedge, Franklyn, Comp. Hist. of McLeod Co. 1917. Cooper. Chi. Winona.
- Illus. Album of Biog. of Meeker & McLeod Co. 1888 Alden, Ogle, Chi.

Martin
- Budd, Wm. H. Hist. of Martin Co. 1897. Fairmount.
- Martin Co. & Other Border Cos. of S. Minn. & Upper Iowa. London 1878. 8 V. 47 pp.
- Memorial Record of The Counties of Faribault, Martin, Watonwan, and Jackson, Minn. 1895. Lewis. Chi.
- Moore, Allen L. Comp. Martin Co. Before 1850. 1932. Martin, Fairmount Hist. Socy.

Meeker
- Album of Hist. & Biog. of Meeker Co. 1888 Alden, Ogle. Chi.
- Illus. Biog. of Meeker & McLeod Cos. 1888 Alden, Ogle. Chi.
- Lamson, Frank B. Comp. & Pub. Hist. of Meeker Co. 1855-1939 Brown Litchfield.
- Peterson, Clarence Stewart. Meeker Co., Minn. Territorial Pioneers Centennial 1849-1949.
- Smith, Abner C. Meeker Co. 1877 Belfoy & Joubert. Litchfield.

Morrison
- Fuller,Clara K. Hist. of Morrison & Todd Co. 2V 1915. Bowen, Indpls.

Mower
- Curtiss-Wedge, Franklyn. Hist. of Mower Co. 1911. Cooper, Jr. Chi.
- The Interstate Hist. Co.Comp. Hist. of Mower Co. 1884 Free Press Mankato.
- Paden, R.N. Comp. Early Hist. of Mower Co. 1876. Hitchkiss. Austin.

Nicollet
- Gresham, Wing, ed. Hist. of Nicollet & LeSueur Co. 2V 1916 Bowen. Indpls.

Nobles
- Nobles Co. Hist. ed by Al Goff. Pub. by Nobles Co. Hist. Socy 1958. 280 pp. Worthington.
- Nobles Co. Hist. 1958.
- Rose, Arthur P. Illus. Hist. of Nobles Co. 1908. Northern Hist. Pub. Worthington.

Norman
- Norman Co. Statehood Cent. Com. A Short Hist. of Norman Co. Minn. Centennial ed. Ada, Minn. 1958. 124 pp.
- Turner, John & Semling, C.K. eds. Hist. of Clay & Norman Co. 2 V. 1918. Bowen, Indianapolis.

Olmstead
- Hist. of Winona & Olmstead Co. 1883. Hill. Chi.
- Hist. of Winona, Olmstead & Dodge Co. 1884. Hill. Chi.
- Leonard, Jos. A. Hist. of Olmstead Co. Minn. 1910 Goodspeed Chi.
- Mitchell, W.H. Hist. of Co. of Olmstead, 1866. Shaver & Eaton Rochester. 121 pp.

MINNESOTA (continued)

Otter Tail — Mason, John W. ed. Hist. of Otter Tail Co. 2V 1916 Bowen Indpls.

Pipestone — Rose, Arthur P. Illus. Hist. of Counties of Rock & Pipestone
1911. Northern Hist. Pub. Co. Luverne.

Polk — Holcombe, R.I. ed. Hist. & Biog. of Polk Co. 1916 Bingham, Minn.

Pope — Illus. Biog. Pope & Stevens Cos. 1888. Alden, Ogle. Chi.

Ramsey — Werner, Geo. E. & Foote, Chas. M. Hist. of Ramsey Co. & St. Paul
1881 North Star Pub. Co. Minneapolis.
— Williams, J. Fletcher. Hist. of St. Paul & Co. of Ramsey. 1876.
Minn. Hist. Socy. St. Paul
— Biog. of Early Settlers. Minn. 1881   650 pp.

Red River
Valley — Peterson, Clarence Stewart. Red River Valley Territorial
Pioneers. Balto. 1949.

Redwood — Curtiss-Wedge, Franklyn, Comp. Hist. of Redwood Co. 1916.
Cooper. Chi. 2V.

Renville — Curtiss-Wedge, Franklyn, Comp. Hist. of Renville Co. 1916
Cooper. Chi. 2V

Rice — Berg, Tillie Clara. Early Pioneers & Indians of Minn. & Rice
Co. San Leander, Calif. 1959.
— Curtiss-Wedge, Franklyn, Comp. Hist. of Rice & Steele Cos.
2V. 1910 Cooper. Chi.
— Hist. of Rice Co. 1882 Minn. Hist. Co. Minn.
— W.P.A. Project Rice Co. 1938 Minn.

Rock — Rose,Arthur P. Illus. Hist. of the Counties of Rock & Pipestone.
1911. Northern Hist. Pub. Co. Luverne.

St. Croix
River Valley— Peterson, Clarence Stewart. St. Croix River Valley Territorial
Centennial 1849-1949.

St. Louis — Van Brunt, Walter. Duluth & St. Louis Co. 3V 1921 Amer.
Hist. Socy. Chi. & N. Y.
— Woodbridge, Dwight E. & Pardee, John S. eds. Hist. of Duluth
and St. Louis Cos. 2 Vols. 1910 Cooper. Chi.

Stearns — Mitchell, Wm. Bell. Hist. of Stearns Co. 2V 1915 Cooper Chi.

Steele — Curtiss-Wedge, Franklyn. Hist. of Rice & Steele Co. 2 V. 1910
Cooper. Chi.
— Hist. of Steele & Waseca Co. 1887. Union Pub. Co. Chi.
— Mitchell, W.H. Hist. of Steele Co. 1868. Tribune Print. 97 pp.

MINNESOTA (continued)

Stevens   - Brown, Calvin L. Stevens Co. & City of Morris. 1923. Morris Tribune.

                   - Illus. Biog. of Pope & Stevens Co. 1888 Alden, Ogle. Chi.

Swift   - Anonsen, Stanley H. Hist. of Swift Co. 1929 Swift Co. Hist. Socy. Benson.

                   - Peterson, Clarence Stewart. Swift County's First Pioneers. Minn. Territorial Centennial 1849-1949.

Todd   - Fuller, Clara K. Hist. of Morrison & Todd Co. 2V 1915 Bowen, Indpls.

Traverse   - Barrett, Jos. O. Hist. of Traverse Co. 1881. Browns Valley, Minn.

Wabasha   - Mitchell, W.H. & Curtis U. Wabasha Co., 1870. Fed. Union Pr. 164 pp. Rochester.

                   - Hist. of Wabasha Co. & Winona Co. 1884. Hill. Chi.

                   - W.P.A. Minnesota. Wabasha Co. 1938. Minneapolis.

Waseca   - Child, James E. Waseca Co. 1905. Owatonna Chronicle.

                   - Hist. of Steele & Waseca Co. 1887. Union Pub. Co. Chi.

Washington   - Hist. of Wash. Co. and St. Croix Valley with Explorers & Pioneers of Minn. by Rev. E. D. Neill, Hist. of Minn. by J. F. Williams 1881. North Star Pub. Co. Minn. 636 pp.

Watonwan   - Brown, John A. Hist. of Cottonwood & Watonwan Co. 2V 1916 Bowen Indpls.

                   - Memorial Record of The Counties of Faribault, Martin, Watonwan & Jackson 1895 Lewis. Chi.

Winona   - Curtiss-Wedge, Franklyn Comp. Hist. of Winona Co. 2V 1913 Cooper Chi.

                   - Gravestone Records of Winona Co. 1934 126 pp. Typed.

                   - Hist. of Winona & Olmstead Co. 1883 Hill. Chi.

                   - Hist. of Winona & Olmstead & Dodge Co. 1884. Hill. Chi.

                   - Hist. of Wabasha Co. & Hist. of Winona Co. 1884. Hill. Chi.

                   - Hist. of Winona Co. 1883. Hill. Chi.

                   - Port. & Biog. Record of Winona Co. 1895. Chapman. Chi. 423 pp.

                   - Johnson, Syvert H. Biog. of Earliest Settlers. Rush Creek Valley Winona. 1940.

Wright   - Curtiss-Wedge, Franklyn. Hist. of Wright Co. 2V 1915 Cooper. Chi.

                   - French, C.A. & Lamson, F.B. Hist. of Wright Co. 1851-1935. Eagle Pr. Deland.

MINNESOTA (continued)

Yellow
Medicine
- Dirnberger, Ethel (Erickson) Pioneers In Sandness, Yellow
  Medicine Co. Echo. 1958.
- Rose, Arthur P. Illus. Hist. of Yellow Medicine Co. 1914.
  Northern Hist. Pub. Co. Marshall.
- W.P.A. Inventory of County Archives of Minnesota.
- Brief County Histories of all Minnesota Counties in "Who's
  Who In Minnesota", pub. in 1941 by Minn. Editorial Assn.,
  Minneapolis & prepared by Historians for each County.
- St. Paul Institute - Spring Lake Archeology Pt. 3, 1959.

MISSISSIPPI - 82 Counties

Adams
- W.P.A. Archives No. 2 Adams Co. Ct. of Gen. Sess. 1799-
  1801. (1942).
- W.P.A. Archives No. 2 Adams Co. Ct. of Gen. Sess.
  1802-04. Jackson. 1942.

Amite
- Casey, A. E. Amite Co. Miss. 1699-1865. Vol. 2 1950.
- Casey, A.E. Amite Co. Miss. 1699-1890 Birmingham Hist.
  Fund. 1957.

Bolivar
- Gray, W.F. Bolivar Co. 94 pp. Cleveland 1923.
- Sillers, F.W. Bolivar Co. 634 pp. Jackson 1948.

Calhoun
- Ryan, J.S. & Murphree, T.M. Hist. of Calhoun Co. Pittsboro,
  Monitor, 1904 49 pp.

Clay
- Miller, A.E. Gravestone Records Clay Co. 414 pp. 1936. Type.

Copiah
- Upton, Marie Luter. Marriage Records. Copiah Co. Miss.
  1823-43. Madison 1958.

Hancock
- Claiborne, J.F.H. Hist. of Hancock Co. New Orleans 1876 16 pp.

Hinds
- Berry, Mary Josephine. Marriage & Cemetery Records. Hinds
  Co. Miss. D.A.R. 1951.
- Rowland, Mrs. D. Hist. of Hinds Co. 1821-1922. Jackson, Jones.
  1922. 63 pp.

Jackson
- Four Centuries In The Pascagouda, by C. E. Cain State Coll.
  Miss. 1953.

Lowndes
- Cemeteries of Lowndes Co. 35 pp. 1949 Typed.

Madison
- Upton, Robert C. Marriage Records, Madison Co. Miss. 1958.
  F1835-47. E1830-6.

Monroe
- Evans, W.A. & Shell, J.L. Cemeteries In Monroe Co. 271pp.
  1938. Typed.
- Rollins, B.S. Brief Hist. of Aberdeen & Monroe Cos., Miss.
  1821-1900 Aberdeen, Miss. 1957

MISSISSIPPI (continued)

__Newton__   - Brown, A.J. Hist. of Newton Co. 1834-1894. Jackson 1894. 472 pp.

__Oktibbeha__ - Carroll, T.B. Hist. of Oktibbeha Co. Butts, Garner & Mellen,
             ed. Gulfport Dixie Pr. 1931 263 pp.

__Pike__   - Conerly, L.W. Pike Co. 1798-1876. Nashville. Brandon Pr. 1909.
             368 pp.

            - Gillis, Miss N. Hist. of Pike Co., & McComb.

__Prentiss__ - Bouton, R. L. Hist. of Prentiss Co. U. of Miss. M.A. Thesis
             1935. 131 pp.

            - Nabors, S.M. Hist. of Old Tishomingo Co. Corinth. 1930 108 pp.

__Tishomingo__ - D.A.R. Tishomingo Co. (now Alcorn, Prentiss & Tishomingo Cos.)
             1836-70. 202 pp. Typed.

__Union__   - Smith, J.I.S. Cemetery Rec. Union Co. 82 pp. 1944. New Albany.

__Warren__   - King. J.E.S. Warren Co. Wills and Marriages (Court Records.
             1936 pp. 127-143.

Washington - McCain, William David. Memoirs of Henry Tillinghast. Ibreys.
             Papers of Wash. Co., Miss. Hist. Socy Edited by W. D. McCain &
             Charlotte Capers, Jackson. State Archives. 1954.

__Yazoo__   - Yazoo Hist. Assn. Yazoo Co. Story. A Pictorial Story of Yazoo Co.
             Miss. (Fort Worth Univ. Supply & Equipment Co. 1958). 148 pp.

MISSOURI - 114 Counties

__Adair__   - Violette, E.M. Hist. of Adair Co. 1911. Denslow. 1168 pp.

            - Hist. of Adair, Sullivan, Putnam & Schuyler Co. Chi. Goodspeed.
             1888. 1225 pp.

__Andrew__   - Hist. of Andrew & DeKalb Cos. St. Louis & Chi. Goodspeed.
             1888 591 pp.

__Andrain__ - Robertson G. Hist. of Andrain 1913.

            - Schooley, H. Cent. Hist. of Andrain, McIntyre. 1917 304 pp.

            - Andrain Co. Illus. St. Louis Nat'l Hist. Co. 1884. 978 pp.

__Barry__   - Mills, Nellie Alice. Hist. Spots In Old Barry Co. Mo. Monett, Mo.
             1952.

__Bates__   - Atkeson, W.O. Hist. of Bates Co. Hist. Pub. Topeka. 1918. 983 pp.

            - Hist. of Bates & Cass Cos. Natl. Hist. Co. St. Joseph 1883. 1414pp.

            - Old Settlers' Hist. of Bates Co. 1897. Tathwell & Maxey.
             Amsterdam. 212 pp.

MISSOURI (continued)

Benton — Lay, J.H. Hist. of Benton Co. Cent. Cel. July 4, 1876.
Warsaw. Hannibal. Winchell & Ebert Pr. 1876. 76 pp.

Boone — Hist. of Boone Co. St. Louis. West. Hist. Co. 1882. 1144 pp.
— Ramsay, Robert Lee. The Place Names of Boone Co., Mo.
Gainesville, Fla. Amer. Dialect Socy. 1952.

Buchanan — Hist. of Buchanan Co. Cities. Biog. Mil. Union Hist. Co.
St. Joseph 1881. 1073 pp.
— Hist. of Buchanan Co. & St. Joseph & Mo. to 1915. Midland.
St. Joseph 567 pp.
— Port. & Biog. Rec. Buchanan and Clinton Cos. 675 pp.
Chi. 1893.
— Rutt, C.L. ed. Buchanan Co. & St. Joseph to 1898. St. Joseph
Pub. 1899. 569 pp.
— Rutt, C.L. ed. Buchanan Co. & St. Joseph to 1826-1904. Biog.
Pub. Chi. 1904. 723 pp.
— News Hist. of Buchanan Co. & St. Joseph. St. Joseph Pub. Co.
569 pp.

Butler — Deem, D.B. Hist. of Butler Co. Poplar Bluff. 1940.

Caldwell — Johnston, C.P. & McGlumphy, W.H.S. Clinton & Caldwell Cos.
836 pp. Topeka 1923.
— Richards, F.D. Hist. of Caldwell & Livingston Co. Biog.
St. Louis 1886. 241 pp.
— Hist. of Caldwell & Livingston Co. St. Louis. Natl. Hist.
Co. 1886. 1227 pp.

Callaway — Bell, O. Callaway Co. 32 pp. 1923.
— Hist. of Callaway Co. Rec. Illus. Natl. Hist. Co. 1884 954 pp.

Carroll — Carroll Co. 694 pp. 1876.
— Port. & Biog. Rec. Clay, Ray, Carroll Charitan & Linn Cos.
740 pp. Chi. 1893.
— Illus. Hist. Atlas Map Carroll Co. 103 pp. 1876.

Cass — Hist. of Cass & Bates Cos. Illus. St. Joseph. Nat'l Hist. Co.
1883. 1414 pp.

Chariton — Nat'l. Hist. Co. Howard & Chariton Co. 1225 pp. St. Louis 1883.
— Hist. Pict. & Biog. of Chariton Co. Salisbury. Pictorial
& Biog. Pub. 1896. 248 pp.

Clay — Port. & Biog. Rec. Clay, Ray, Carroll, Chariton & Linn Cos.
740 pp. Chi. 1893.
— Hist. of Clay & Platte, St. Louis Hist. Pub. Co. 1885 1121 pp.
— Woodson's Hist. of Clay Co. Hist. Pub. Co. Topeka 1920 777 pp.

MISSOURI (continued)

Clinton
- Port. & Biog. Rec. Buchanan & Clinton Cos. 675 pp. Chi. 1893.
- Hist. of Clinton Co. St. Joseph Natl. Hist. Co. 1881 264 pp.
- Marriage Records of Clinton Co. Mo. 1833-70. Mimeo 1955 Wills and Administrations of Clinton Co. Mo. 1833-70 K.C. Mo. Mimeo 1954; Both by Carr Nanon Lucille.

Cole
- Hist. of Cole, Moniteau, Morgan, Benton, Miller, Maries, & Osage Cos. Illus. Chi. Goodspeed 1889 1172 pp.

Cooper
- Johnson, W.F. Hist. of Cooper Co. Hist. Pub. Co. 1919 1167 pp.
- Hist. of Cooper and Howard Cos. Natl. Hist. Co. Nixon. St. Louis 1883. 1162 pp.
- Levens, H.C. Drake, N.M. Hist. of Cooper Co. Perrin. St. Louis 1876. 231 pp.
- Melton, E.J. Hist. of Cooper Co. Columbia. Stephenson 1937. 584 pp.

Daviess
- Jordin, J.F. Early Daviess Co. Gallatin, N. Mo. Pr. Mo. 206 pp.
- Hist. of Daviess Co., K.C. Mo. Birdsall. 1882 868 pp.

Douglas
- Early Settlers of Douglas Co. Mo. by Selleck, Bessie J. Woods, Berkeley, Calif. Prof. Press 1952.
- Selleck, Bessie Janet. Early Settlers of Douglas Co. Mo. Berkeley 1952.

Dunklin
- Papers, Vol. 1 Kennett, Mo. Dunklin Co. Hist. Socy. Thrower 1951.
- Smyth, Davis Mary F. Hist. of Dunklin Co. 1845-95. St. Louis. Nixon. 1896. 290 pp.

Franklin
- Goodspeed Bros. Goodspeed's Hist. of Franklin etc. Cos. 1958.
- Ramsay, Robt. Lee. Place Names of Franklin Co., Mo. Columbia Mo. 1954.
- Hist. of Franklin, Jefferson, Washington, Crawford, Gasconade Co. Chi. Goodspeed 1888. 131 pp.

Gentry
- Hist. of Gentry & Worth Co. St. Joseph Natl. Hist. Co. 1882 837 pp.

Greene
- Atlas of Greene Co. Brink 1876 75 pp.
- Fairbanks, J. Early Greene Co. Indpls. Bowen.1915 & 1933. 2 Vols.
- Hist. of Greene Co. Towns. Biog. St. Louis. West Hist. Socy. 1883. 919 pp.
- Hubble, M.J. Early Hist. of Springfield & Greene Co. 1909 34 pp.
- Hubble, M.J. Early Hist. of Springfield & Greene Co. Springfield Inland 1914 96 pp.
- Honor Roll of Greene Co. Biog. Faithorn. Chi. 1919 427 pp.

MISSOURI (continued)

Grundy
- Ellsberry, Elizabeth P. Marriage Records of Grundy Co. Mo. 1841-64. Chilicothe.
- Ford, J. E. Hist. of Grundy Co. Trenton 1908. 875 pp.
- Grundy Co. 739 pp. Kan. City 1881.

Harrison
- Harrison & Mercer Cos. 758 pp.   St. Louis 1888.
- Wanamaker, G. W. Hist. of Harrison Co. Topeka 1921 855 pp.

Henry
- Hist. of Henry & St. Clair Co. St. Joseph Natl. Hist. Co. 1883. 1224 pp.

Hickory
- Donnavan, Albert Thomas, Allen Faye (Smith) & Jenkins Mamie (Bandel). Hickory Co., Mo. Happenings For 79 Yrs. Not in Books. Mimeo.
- Hist. of Hickory, Polk, Cedar, Dade & Batton Co., Chi. Goodspeed. 1889. 967 pp.

Holt
- Hist. of Holt & Atchison Co., St. Jo. Natl. 1882 1036 pp.

Howard
- Ellsberry, Elizabeth P. Marriage Records of Howard Co., Mo. 1818-36. 1948.
- Hist. of Howard & Chariton Cos. St. Louis Natl. 1883. 1225 pp.
- Hist. of Howard & Cooper Co. Natl. 1883. 1167 pp.

Jackson
- Marshall & Morrison. Polit. Hist. of Jackson Co. Biog. K.C., Mo. 1902 247 pp.
- Hist. of Jackson Co. Biog. Mil. Union. Birdsall 1881 1006 pp.

Jasper
- Hist. of Jasper Co. Carthage. Banner. 1887. 28 pp.
- Hist. of Jasper Co. Des Moines. Mills. 1883. 1065 pp.
- Livingston, Jasper Co. Chi. Lewis. 2 V. 1912.
- McGregor, M.G. Biog. Rec. Jasper Co. 526 pp. Chi. 1901.

Jefferson
- Atlas of Jefferson Co. Illus. Brink. 1876. 79 pp.

Johnson
- Cockrell, E. Hist. of Johnson Co. Topeka 1918 1144 pp.
- Hist. of Johnson Co. Biog. K.C. Mo. K.C. Hist. Co. 1881 989 pp.
- Port. & Biog. Rec. Johnson & Pettis Cos. 665 pp. Chi. 1895.

Knox
- Early Hist. of Knox Co. Edina Sentinel. 1916. 162 pp.

Laclede
- Nyberg, L. Hist. of Laclede Co. 1820-1926. 1926. 176 pp. Rustic. Lebanon.
- Hist. of Laclede, Camden, Dallas, Webster, Wright, Texas. Pulaski, Phelps & Dent Co., Chi. Goodspeed. 1889. 1219 pp.

MISSOURI (continued)

Lafayette — Young's Hist. of Lafayette Co. Bowen. Indpls. 1910 2V 837 pp.
— Hist. of Lafayette Co., Mo. Hist. Co. St. Louis 1881 702 pp.

Lawrence — Hurley, Mrs. L.S. Hist. of Mt. Vernon & Lawrence Co. 1831-1931.
Record. Mt. Vernon.
— Lawrence Co. Interstate Hist. Socy. Springfield. 3V.

Lewis — Hist. Lewis, Clark, Knox & Scotland Co., St. Louis. Goodspeed
1887. 1229 pp.

Lincoln — Hist. of Lincoln Co. Chi. Goodspeed 1888 637 pp.

Linn — Ellsberry, Elizabeth P. Cemetery Records N.W. Linn Co., Mo.
Chillicothe. 1957.
— Ellsberry, Elizabeth P. Will Records, Linn Co., Mo. 1830-78.
Chillicothe.
— Ellsberry, Elizabeth P. Marriage Records, Linn Co., Mo. 1842-57
1936.
— Comp. of Hist. & Biog. of Linn Co., Mo. Chi. H. Taylor & Co. 1912.

Livingston — Boehmer, Grace A. Hist. of Livingston Co. Cent. Com. Chillicothe
1937 167 pp.
— Ellsberry, Elizabeth P. Cemetery Records. N. Livingston Co.
Chillicothe.
— Ellsberry, Elizabeth P. Marriage Records. N. Livingston Co.
Chillicothe.

Marion — Perkins, E. F. Hist. of Marion Co. 1884. Nixon. St. Louis 1003 pp.
— Hist. of Marion, Ralls & Pike Co. Owen. 1895

McDonald — Sturges, J. A. Hist. of McDonald Co. Pineville 1897. 344 pp.

Mercer — Harrison & Mercer Cos. 758 pp. St. Louis. 1888.

Miller — Schultz, G. Miller Co. 176 pp. Jefferson City 1933.

Moniteau — Ford, J.E. Hist. of Moniteau Co. Calif. Crawford Co. 528 pp.
— Hist. of Monroe & Shelby Co. St. Louis. Nat'l. Hist. Co.
1884. 1176 pp.

Monroe — Monroe & Shelby Cos. 1176 pp. St. Louis 1884.

Montgomery — Thompson, L.A. Montgomery Co. Montgomery City 1879.

Morgan — Yarnell, Ilene Sims. Morgan Co., Mo. Inscriptions. Versailles.
Mo. 1954.

MISSOURI (continued)

Newton
- Newton, Lawrence, Barry & McDonald. 1082 pp. Chi. 1888.
- Lackey, Walter Fowler. Hist. of Newton, Independence. Zion 1950.
- Hist. of Newton, Lawrence, Barry & McDonald Co., Chi. Goodspeed. 1888. 1092 pp.

Nodaway
- Nodaway Co. Bowen 1910. 1184 pp.
- Biog. Hist. of Nodaway & Atchison Co. Lewis 1910 630 pp.
- Hist. of Nodaway. Natl. Hist. Socy St. Jo. 1882 1034 pp.

Ozark Region- Each Co. Biog. Goodspeed. 1894. 787 pp.

Pettis
- Hist. of Pettis Co. Biog. Mil. 1882 1108 pp.
- Demuth, Y.M. Hist. of Pettis Co. 1882 1018 pp.
- McGruder, M. Hist. of Pettis Co. 1919. Hist. Pub. Co. Topeka. 850 pp.
- Sampson, F.A. Pettis Co. & Sedalia, Smalley 1886 16 pp.

Pike
- Hist. of Pike Co. Biog. Des Moines. Mills 1883 1038 pp.

Platte
- Paxton, W.M. Annals of Platte Co. K.C. Hudson-1897. 1182 pp.

Ralls
- Norton, N.D. Early Ralls Co. 104 pp. New London 1945.

Randolph
- Hist. of Randolph & Macon Co. Natl. Hist. Co. 1884 1223 pp.
- Waller, A.H. Randolph Co. 852 pp. Topeka 1920.

Ray
- Hist. of Ray Co. Biog. St. Louis, Mo. Hist. 1881. 818 pp.

Saline
- Hist. of Saline Co. St. Louis, Mo. Hist. Co. 1881. 966 pp.
- Port. & Biog. Rec. Lafayette & Saline Cos. 650 pp. Chi. 1893.

St. Charles
- Hist. of St. Charles, Montgomery & Warren Co., St. Louis Natl. Hist. Co. 1885 1131 pp.

St. Louis
- Gross, Henry Emmett. Street Guide to St. Louis Co. Mo. St. Louis 1959.
- Scharf, J. T. Early Hist. of St. Louis City & Co., Phila. Everts 988 pp.
- Thomas, W. L. St. Louis Co. 2V St. Louis 1911.

Sullivan
- Ellsberry, Elizabeth P. Marriage Records of Sullivan Co., Mo. 1845-9. Chillicothe.
- D.A.R. Gen. John Sullivan Chap. Cemetery Inscriptions of Sullivan Co., Mo. Milan 1951.

Ste. Genevieve- Hist. of Counties of S.E. Mo. Goodspeed 1888 1215 pp. Same historical works containing historical material on groups of counties are: Hist. of S.E. Mo. 1888., Hist. of N.E. Mo. 3 vols. 1913. Hist. of N.W. Mo. 3 Vols. 1915; Reminiscent Hist. of The Ozark Region.

MISSOURI (continued)

Ste. Genevieve- (cont'd)
- Dr. Walter Williams & Floyd C. Shoemaker. Missouri Mother of the West. Pub. by Amer. Hist. Socy. Inc. Chi. 1930 Vols 1 & 2 on Mo. Hist. & Vols. 3, 4 & 5 Biog.
- Walter B. Steven's Centennial Hist. of Mo. 6 Vols. St. Louis-Chi. Clarke 1921

County Archives
- Inventory of County Archives of Mo.

Webster
- George Floy Watters. Hist. of Webster Co. 1855 to 1955. Marshfield, Mo. 1955.
- The Collection of Mo. County Histories were published mostly in the 1880's by Hist. Pub. Companies and the compiler's or author's names seldom appear on the title pages of the volumes. Histories of some thirty Missouri Counties have been published since 1900, most of them of counties which had an earlier county history.

MONTANA - 56 Counties

Blaine
- Noyes, A.J. Blaine Co. 152 pp. Helena 1917

Carbon
- Western Hist. Pub. Co. Illus. Hist. Counties of Park, Sweet Grass, Carbon, Yellowstone, Rosebud, Custer & Dawson 669 pp. Spokane, Wash.

Gallatin
- Houston, Lina E. Early Hist. of Gallatin Co. Chronicle. Bozeman 1933.

Treasure
- Treasure Co. Mont. Booster. By Geo. O. Criswell. Nov. 1948. Part of Co. Covered.

Yellowstone
- Valley Hist. of Yellowstone Valley Mont. Park, Sweetgrass, Carbon, Yellowstone, Rosebud Custer, Dawson Counties. Pub. by Western Hist. Pub. Co. Spokane, Wash.
- M. B. Milligan - Articles on Each County in Mont. Pub. in the Helena Independent In 1931.

Mont. Frontier
- Davis, William Lyle. A Hist. on St. Ignatius Mission on Outpost of Catholic Culture on the Mont. Frontier Spokane. 1954.
- W.P.A. Inventory of The County Archives of Mont.

NEBRASKA   93 Counties

- Biog. & Hist. Memoir of Adams, Clay, Webster & Nickolls Cos., Chi. 1890. 810 pp.
- Biog. Album of Northeastern Nebr. Phila. 1893 599 pp.
- Biog. Souvenir of Buffalo, Kearney & Phelps Cos. Battey. Chi. 1890. 716 pp.

NEBRASKA (continued)

- Port. & Biog. Album of Gage Co., Nebr. Chi. 1888. 778 pp.
- Port. & Biog. Album of Johnson & Pawnee Cos. Chapman, Chi. 1889. 630 pp.
- Port. & Biog. Album of Lancaster Co., Chi. 1888 796 pp.
- Port. & Biog. Album of Atol & Cass Cos. Chapman Bros. Chi. 1889.

Adams
- Burton, Wm. R. and Lewis, David. Hist. of Adams Co. Clarke. Chi. 1916. 2 V 475 pp.

Antelope
- Leach, A.J. Hist. of Antelope Co. 1909. 261 pp.

Blaine
- Dunn, Pella J. Hist. & Dev. of Blaine Co. Typed 1927 27 pp.

Box Butte
- Phillips, Anna N. and Boll, Velma D. Hist. of Box Butte Co. Private 1929 233 pp.

Boyd
- Snider, Luree. Hist. of Boyd Co. Lynch, Nebr. Herald. 1938 99 pp. Pamphlet.

Brown
- Jones, Lillian L. Days of Yore, Early Hist. of Brown Co. Pamphlet. Ainsworth. 1937. 56 pp.
- Progress On The Prairies - Ainsworth-Brown Co. Diamond Jubilee Aug. 6-9, 1958. Ainsworth, Nebr. Star Journal 64 pp. 1958.

Buffalo
- Bassett, S.C. Hist. of Buffalo Co. Clarke. Chi. 1916 2 Vols. 392 & 451 pp.

Burt
- Brookings, Eugene. Burt Co. & Her Schools. Pamphlet n.d. n.p. Cir. 1906.

Butler
- Brown, George L. Centennial Hist. of Butler Co. Pamphlet 1876 34pp

Cass
- Child, A.L. Centennial Hist. of Plattsmouth City & Cass Co. Herald 1877 84 pp.
- Cass Co. Hist. Socy. Mag. Pioneer Stories of Cass Co. Pamphlet 100 pp. Circa 1940.
- Port. & Biog. Otoe & Cass Cos. 1307 pp. Chi. 1889.

Cedar
- Jones, L.E. Hist. of Cedar Co. St. Helena 1876. 18 pp Wraps.
- McCoy, J. Mike. Hist. of Cedar Co. Private 1937 189 pp.

Chase
- Hist. of Chase Co. Comp. by Chase Co. Hist. Socy 1938 40 pp Mimeo.

Cheyenne
- Cheyenne Co. by Cheyenne Co. Real Estate Assn. Pamphlet 39 pp. Cir. 1887.

Clay
- Cent. Sketch of Clay Co. Comp. 1876. Reprint. 1933. Clay Co. Sun Clay Center 19 pp. Pamphlet.
- Stough, Dale P. Hist. of Hamilton & Clay Cos. Clarke. Chi. 1921. 2 Vols. 850 & 650 pp.

NEBRASKA (continued)

Colfax — Schuyler Sun Souvenir Number Colfax Co., Pam. 1902.

Cuming — O'Sullivan, Bartlett. Hist. of Cuming Co. West Point, Nebr. 1884. 178 pp. Hist. & Dir.

— Sweet, E. N. Hist. of Cuming Co. Lincoln 1876 Pamph. 52 pp.

Custer — Gaston, W. L. and Humphrey, A.R. Hist. of Custer Co. Western. Lincoln 1919. 1175 pp.

— Butcher, S.D. Pioneer Hist. of Custer Co. Broken Bow. 1901 403 pp.

— Purcell, Emerson R. ed. Pioneer Stories of Custer Co. Broken Bow. 1936. Pamphlet 193 pp.

Dakota — Warner, W.M. Hist. of Dak. Co. Lyons. 1893.

Dawson — Stuckey, Gertrude Comp. Early Hist. of Dawson Co. 1931.

Dixon — Huse, William. Hist. of Dixon Co. Norfolk 1896 372 pp.

Dodge — Buss, William H. & Osterman, Thomas T. Hist. of Dodge & Washington Cos. Amer. Hist. Socy. Chi. 1921 2 Vols. 455 & 921 pp.

Douglas — Wakeley, Arthur C. Omaha & Douglas Co. Clarke Chi. 1917 2 Vols. 472 & 997 pp.

— Burkley, Frank J. Faded Frontier. Omaha. 1935. 436 pp. Sketches of Omaha Hist.

— Savage, James W. & Bell, John T. Hist. of City of Omaha & South Omaha. N.Y. 1894. 699 pp.

— Sorenson, Alfred. Hist. of Omaha. Omaha 1889. 327 pp.

Fillmore — McKeith, G.R. Pioneer Stories of Fillmore & Adjoining Cos. Pamphlet n.p. 1915.

Franklin — O'Sullivan, M. Hist. of Franklin Co. Lincoln 1873. Pamphlet 74 pp.

Gage — Dobbs, Hugh. Hist. of Gage Co. Lincoln 1918. 1098 pp. Western & Engraving. Lincoln.

Greeley — McDermott, Edith S. Pioneer Hist. of Greeley Co. Private 1939. 174 pp.

Hall — Buecher, A.F. & Barr, R.J. Hist. of Hall Co. Western Pub. Lincoln 1920 965 pp.

— Hist. of First Settlement of Hall Co. Nebr. Stotley. W. Lincoln, Nebr. Hist. Socy.

Hamilton — Hastings, L.W. Cent. Hist. of Hamilton Co. Aurora 1876 Pamphlet 15pp

— Stough, Dale P. Hist. of Hamilton & Clay Cos. Clarke. Chi. 1921. 2 V. 850 & 650 pp.

NEBRASKA (continued)

Hooker
- Motl, Mary Erna. Geographic Interpretation of Mullen. M.A. Thesis. U. of Nebr. 1939. 150 pp. Typed.

Jefferson
- Dawson, Charles. Pioneer Tales of the Ore. Trail & Jefferson Co. Topeka. 1912. 488 pp.
- Hist. of Jefferson Co. Bloyd, Levi, Fairbury, Nebr.

Johnson
- Port. & Biog. Johnson & Pawnee Cos. 626 pp. Chi. 1899.
- Johnson Co. Centennial 1856-1956. Tecumseh Chieftain 1956. 50 pp. Illus.

Kearney
- Bang, Roy T. Heroes Without Medals; A Pioneer Hist. of Kearney Co., Nebr. Minden Warp. 1952.

Keya Paha
- Early Settlers of Keya Paha Co., Nebr. Decker, Beryl & H.S. Students 1950-1.

Knox
- Durbin, Mrs. Mae. Hist. of Knox Co. 1940. Nebr. Press. Assn.

Lancaster
- Hayes, A.B. & Cox, Samuel D. Hist. of The City of Lincoln. Lincoln. 1889. 380 pp.
- Port. & Biog. Lancaster Co. 796 pp. Chi. 1888.
- Sawyer, Andrew J. Hist. of Lincoln & Lancaster Co. Clarke. Chi. 1916. 2 Vols. 358 & 811 pp.

Lincoln
- Bare, Ira L. & McDonald, Will H. Hist. of Lincoln Co. Amer. Hist. Socy. Chi. 1920. 2 Vols.
- Breternitz, Louis. Settlement & Economic Dev. of Lincoln Co., M.A. Thesis. U. of Colo. 1931. 161 pp. Typed.

Merrick
- Merrick County's 100th Year. 1858. 1958 Central City. 1958- 72 pp. Illus.

Nemaha
- Dundas, J.H. Hist. of Nemaha Co. 1902. 220 pp.
- Garrett, Hubert. Hist. of Brownville, Nebr. M.A. Thesis. U. of Nebr. 1927. 158 pp. Typescript.

Nuckolls
- Wilcox, V.R. Hist. of Nuckolls Co., Nebr. M.A. Thesis Colo. St. Coll. 1935. 178 pp. Typed.

Otoe
- Otoe Co. In World War, 1917-1919. n.p. n.d.

Pawnee
- Edwards, Jos. L. Cent. Hist. of Pawnee Co. Pawnee City, Nebr. 1876. Wraps. 50 pp.

Phelps
- Arnold's Complete Dir.of Phelps Co. 1909. Sketch of Co.& Towns. Comp. & Pub. by W. H. Arnold, Kearney, Nebr. 1909.

Pierce
- Hansen, Mrs. Esther (Kotterman) Along Pioneer Trails In Pierce County, Nebr. 1940. 114 pp. Privately Pr.

NEBRASKA (continued)

Platte
- Hist. of Platte Co. Nebr. Curry, Margaret, Culver City, Calif. Murray & Gee. 1950. 1011 pp.
- Phillips, C.W. Hist. of Platte Co. Clarke. Chi. 1915 2 Vols. 396 & 668 pp.
- Taylor, I.N. Hist. of Platte Co. Columbus 1876 Pamphlet 18 pp.
- Turner, Martha M. Our Own History; Columbus 1541-1860. Columbus. 1936. Wraps. 106 pp.

Polk
- Nance, Albinus. Centennial Hist. of Polk Co. 1876. Pamphlet.
- Nuquist, Jos. E. Social Processes & Social Trends In Osceola, Polk Co., Nebr. 1867-1935. M.A. Thesis. U. of Nebr. 234 pp. Typed.

Richardson
- Edwards, Lewis C. Hist. of Richardson Co. B. F. Bowen, Indpls. 1917. 1417 pp.

Saline
- Gregory, Annadora F. Pioneer Day In Crete, Nebr. Chadron 1937 243 pp.

Sarpy
- Old Bellevue, Federal Writers. 1937. Pamphlet 32 pp.
- Cent. Hist. of Sarpy Co. 1876. Pamphlet.

Saunders
- Perky, Charles. Hist. of Saunders Co. Clarke. Chi. 1915. 2V.
- Stories of The Early Days of Valparaiso, Comp. by Nellie F. Magee. 1940. 272 pp. Typed.
- Hist. of Prague 1887-1937. Pamphlet 52 pp.

Scotts Bluff
- Scotts Bluff & The North Platte Valley. Green, Thos. L. Scotts Bluff Star. Herald Pr. 1950. 99 pp.

Seward
- Cox, W.W. Hist. of Seward Co. Lincoln. 1888. 290 pp. 2nd ed. rev. 1915. 4555pp.
- Smith, Wm. H. Early Days In Seward Co. Nebr. Wraps 1937 112 pp.
- Waterman, John H. General Hist. of Seward Co., Nebr. Beaver Crossing, Nebr. 1915. 294 pp.
- Williams, O.B.T. Seward Co., Nebr. Hist. Des. & Resources. Milford 1872. Pamphlet.

Sherman
- A. Brief Hist. of Sherman Co., Nebr. Owen. Norfolk Daily News. 1952. 258 pp.
- The Story of Our First Century, Arrows To Airpower. 1857-1957. Bellevue. Aug. 4-10, 1957. Souvenir Program 24pp.
- Owens, Meroe J. A Brief Hist. of Sherman Co. Nebr. Norfolk. 1952.

Stanton
- Outhouse, M.J. Stanton Co. 165 pp. 1944.

Thayer
- Brief Des. of Thayer Co. Hebron Journal Print. 1885 48pp. Pamphlet.

NEBRASKA (continued)

Thomas
- Smith, Carl. Natural Hist. of Thomas Co., Nebr. Halsey, Neb. 1958

Tri-County
Pioneers
- Halderson, H. Newman Grove, Nebr. 1946.

Valley
- Hist. of Valley Co. Elizabeth Shaver, M.A. Thesis. U. of Nebr. Typed.

Washington
- Bell, John T. Hist. of Washington Co. Omaha 1876. 64 pp. Pamphlet.
- Buss, William H. & Osterman, Thomas T. Hist. of Dodge & Washington Counties. Amer. Hist. Socy. Chi. 1921. 2 Vols. 455 & 921 pp.
- Fuhlrodt, Verne C. Pioneer Hist. of Fontanelle. M.A. Thesis U. of Nebr. 1930. 177 pp. Typed.

Wayne
- Crawford, P.B. Hist. of Wayne Co. 1902. Pamphlet.
- Nyberg, Dorothy Husel. Hist. of Wayne Co. Herald 1938. 306 pp.
- Jones, F.M. Hist. of Winside, Wayne Co. 1942. Wraps. 249 pp.

Webster
- Peters, E. Early Hist. of Webster Co. Guide Rock Signal 1915 Pamphlet. 27 pp.
- Eighty years In Webster Co. Thomas, Elmer Alonzo. Hastings. 1953. 148 pp.

York
- Old Settlers Hist. of York Co. Nebr. Biog. 175 pp. 1914.
- Cradle Days In York Co., Nebr. 1937. Wraps. 108 pp.
- Old Settlers Hist. of York Co. 1913. 175 pp.
- Sedgewick, T.E. Hist. of York Co., Nebr. Clarke. Chi. 1921 2 Vols.

NEVADA
(No County Histories) - 17 Counties

NEW HAMPSHIRE - 10 Counties

Belknap
- Hurd, D.H. Merrimack & Belknap Cos. N.H. 915 pp. Phila. 1885

Carroll
- Merrill, Georgia D. Carroll Co. Boston 1889 987 pp.

Cheshire
- Child, H. Gaz. of Cheshire Co. 1736-1885. Roy. Syracuse 1885 272 pp.
- Hillsborough & Cheshire Co. Biog. Boston 1897 481 pp.
- Hurd, D. H. Cheshire & Sullivan Co. Phila. 1886. 995 pp.

Coos
- Merrill, Georgia D. Coos Co. Syracuse 1888. 956 pp.
- Powers, G. Coos Co. 1754-85. 240 pp. Haverhill. 1841.

NEW HAMPSHIRE (continued)

Grafton   - Child, H. Gazeteer. Syracuse. 1886. 1024 pp.
     - Grafton Co. Biog. Buffalo 1897. 432 pp.

Hillsborough- Boylstron, E.D. Congresses 1774-5. Amherst. 1884. 8 Vols.
     - Hurd, D.H. Hillsborough Co. Lewis. Phila. 1885. 748 pp.

Merrimack &
Belknap   - Hurd, D.H. Hist. Phila. 1885. 915 pp.
     - Sullivan Co. Hist. Biog. Boston 1897 595 pp.

Rockingham - Hazlett, C.A. Co. Hist. Chi. 1915 1306 pp.

Rockingham
& Strafford - Hurd, D.H. Hist. Phila. 890 pp.
     - Co. Biog. Boston. 1896. 646 pp.

Strafford   - Scales, J. Hist. Chi. 1914. 953 pp.

Strafford &
Belknap Co. - Biog. Boston. 1897. 605 pp.
     - Hammond, O.G. List of N.H. Local Hist. Concord. Hist. Socy 1925.

NEW JERSEY - 21 Counties

Atlantic   - Atlantic Co. Hall Daily Union Hist. of Atlantic City & Co. 1899.
     - Wittis, L.L. & Others. Early Atlantic Co. 179 pp. Kutztown 1915.

Bergen   - Minutes of Justices 1715-95. Hist. Socy. Hackensack 1915.
     - Proceedings 1902-2. Hist. Socy. Hackinsack. 1922.
     - Clayton, W.W. Bergen & Passaic Co. Biog. Everts. Phila. 1882.
     - Nelson, W. Bergen & Passaic Co. Biog. Everts. Phila. 1882 577 pp.
     - Van Dalen, J.M. Bergen Co., N.Y. Pub. 1900 691 pp.
     - Westervelt, Mrs. F.A. Bergen Co. 1620-1923. N.Y. Lewis 1923 2V.
     - W.P.A. Bergen Co. Panorama Hackensack 1941 356 pp.

Burlington - Bisbee, Henry Harold. Place Names In Burlington Co. Burlington
     Co. Pub. Co. 1955.
     - Woodward, E.M. Hageman, J.F. Burlington & Mercer Co. Phila.
     Everts. 1883. 888 pp.

Camden   - Biog. Rev. of Camden & Burlington Co. Rev. Pub. Boston 1879 535pp
     - Cranston, P.F. Camden Co. 1681-1931. Cham. of Com. 1931 200pp.
     - Camden Co., Godfrey. Hist. of Medical Profession of Camden Co. 1896.
     - Prowell, G.R. Camden Co. Phila. Richards. 1886. 769 pp.
     - Revolutionary Reminiscences of Camden Co. S. Chew. Camden
     1876. 38 pp.

NEW JERSEY (continued)

Cape May
- Boesley, Early Hist. of Co. of Cape May. 1856.
- Gandy, L.M. Cape May Co. Cem. Rec. 3 V 1939-41.
- Howe, Mayflower Descendants In Cape May Co. 1921.
- Post, E.M. Cape May Co., N.J. 1940. 16 pp.
- Stevens, L.T. Cape May Co. War Records. Author Pub. 1897 479pp.
- Stevens, L.T. Cape May Co. 479 pp. Cape May City 1897

Cumberland
- Elmer, L.G.C. Early Cumberland Co. Bridgeton, Nixon 1869 142pp.
- Mulford, W.C. Tales of Cumberland Co. Bridgeton Eve News. 1941.

Essex
- Folsom, Municipalities of Essex Co. 1925 4 Vols.
- Ricord. Newark & Essex Co. 1898. 2 Vols.
- Shaw, W.H. Essex & Hudson Co. Phila. Everts. 1884. 2 Vols.

Gloucester
- Cushing, T. Sheppard, C.E. Gloucester, Salem & Cumberland, Phila. Everts, 1883.
- Mickle, I. Old Gloucester, Atlantic & Camden, Phila. Ward 1845 617 pp.

Hudson
- Harvey, C.B. Hudson & Bergen Co. N.Y. Gen. Pub. 1900 617 pp.
- Stinson, R.R. Hudson Co. Dispatch. 1914. 162pp.
- Trust Co. of N.J. Hudson Co. & Bergen, Orr. 1921. 59 pp.
- Van Winkle, D. Municipalities of Hudson Co. 1630-1923 Lewis 1924 534 pp.
- Winfield. Land Titles In Hudson Co. 1609-1871. 1872.
- Winfield, C.H. Co. of Hudson. Hayl. 1874. 568 pp.
- Van Winkle, D. Hudson Co. Hist. Socy. 1916. 1918. 2 Vols. 111pp.

Hunterdon
- Deats, Marriage Records of Hunterdon Co. 1795-1875.
- Mott, G.S. First Century of Hunterdon Co. Flemington, Vaseller 1878. 54 pp.
- Port. & Biog. Hunterdon & Warren Cos. 578 pp. N.Y. 1898.
- Snell, J.P. Hunterdon & Somerset Co. Phila. Everts. 1881 1864 pp.

Mercer
- Lee, F.B. Mercer Co. N.Y. Chi. Lewis. 1907 2V 916 pp.
- Freeholders, Mercer Co. 1838-1928. McGoldrick 1928. 40 pp.

Middlesex
- Crowther, S. Middlesex Co. Country Life Pr. 1926. 64 pp.
- Wall, J.P. & Pickersgill, H.E. Middlesex Co. 1664-1920 Lewis 1921 1041 pp.
- Wiley, S.T. Middlesex, Monmouth & Somerset Biog. Biog. Pub.Co. Phila. 1896. 1039 pp.

Monmouth
- Hist. of Monmouth Co. Ellis 1885.
- Beekman, Early Dutch Settlers 1901.
- Franklyn, E. Monmouth Co. Peck Phila. 1885 902 pp.
- Horner, W.S. Old Monmouth. Moreau. Freehold. 1932 444 pp.
- Monmouth. Hist. of Monmouth Co. 1664-1920. 1922 3 Vols.
- Parker, J. Monmouth Co. To 1702. Newark. Bailey 1872. 32 pp.
- Stilwell, J.E. Hist. Miscellany. N.Y. 1906. 4 Vols.
- Salter, E. Monmouth & Ocean Co. Gardner. Bayonne 1880 442 pp.
- Old Monmouth. Freehold. 1887. 318 pp.

Morris
- Amer. Rev. & Morris Co. 110 pp. Rockaway 1926.
- Crayon, J.P. Morris Co. Biog. Rockaway. 1902. 300pp.
- Morris Co. 1710-1913. Lewis, N.Y. 1914. 2 Vol.

NEW JERSEY (continued)

Morris
(cont'd)
- Munsell, W.W. and Co. Morris Co. 407 pp. N.Y. 1882.
- Nelson, W. Morris Co., N.Y. 1882. 8 Vol.
- Tuttle, J.F. & Nelson, W. Cent. Celebration of Morris Co. 8 Vol. 54pp
- Tuttle, J.F. Morris Co. Read Before N.J. Hist. Socy May 20 1869 127pp
- W.P.A. Records Survey. Freeholders. Morristown 1937. 135pp.

Ocean
- Ocean Co. Principal's Council. 1940. 192 pp.

Passaic
- Clayton, W. Bergen & Passaic Co. Biog. Phil. Everts 1882. 572 pp.
- Dietz, C.E. Paterson & Passaic Co. Paterson Schools 1937. 16pp.
- Graf, E.M. Passaic Co. Paterson. Privately Pr. 1935. 27 pp.
- Nelson, W. Co. of Passaic, N.J. Paterson. Chiswell. 1877. 39pp.
- Nelson, Hist. of The City of Paterson & The County of Passaic. 1901

Salem
- Sickler, J.S. Salem Co. Sunbeam Pub. 1937. 390pp.

Somerset
- Messler, A. Cent. Hist. of Somerset Co. Somerville. Jameson 1878. 190pp.
- Somerset Co. 250 Years Messenger. Somerville. 1938. 192pp.
- Hist. of Reformed Dutch Church In Somerset Co., N.J. 1873.
- Labow. Preakness & Preakness Reformed Church, Passaic, N.J. A Hist. 1695-1902.
- Mossler, Forty Years at Rariton. Eight Memorial Sermons with Notes
- Hist. of The Oranges - 1666-1806. 1892.
- Ackerman, H.S. - N.Y. & N.J. Cemeteries. 1947.
- Wilson, Harold Fisher. The Jersey Shore, N.J. Social & Econ. Hist. of Atlantic, Cape May, Monmouth, & Ocean, N.J. N.Y. Lewis Hist. Pub. Co. 1953.
- Traditions of Hunterdon, by John W. Lequear. Ed. & Pub. by D.H. Moreau at Flemingtoh, N.J. 1957. 210 pp. First pub. 1869-70. In Hunterdon Republican
- McGinnis, W.C. Hist. of Perth Amboy. N.J. 1959.

Sussex
- Bunnell, J.L. Sussex Co. Sesqui. Edsall. 1903. 157pp.
- Honeyman, A.V. Somerset, Morris, Warren & Essex Co. Lewis 1927 962pp.
- Schaeffer, Rev. C. Memoirs & Early Hist. of Sussex Co. Johnson. 1907. 187 pp.
- Schrabisch, M. Indians In Sussex Co. Geol. Bull. 1915. 107 pp.
- Snell, J.P. Sussex & Warren Co. Everts. Phila. 1881. 748 pp.
- Swayze, F.J. Sesqui. of Sussex Co. N.J. Herald 1903. 67 pp.
- Webb, E.A. Hist. Dir. of Sussex Co. Andover 1872. 143pp

Union
- Clayton, W.W. Union & Middlesex Co. Biog. Evarts Phila 1882. 885pp
- Hatfield, Rev. E.F. Elizabeth & Union Co. N.Y. Carlton 1868. 701pp.
- Union Co. Pageant. June 1928. Interstate. Plainfield. 1928. 64pp.
- Honeyman, A.V. Union Co. 1664-1923. Lewis 1923. 3V. 1123pp.
- Ricord, F.W. Union Co. Newark. E. Jersey Hist. Co. 1897. 656 pp.

Warren
- Cummins. Warren Co. 1911.
- Shampanore, F. Hist. & Dir. of Warren Co. Shampanore Pub.
- Honeyman, A.V. n.w. N.J. Hist. of Somerset, Morris, Hunterdon, Warren & Sussex Co. N.J. Chi. Lewis. 1927.
- Nelson, W. Hist. of Counties of N.J. Hist. Socy of Newark 1934. 87 pp.

NEW MEXICO - 32 Counties

Santa Fe
- Frost, Max and Walter, Paul A. F., Santa Fe Co. N. Mex. Bureau of Immigration, 1906. For County Histories.
- Coan, Charles Flores. A Hist. of N. Mex. 3 vols. Chicago American Hist. Socy. 1925. Vol I For County Histories.
- Twitchell, Ralph E. Leading Facts of New Mexican History. 5 vols. Cedar Rapids, Iowa. Torch Press, 1911-17.

Socorro
- Hist. of Socorro Co., Santa Fe., 1901. 24 pp.

NEW YORK - 62 Counties

Adirondack
- Adirondack County. White, William Chapman. Ed. by Erskine Caldwell. N.Y. Duell, Sloan & Pierce, 1954. 315 pp. 22 Cm. Amer. Folkways.

Albany
- Parker, A. J. Albany Co. Syracuse, 1897, 1153 pp.

Allegany
- Allegany Co. 392 pp. 1879. Allegany Co. Cent. 941 pp. Alfred, 1896.

Baldwin
- A Brief Hist. of Baldwin Co. N. Y. by Comings, Lydia Jane Newcomb.

Broome
- Seward, W. F., Binghamton & Broome Co., Lewis, 1924, 1145 pp.
- Smith, H. P., Broome Co., Syracuse, Mason, 1885. 630 pp.
- Broome Co. 1806-67, Syracuse, 1867, 8 vol.

Cattaraugus
- County Hist. Biog. Phila. Everts, 1879. 512 pp.
- Some Early Homes Located In Cattaraugus Co. N. Y. Comp. by Julia G. Pierce, Chap. Hist. Olean Chap. D.A.R. N. Y. 1951, Illus. Photo. 29 Cm. unpaged.
- Ellis F. Cattaraugus Co. 512 pp. Phila. 1879.
- Manley, J. Cattaraugus Co., 128 pp. Little Valley 1857.

Cayuga
- Storke, E. G., 1789, Cayuga Co. Syracuse, Mason. 1879. 518 pp.
- Cayuga Co. Hist. Socy. Rochester, Smith. 1908. 598 pp.

Chautauqua
- McMahon, Helen Grace, Chautauqua Co. A. Hist. 1958. B. H. Stewart.
- Downs, J. P., Hedley, F. Y., Chautauqua Co., 3 v. Boston. 1921.
- Merrill, J. D., Chautauqua, 975 pp. Boston, 1894.
- Warren, E. F., Chautauqua, 159 pp. Jamestown, 1846.
- Young, A. W., Chautauqua Co., Buffalo. Matthews. 1875. 672 pp.

Chemung
- Tioga, Chemung, Tompkins, and Schuyler Cos. 2 v. Phila. 1879,
- Towner, A., Chemung, Syracuse. 1892.

Chenango
- Barber, Gertrude Audrey. Index To Wills of Chenango Co., N. Y.
- Clark, H. C., Chenango Co., Thompson, Norwich, 1850. 120 pp.
- Smith, J. H., Chenango & Madison Co. Mason. 1880. 760 pp.
- Chenango Co. Biog. Pub. Buffalo. 1898. 635 pp.

Clinton
- Hurd, D. H., Clinton & Franklin Co. Phila. Lewis. 1880. 508 pp.

Columbia
- Columbia Co. 447 pp. Phila. 1878.
- Co. in 1900. Hudson. 2 vols.

Cortland
- Blodgett, Mrs. B. E., Cortland Co. Youth. 1932. 287 pp.
- Cornish, C. B., Cortland Co. 1929. 135. 60 pp.
- Cortland Co. 1876-1927. 47 pp.
- Stories of Cortland Co. Blodgett, Bertha Evelette. Notes, Indexes. Cortland Co. Hist. Socy. Cortland 1952. 307 pp. Illus. Maps. 20
- Cortland Co. Cemetery Records, 173 pp. 1944. Typed.
- Goodwin, H. C., Pioneer Hist. 1859. 456 pp.
- Grips, Hist. Souvenir of Cortland. 1899. 240 pp.
- Reusswig, Harriett M., Cortland. 1792-1854. Thesis 1934. 30 pp.
- Smith, H. P., Cortland Co. 1885. 543 pp.
- Whitmore, Mrs. F. E., 100th Anniv. of Cortland Co. 1808-1908, 100 pp.

Delaware
- Gould, J., Del. Co. & Wars of N. Y. Roxbury, Keenly. 1856. 426 pp.
- Munsell, W. W., Early Del. Co. Biog. 1880. 362 pp.
- Murray, D., Delaware Co. 1797-1897. 604 pp. Delhi. 1898.
- Delaware Co. Illus. N. Y. 1880. 363 pp.

Dutchess
- Bailey, H.D.B., Dutchess Co. N. Y. Hist. Socy. 1874.
- Dutchess Co. Hist. Socy. Coll. 6 v. 1924-40.
- Biog. Rec. of Dutchess Co. Chi. Beers. 1897. 941 pp.
- "   "   "   "   & Putnam Cos. Chi. Beers. 1897. 1149 pp.
- Dutchess Co. Am. Guide Ser. Women's Club, Phila. 1937. 166 pp.
- Hosbrouck, F., Dutchess Co. Poughkeepsie, Matthien, 1909. 418 pp.
- King, Charles Donald, Hist. of Education in Dutchess Co. N. Y. 1959.
- MacCracken, Henry Noble. Blithe Dutchess, The Flowering of An American Co. From 1812. N. Y. Hastings House. 1958.
- Smith, P. H., Dutchess Co. 1609-1876. Pawling. 1877. 508 pp.
- "   J. H.,   "   " 1683. Biog. Syracuse. Mason, 1882. 562 pp.

Erie
- Boots, James Franklin, Reminiscences of Niagara & Erie Cos., N. Y. Riverside, Calif. 1942.
- Johnson, C., Cent. Erie Co., 512 pp. Buffalo. 1876. Matthews.
- Smith, H. P., Buffalo & Erie Co. Syracuse. Mason. 1884. 776 pp.
- Sweetney, D., Buffalo & Erie Co. 1914-19, Buffalo, 1920,733 pp.

NEW YORK (Continued)

Erie
(cont'd)
- White, T. C., Our County. Boston. 1898. 854 pp. 2 vols.
- Doty, L. R., The Genesee Country. Cos. of Allegany, Cattaraugus, Chautauqua, Chemung, Erie, Genesee. Clir. Clarke. 1925. 4 vols.

Essex
- Cook, F. J., Essex Co. Keeseville, Lansing. 1858. 140 pp.
- Smith, H. P.   "   "   Syracuse. Mason. 1885. 754 pp.
- Watson, W. C. "   "   Mil. & Civil Hist. Albany. Munsell. 1869. 504 pp.

Franklin
- Clinton & Franklin Co. Phila. Lewis. 1880. 508 pp.
- Hough, F. B., St. Lawrence & Franklin Co. Albany. Little. 1853. 819 pp.
- Leavi, F. J., Franklin Co. & Towns, Albany. Lyons. 1918. 819 pp.

Fulton
- Frothingham, W., Early Fulton Co., Syracuse. Mason. 1892. 635 pp.

Genesee
- Cent. Genesee. 1839-1939. 69 pp. 1939.
- North, S. E., Des. & Biog. Genesee Co. 199 pp. 1899.
- Cooley, LaVerne C., Tombstone Inscriptions From Abandoned Cemeteries & Farm Burials of Genesee Co. N. Y. Batavia. 1952.

Greene
- Beers, J. B., Greene Co. 1884. 462 pp.
- Vedder, J. V. V., "   " Recorder. 1927. 207 pp.

Herkimer
- Beers. Herkimer Co. 1879. 289 pp.
- Benton, N. S. "   " Munsell, Albany. 1856. 497 pp.
- Hardin, G. A. "   " Mason. 1893. 876 pp.

Jefferson
- Child, H. Dir. of Jefferson Co. 1866-7. Watertown. Ingalls. v. I-208 pp., v. II-365 pp.
- Coughlin, J., Jefferson Co. Cent. 1905.
- Durant, S. W., 1797. Jefferson Co. Biog. Phila. Evarts. 1878. 593 pp.
- Emerson, E. C., Jefferson Co. 318 pp. Boston. 1898.
- Gould, Ernest C., Jefferson Co. N. Y. Sesqui-Centennial Prog. & Hist. Almanac 1805-1955. Carthage Press.
- Haddock, J. A., Jefferson Co. 1793-1894. Phila. 1894.
- Horton, W. H.,   "   "   1684-1890. Syracuse. 1890. 887 pp.
- Hough, F. B. Early Jefferson Co. Albany. Munsell. 1854. 601 pp.
- Jefferson Co. Illus. 1878.
- Landon, H. F. Jefferson Co. St. Lawrence & Franklin Co. Indpls. Hist. Pub. Co. 1932. 1647 pp.
- Oakes, R. A. Jefferson Co. Geneal. N. Y. 1905. 2 v.
- Ralph, Alta. Early French In Jefferson Co. LeRays, Hist. Journal Nov. '08.
- Reeves, G. W. Jefferson Co. In World War. Watertown. 1920.

Kings
- Bergen, T. G. Early Kings Co. Biog. N. Y. 1881. 552 pp.

Lewis
- Hough, F. B. Lewis Co. Biog. Mason. Syracuse. 1883. 606 pp.
   "   " "   "   Albany. Munsell. 1860. 319 pp.

NEW YORK (continued)

Lewis
- Hough, F. B. Lewis Co. Biog. Mason. Syracuse. 1883. 606 pp.
-    "   "   "   "   Albany. Munsell. 1860. 319 pp.

Livingston
- Biog. Rev. Livingston & Wyoming Co. Boston. 1895. 684 pp.
- Doty, L. L. Livingston Co. Doty 1876. Genesee. Clements. 685 pp.
- Doty, L. L. Livingston Co. Van Deusen. 1905. Jackson, Mich. 1016 pp.
- Doty, L. L. Allegany, Cattaraugus, Chatauqua, Chemung, Erie, Genesee, Livingston, Monroe, Niagara, Ontario, Orleans, Schuyler, Steuben, Wayne, Wyoming & Yates Co. Clarke. Chi. 1925. Biog. 4 v.
- Smith, J. H. Livingston Co. Mason. Syracuse. 1881. 490 pp.

Madison
- Hammond, Mrs. L. M. Madison Co. Smith. 1872. 775 pp.
- Lehman, Karl H. Madison Co. Today. Oneida Castle, N. Y. 1943.
- Madison Co. Boston Biog. Rev. 1894. 706 pp.

Mohawk
- Forts & Firesides of The Mohawk Country, N. Y. Vroonan, John J. Stories of Pre-Revolutionary War Period including some history and genealogical mention during post-war period. Rev. ed. Johnstown, N.Y. Baronet Litho. Co. 1951, XV, 320 pp.illus.maps 24 cm. Bib. pp. 307-8. The Mohawk Dutch and The Palatines, their background and influence in the dev. of the U.S.A. St. Johnsville, N.Y., 1951, 90 pp. Illus. map 22 cm. Bib.

Monroe
- Crapsey, Arthur H. Hist. Almanac of The County of Monroe In N.Y. 1949-1950. Rochester, N. Y. 1954.
- D.A.R. 1850 Census. Monroe Co. 6 v. 1934-6.
- Fisher, G.W. Early Rochester 1810-1860. Rochester. Fisher 1860.
- Hanford, F. Names in Monroe, Scottsville, Van Hooser, 1911-54 pp.
- McIntosh, W. H. Monroe Co. Phila. Everts. 1877, 32 pp.
- Peck, W. E. Monroe Co. Boston Hist. Co. 1895. 934 pp.
- Peck, W. E. Rochester & Monroe Co. To 1907. N.Y. & Chi. Pioneer, 1908, 2 vol.
- Turner, O. Early Monroe, Ontario, Livingston, Yates, Steuben, Wayne, Allegany, parts or Orleans, Genesee & Wyoming, Rochester. Alling, 1851.
- Wright, A. H. Northampton In W. N.Y. Hist. Soc. Rochester,1927, 424 pp.
- Rochester and Monroe Co. W.P.A. Project. Scranton's 1937. 460 pp.

Montgomery
- Montgomery & Fulton Co., N.Y. Beers. 1878. 252 pp.
- Frothingham, W. Montgomery Co., Syracuse. Mason 1892. 805 pp.

Nassau
- Darlington, O. J. Glimpses of Nassau Co. Hist. 1949.

New York
- St. Thomas' Church In the City & County of New York, 1958.

NEW YORK (Continued)

Niagara
- Pool, W. Landmarks of Niagara Co., 1897.
- Porter, B. A. Niagara Co., 1902.
- Sanford & Go. Niagara Co., 397. pp. 1878.
- Wiley, S. T. & W. S. Cyclopedia of Niagara Co., Garner. 1892. 640 pp.
- Williams, E. T. Niagara Co. 1821-1921. 2 v. Chi. -
- Hist. of Niagara Co., N. Y.

Oneida
- Canfield, W. W. & Clark, J. E. Oneida Co. Utica. Griffiths. 1909. 148 pp.
- Cookingham, N. J. Oneida Co. 1700-1912. Chi. Clarke. 1912.
- N. Y. D. A. R. Oneida In Amer. Rev. Mrs. Sanford & Mrs. Cronin. Utica. 1927-8.
- N. Y. D. A. R.   "   "   "   " Mrs. E. G. Smith, Utica. 1937.
- Durant, S. W.   " Biog. Phila. Everts. 1878. 678 pp.
- Galpin, W. F. Cent. N. Y. Oneida, Madison, Onondaga, Cayuga, Tompkins, Cortland & Chenango Co. Lewis, 1941. 4 vol.
- Pouroy, J. Annals of Oneida Co. Rome. Jones. 1851. 893 pp.
- Mowris, J. A. 117th Reg. (4th Oneida) 1862 to June 1865. Hartford. 289 pp. Case. 1866.
- Oneida Hist. Socy. Trans. 1881-98. Utica. Roberts. 1881-98.
- Wager, D. E. Our County. Boston Hist. Co. 1896.

Onandaga
- Beauchamp, W. M. Syracuse & Onandage Co. Clarke. 1908. 1000 pp.
- Bruce, D. H. Onandaga's Cent. Boston. Hist. Co. 1896. 2 vols. 546 pp.
- Clayton, W. W. Onandago Co. Mason. Syracuse. 1878. 430 pp.
- Clark, J. V. H.   " Stoddard, Syracuse. 1849. 794 pp.
- Smith, C. E. Pioneer Onandaga Co. Bardeen, Syracuse. 1904. 415 pp.
- Smith, R. B. ed. Syracuse & Onandaga Co. Syracuse. 1923. 218 pp.

Ontario
- Aldrich, L. C. Ontario Co. 396 pp. Syracuse. 1893.
- Milliken, C. F. Ontario Co. 2 v. 1911.

Orange
- Akers, D. Outposts of Orange Co. Washingtonville, D.A.R. 1937. 114 pp.
- Biog. Rec. of Orange Co. N. Y. 1895. 1548 pp.
- Denniston, G. Early Orange Co. Albany. 1863. 100 pp.
- Eager, S. W.   "   "   " Newburgh, Callahan. 1846-7. 652 pp.
- Orange Co. Biog. Phila. Everts. 1881. 820 pp.
- Ruttenber, E. M. County Orange. Newburgh. Author. 1875.422 pp.
- Seese, M. P. Orange Co. 2 v. Middletown. 1941.

Orleans
- Signor, I. S. ed. Orleans Co. Mason. Syracuse. 1894. 930 pp.
- Thomas, A. Pioneer Orleans Co. Albion. Bruner. 1871. 463 pp.
- Album of Orleans Co. Sanford. 1879. 320 pp.

Oswego
- Churchill, J. C. Oswego Co. Syracuse. Mason. 1895. 1201 pp.
- Johnson, C. Oswego Co. Everts. 1877. 449 pp.

Otsego
- Bacon, E. F. Otsego Co. To 1902. Oneonta. Herald. 1902. 85 pp.
- Biog. Rev. of Otsego Co. Biog. Rev. Pub. 1893. Boston.
- Otsego Co. Everts. 1878. Phila.

NEW YORK (Continued)

Putnam
- Blake, W. J. Putnam Co. N. Y. Baker. 1849. 368 pp.
- Westville Cemetery. Otsego Co. N. Y. Putnam Co. N. Y. 1959.
- Putnam Co. Hist. N. Y. Work Shop 1955-7. Patterson, N. Y.
- Pelletrean, W. S. Putnam Co. 771 pp. Phila. 1886.

Queens
- Rev. Era In Queens Co. Leavitt. 1846. 264 pp. 1884.
- Queens Co. In Older Times. Jamaica. Welling. 1865. 122 pp.
- Queens Co. Illus, 1882. 576 pp.

Rensselaer
- Anderson, G. B. Rensselaer Co. Syracuse. Mason. 1897. 1195 pp.
- Craib, Stephanie Hicks & Roderick Hill Craib. Our Yesterdays.
  A Hist. of Rensselaer Co. N. Y. Troy. 1948.
- Hayner, R. Troy & Rensselaer Co. Lewis. 1925. 3 v.
- Sylvester, N. B. Troy & Rensselaer Co. Phila. Everts. 1880. 564 pp.
- Weise, A. J. Towns of   "   "   Troy. Francis. 1880. 158 pp.

Richmond
- Leng, C. W. & Davis, W. T. Staten Is. 1609-1929.
- Lewis. N. Y. 1930. 4 v.
- Bayles, R. M. ed. Richmond Co. To 1887. Preston, N. Y. 750 pp.
- Clute, J. J. Staten Is. To 1877. Vogt. N. Y.
- Morris, I. K. Mem. Hist. of Staten Is. Mem. Pub. Co. N. Y.
  1898. 2 v.

Rockland
- Barber, Mrs. Gertrude Audrey. Abstracts of Wills of Rockland
  Co. N. Y. 1953.
- Bedell, C. F. Rockland Co. 368 pp. Suffern. 1941.
- Cole, D. Rockland Co. Biog. N. Y. 1884. 419 pp.
- Conover, Amanda A. Rockland Co. D.A.R. Chap. 1936.
- Green, F. B. Rockland Co. N. Y. 1886. 450 pp.

St. Lawrence
- St. Lawrence Co. 1749-1878. 521 pp. Phila. 1878.
- Curtis, G. St. Lawrence Co. 372 pp. Syracuse. 1894.
- Durant, S. W. & Pierce, H. B. 1749. Hist. of St. Lawrence Co.
  Biog. Everts. Phila. 1878. 521 pp.
- Hough, F. B. St. Lawrence & Franklin Co. Albany. Little.
  1853. 719 pp.
- Mem. Rec. of St. Lawrence Co. Mason. Syracuse. 1894. 1092 pp.

Saratoga
- Anderson, G. B. Saratoga Co. Biog. Boston Hist. Co. 1899.
  787 pp.
- Scott, G. G. L'Amoreaux, J. S. Saratoga Co. Cent. Address.
  Ballston Spa. July 4, 1876.
- Stone, W. L. Saratoga, Ballston, Virtue & Yorstan, 1875.
  451 pp.
- Sylvester, N. B. Saratoga Co. Everts. 1787. 514 pp.

Schoharie
- Barber, Gertrude Audrey. Schoharie Co. N. Y. Cem. Rec. 1932.
- Brown's Hist. of Schoharie Co. Hist. Socy. Bouck. Middlebrogh.
- Simms, Jeptha R. Frontiersmen of N. Y. With Early Hist. of
  Schoharie Co. Riggs, Albany. 1883. 2 vols.
- Sias, S. Schoharie Co. Danforthis Middleburgh. 1904. 154 pp.

NEW YORK (Continued)

Schoharie   — Simms, Japtha R. Schoharie Co. & Border Wars of N. Y. Munsell.
(cont'd)   Albany. 1845.   672 pp.
                Warner, G. H. Schoharie Co. In Four Wars, Weed, Albany.
                1891. 428 pp.

Seneca   — Seneca Co. 1786. 170 pp. Phila. 1876.

Shelter   — The Hist. of Shelter Island, 1652-1932 with Supplement 1932-52
Island   by Jean G. Schlodermundt. 270 pp. Illus.

Steuben   — Clayton, W. W. Steuben Co. 460 pp. Phila. 1879.
            — McMaster, G. H. Steuben Co. 207 pp. Bath. 1863.
            — Near, I. W. Steuben Co. 2 v. Chi. 1911.

Suffolk   — Bayles, R. M. Suffolk Co. 1874. Port Jefferson.

Sullivan   — Heidt, William, Jr. Francis Knapp's 103 yrs. of Brief History
                of The Deve. of Sullivan Co. N. Y. Hist. Socy. 1956.
            — Quinlan, J. E. Sullivan Co. 700 pp. Liberty 1873.

Sunrise   — Howell, Nathaniel Robinson. Know Suffolk & Sunrise Co. N. Y.
                Then & Now. Islip, N. Y. Bwys. Bros. 1952.

Tioga   — Gay, W. B. Tioga Co. 1785-1888. Dir. '88. Syracuse. 1887. 493 pp.
            — Kingman, L. W. Tioga Co. 800 pp. Elmira.
            — Peirce, H. B. & Hurd, D. H. Tioga, Chemung, Tompkins & Schuyler
                Cos. Everts, Phila. 1879. 687 pp.

Tolland   — Cole, J. R. Tolland Co. 1888. 992 pps.

Tompkins   — Selkreg, J. H. Tompkins Co. Syracuse. Mason. 1894. 704 pp.

Tryon   — Campbell, W. W. Tryon Co. & Border Warfare. Harper. 1831. 191 pp.
            —   "   " "   "   " & Rev. Baker 1849. 396 pp.

Ulster   — Clearwater, A. T. Ulster Co. Van Deusen. Kingston. 1907. 712 pp.
            — Sylvester, N. B.   "   " Biog. Everts. Phila. 1880. 339 pp.
            — Van Buren, A. H.   "   " Under The Dutch, Kingston, 1923.
                146 pp.

Warren   — Smith, H. P. ed. Warren Co. Mason. Syracuse. 1885. 702 pp.

Washington — Corey, A. Co. of Washington, Schuylerville, 1849. 246 pp.
            — Johnson, C. Hist. of Wash. Co. Phila. Ensign. 1878. 504 pp.
            —   "   " Wash. Co. To 1900, 1901. 888 pp.
            — Stone, W. L. "   " To End of 19th Cent. N. Y. Hist. Co. 1901.
            — Washington Co. & Queensbury Biog. N. Y. Gresham. Chi. 1894. 436 pp.

Wayne   — Clark, L. H. Inil. Hist. of Wayne Co. Clark. 1883. 691 pp.
            — Cowles, G. W. Wayne Co. Mason. Syracuse. 1895. 776 pp.
            — Bolton, R. Westchester Co. 2 v. N. Y. 1848.

NEW YORK (Continued)

Westchester — Dawson, H. B. Westchester Co. In Amer. Rev. Morrisiano, N.Y.C.
1886. 281 pp.
— Biog. Hist. Westchester Co. 2 v. Chi. 1899.
— French, A. P. Westchester Co. 5 v. N. Y. 1925-7.
— Haacker, F. C. F. Muster Rolls of Westchester Co. N. Y.
U. S. Census Office. 7 Census 1850. Westchester Co. N. Y.
French & Indian Wars. Col. Serv. 1896-7. N. Y. 1952.
— Scharf, J. T. Westchester Co. Phila. 1861.
— Shonnard, F., Spooner, W.W. Westchester Co. N. Y. Hist Co.
1900. 638 pp.
— This Is Westchester. Crandell, Richard F. N. Y. Sterling 1954.
240 pp. Illus, Parts. Maps, Bib. pp. 238.
— North & Manhattan; Persons & Places In Old Westchester By
Hansen, Henry. 1884. 54 Photos By S. Chamberlain. N. Y.
Hastings House. 1950. 181 pp. Illus.

Yates   — Aldrich, L. C. Yates Co. 671 pp. Syracuse. 1892.
— Bootes, Thelma E. Index to Business Dir. Yates Co. N. Y.
— Cleveland, Stafford Canning. Inscriptions From Three Abandoned
Cemeteries In Yates Co. N. Y. Friends. Stoddard. Thomas.
— Cleveland, S. C. Early Yates Co. Biog. Chronicle. N. Y. 1873.
— Hist. and Dir. of Yates Co. By Cleveland, Stafford Canning.
Reprint. Vol. 1, 1951. Vol. 2, 1950.
— Cleveland, S. C. Early Yates Co. Biog. Chronicle, N. Y. 1873.
— N. Y. State Library Bull. #56. Feb. 1901 By Chas. A. Flagg and
Judson T. Jennings give Co. Hist. of Hudson River Counties,
Mohawk Valley, Northern New York, Central New York, Southern
Central New York, Western New York, Lake Erie and Niagara.
— Melone, Harry R. Hist. of Central N. Y. embracing Cayuga,
Seneca, Wayne, Ontario, Tompkins, Cortland, Schuyler, Yates,
Chemung, Steuben, and Tioga Counties. Indpls. Ind.
Hist. Pub. Co. 1932.
— Hammersley, S. E. The Hist. of Waterfprd, N. Y. 1957.
— Ackerman, H. S. N. Y. & N. J. Cemeteries 1947.
— Lamb, Wallace Emerson. Sec. Hist. Atlas of N. Y. State
Phoenix, N. Y. F. E. Richards 1955-6.

NORTH CAROLINA — 100 Counties

The Bibliography of North Carolina County Histories, Univ. of
N. Car. Library Studies #1 By William S. Powell, Pub. in 1958
at Chapel Hill, U. of N. C. Library, is an excellent bibliography and one of the very best bibliographies of this kind
found in all of the fifty states.

Of North Carolina's one hundred counties, twenty-two published
works cover several counties, and three hundred seventy-four pub.
works cover individual counties according to this publication
published in 1958.

NORTH CAROLINA (Continued)

Allamance — Stockard, Miss S. W., Hist. of Allamance, Raleigh Pr. 1900.

Alexander — Crouse, Rev. A. L. Alexander Co. Hickory-Crouse. 1905.

Anson — Boykin, Mrs. J. G., Anson Co., N.C. Booklet XIII, No. 4.

Beaufort — Paschal, Herbert R., Jr. A Hist. of Colonial Baltimore, Beaufort
Co., Raleigh. Edwards & Broughton. 1955. 69 pp.

Bladen — Crawford, Clifton E. (Bladen Co.) Elizabethtown 1957. Mimeo. 46 pp.

Buncombe — Davidson, T. F., Buncombe Co., Asheville. The Citizen. 1922.
— Digges, G. A., Buncombe Co. 316 pp. 1935.
— Sondley, F.A., Buncombe Co., Asheville. The Advocate. 1930

Caldwell — Scott, W.W., Annals of Caldwell Co. Lenoir News. Topic Pr. 1930.
— Alexander, Nancy. Here Will I Dwell. (Caldwell Co.) Lenoir. 1956
230 pp.

Camden — Three Hundred Years Along The Pasquotank. Biog. Hist. of Camden Co.
Old Traph. C. 1957. 249 pp.

Carteret — Oaksmith, A., Carteret Co. Cent. Address, July 1876. Beaufort Eagle.

Chatham — London, W. A., Rev. Hist. of Chatham Co., Sanford. Cole. 1876.

Cherokee — Hills of Cherokee, N.C., Roach, H. J., 1953.

Chowan — Boyce, W.S., Chowan Co., 1800-1915. N.Y. Col. U.1917.

Cleveland — Weathers, Lee B., The Living Past of Cleveland Co. A History.
Shelby: Star Pub. Co. 1956. 269 pp.

Craven — Brinson, S.M., Early Craven Co., N.C. Book Xth 4.

Cumberland — Myrover, H. J., Cumberland Co. & Cape Fear. Baptist Pub.,
Fayetteville. 1905.

Davidson — Leonard, Rev. Jacob Calvin, Centennial Hist. of Davidson Co.
Raleigh. Edwards.
— Leonard, Rev. J. C., Davidson Co., Raleigh. Edwards. 1927. 523 pp.
— Paul, Hiram W., Hist. of Durham, Raleigh. Edwards & Broughton Co.
1884.

Durham — Paul, H. W. Hist. of Durham. Raleigh. Edwards. 1884.

Edgecombe — Turner, J. K. & Bridges, J. L., Jr., Edgecomb Co. Raleigh.
Edwards. 1920. 486 pp.

Forsyth — Fries, Adelaide L., Forsyth Co. Winston. Stewart's 1898. 132 pp.
— Siewers, C.N., Forsyth Co. U. of N.C. Winston-Salem. 1924.

NORTH CAROLINA (Continued)

Gaston
- Puett, Minnie S., Gaston Co., Charlotte. Observer. 1939.
- Separk, J. H., Gastonia & Gaston Co. Kingsport. 1936. 169 pp.

Guilford
- Stockard, Sallie W., Guilford Co., Knoxville. Gant-Ogden. 1902.
- Arnett, Ethel S., Greensboro, N.C. The County Seat of Guilford. Chapel Hill. U. of N.C. Press. 1955. 492 pp.

Halifax
- Allen, W.C., Halifax Co. Boston. Cornhill. 1918.

Harnett
- Fowler, Malcolm. They Passed This Way: A Personal Narrative of Harnett Co. Cent., Inc. 1955. 167 pp.

Haywood
- Allen, W.C. Cent.of Haywood Co. Waynesville Courier. 1918
- Allen, W.C. Haywood Co. Ashville. Inland Pr.1935. 628 pp.

Henderson
- The State. April 21, 1956. Henderson
- Patten, S. S., Henderson Co. 290 pp. Asheville. 1947.

Hertford
- Moore, J. W., Hertford & Albemarle Co. Inquirer. 1877-8. 3 v.
- Winborne, B. B. Hertford Co. Raleigh. Edwards. 1906.

Hyde
- The State. Aug. 24, 1957. Hyde Co.

Johnston
- The State. September 8, 1956. Johnston Co.
- Bayette, E. T., Johnston Co.
- Saunders, W. M., Jr., & Ragsdale, G. Y., Johnston Co. Raleigh. 1922. 82 pp.

Lincoln
- Nixon, A., Early Lincoln Co., Lincolnton. News. 1908.
- Nixon, A Hist. of Lincoln Co., N.C. Book IX #3.
- Sherrill, W. L., Lincoln Co. 1749-1937. Charlotte. Observer. 1937. 536 pp.

Macon
- Smith, C. D., Macon Co. Franklin Press. 1891.

Mecklenburg
- Alexander, J. B., Mecklenburg Co. 1740-1900. Charlotte. Observer. 1902.
- Tompkins, D. A., Mecklenburg Co. & Charlotte. 1740-1903. 2 vols. Observer 1903. 414 pp.

Moore
- Robinson, Blackwell P., A Hist. of Moore Co., N. C. 1747-1847. Southern Pines. Moore Co. Hist. Assn. 1956. 270 pp.
- Moore, Louis T., Stories Old & New of The Cape Fear Region. Wilmington. Priv. Print. 1956. 261 pp.

New Hanover
- Waddell, A. M., New Hanover Co. & Lower Cape Fear Region, 1723-1800. Wilmington. 1903. 232 pp.

Onslow
- The State. March 26, 1955 (Onslow Co.)

NORTH CAROLINA (Continued)

Orange   - Nash, F. Orange Co. Part I, N.C. Book Xth. #2.

Pasquotank - Pasquotank Hist. Society. Year Book. Elizabeth City. 1955.166 pp.

Perquimans - Winslow, Mrs. W., Perquimans Co. Raleigh. Edwards.1931.

Person   - Foushee, A. R., Early Person Co. Durham. Seeman. 1921.
          - The State. March 10, 1956. Person Co.

Pitt   - King, H. T., Pitt Co. Raleigh. Edwards. 1911. 263 pp.
          - The State. Oct. 5, 1957. Pitt Co.

Randolph - The State. July 14, 1956. Randolph Co.
          - Blair, J. A., Randolph Co. 1880. 71 pp.
          - Burgess, F., Randolph Co. Univ. of N. Car. 1924. Pamp.

Robeson   - Lawrence, R. C., Robeson Co., 279 pp. Lumberton. 1939.

Rockingham - Craig, Marjorie, ed. Home Life in Rockingham Co.
          - In the Eighties and Nineties. In N.C. Hist. Rev. XXX. 4 Act,
            1956 pp. 510-528.
          - Glenn, J. D., Rockingham Co. Leaksville Gazette Pr. 1884. 31 pp.

Rowan   - Rumple, Rev. J., Rowan Co., Salisbury. Bruner. 1881. 508 pp.
          - Rumple, Rev. J., Rowan Co., DAR Charlotte. Observer. 1916.

Rutherford - Griffin, C.W., Old Tryon & Rutherford Co. 1730-1936. Asheville.
            Miller. 1937. 640 pp.

Sampson   - N. C. Abstracts of Sampson Co., N.C. Wills 1784-1895. 1958.
          - Bass, Cora. Sampson Co. Yearbook. Clinton. Boss. 156 pp. 1957.

Surry   - Hollingsworth, J. G., Surry Co. 1935.

Union   - The State. Dec. 1, 1956. Union Co.
          - McNeely, R. N., Union Co. & Waxhaw, N.C., Book XII. #1
          - Stack, A. M. & Beasley, R. F., Union Co. 1902.

Vance   - Peace, Samuel T. "Jeb's Black Baby", Vance Co. N.C. Henderson.
            1955. 457 pp.

          - Watkins, J. B., Jr. Vance Co., Henderson. Daily. 1941.

Wake   - Chamberlain, H. S., Wake Co., Raleigh. Edwards. 1922.

Warren   - Wellman, N. W.,Co. of Warren, N. C. 1959.

Watanga   - Arthur, J. P., Watagna Co., Richmond, Everett. 1915.
          - Chamberlain, H. S., Watanga Co., Richmond, Everett. 1915.
          - The State, Oct. 6, 1956. Watango.

NORTH CAROLINA (Continued)

Wayne
- Daniels, Hon. F.A., Wayne Co. add. at Court House. Nov. 30, 1914.

Wilkes
- Crouch, J., Wilkes Co., Wilkesboro. Chronicle. 1902.
- Battle, K.P., Hist. In Names of N. Car. Counties, Raleigh. 1906.
- Battle, K. P., Names of Co. of N.C. & Their Hist. Winston. Blair. 1888.
- Ferguson, Thomas W., House On The Yodkin. Wilkes Co. Winston-Salem. Clay Printing Co. 1956. 242 pp.
- The State. Jan. 28, 1956. Wilkes Co.
- Henderson, A. The Histories of The Counties. Article In Charlotte Observer. April 4, 1915.
- Collection of Documents. 1664-75. Edited by William S. Powell Raleigh, N.C. 1958. State Dept. of Archives & Hist.

NORTH DAKOTA - 53 Counties

Dickey
- Dickey Co., N. D. Hist. Socy. A Hist of Dickey Co., N.D. P. M. Black, Editor. Ellendale. 1930.

Grand Forks
- Arnold, Henry V. Hist. of Grand Forks Co. & City. Larimore. Pioneer. 1900.

McIntosh
- Wishek, Mrs. Nina Farley. Along the Trails of Yesterday. A Story of McIntosh Co., N.D. Ashley. Tribune. 1941.

McKenzie
- Shafer, G. F., Early McKenzie Co., N.D. Hist. Col. 1913. 57 pp.

McLean
- Williams, Mary A. (Barnes) Fifty Pioneer Mothers of McLean Co., Washburn Leader. 1932.
- Red River Valley, Past & Present of Counties, Cities, Towns, etc., Grand Forks. Herald. Chi. Cooper. 1909.

Mercer
- Heinemeyer, C. B., Mercer Co. Star. 1932.

Pembina
- U. S. Census Pembina Co., Minn. Ter. N.D. Hist. Col. 1906. 405 pp.
- Arnold, H. V., Story of Old Pembina.

Ransom
- Arnold, Henry Vernon. Early Hist. of Ransom Co., N.D. Larimore Pioneer. 1920.

Rolette
- Hist. of Rolette Co. by Laura F. Law. Lind Press. Minneapolis. 1953.

Towner
- Hadler, M. J., Marriage Records of Towner Co., N.D. 1956.
- Hadler, M. Lyles (Jacques) Towner Co., N. D. Families. Loring Beach. 1958.

NORTH DAKOTA (Continued)

Walsh — Walsh Co., N.D. In the World War. Grafton. 1920.

Wells — Spokesfield, Walter Earnest. A Hist. of Wells Co., N.D. Valley City. 1929.
— Hall, Luella J., Hist. of Formation of North Dakota Counties. N.D., Hist Socy. 1923. Vol 5. 169-250 pp.
— Anderson, Oscar. A Brief Hist. of Velva, N.D., Hanff Print. 1955.
— Almont, N.D. 50 Anniversary Hist. of Almont, N.D. Conrad. 1956. Bismarck.
— Arnold, H.V., Early Hist. of The Devils Lake Country. Larimore Pioneer. 1920.
— Buffalo, N.D. 1880-1955. Diamond Jubilee. June 14-15.
— Breeling, Lutie (Taylor) 1882. When the Trail was New In Mountraille. 1956.
— Butte, N. D., Hist. Com. Fiftieth Anniversary July 1956. Bismarck.Tribune.
— Burr, Alexander Carothers. Report on Williston, N.D. and Its Tributary Regions by A.C. Burr & J. A. Assorio. Bismarck Econ. Dev. Com. 1957.
— Bottineau, N.D., June 28,29,30. Diamond Jubilee. 1959.
— Cooperstown Diamond Jubilee. 1882-1957. 1957.
— Center, N. D., Old Settlers' 50th Anniversary Hist. Com. Oliver Co. Hist. 1906-56. Mandan, N.D. Young's 1956.
— Cando, N. D., 1884-1959. Seventy Five Year's Progress. 1959.
— Devils Lakes' Seventy-Five Years. 75th Anniversary Settlement Booklet. Diamond Jubilee Assn., Inc. 1957.
— Egeland 50th Anniversary: Hist. of Egeland Community. 1905-55. 1955.
— Flaten, Mrs. M., The Edinburg Story: Edinburg's 75th Anniversary. June 26-27, 1957. Diamond Jubilee 1882-1957. Grafton Record.Printers. 1957.
— Flem, K. R., Sherwood Golden Jubilee, 1904-1954. Sherwood.Pub. by Community Club. June 1954.
— Laura B.Sanderson.In The Valley of The Jim. N.D. Bismarck Tribune. 1940.
— Garrison 50th Anniversary 1905-55. Souvenir Booklet. Garrison, N.D. 1955.
— Golden Jubilee, 1906-56. Max, N.D. July 1956. Minot, N. D. Print. Co. 1956.
— Hope, N. D. Jubilee Com. Book. Com. Hope of The Prairie, 75th Anniversary. 1882-1957.
— Hatton's Heritage— Hist. of Hatton, N.D. 1884-1959. In connection With the 75th Anniversary Celebration July 1959. Okla. City, Lith. & Color Press. 1959.
— Larimore, N. D., Souvenir Booklet Com. Souvenir Book, Larimore Diamond Jubilee 1881-1956. July 1956.

NORTH DAKOTA (Continued)

Wells
(cont'd)
- Takota's 75 years. Official Souvenir Booklet. Takota. 1958.
- Mandan Jubilee Rodeo Book. 1881-1956. Mandan. 1956.
- New Salem Hist. Com. 75th Anniversary, New Salem. N.D. 1883-1958.
- 50th Anniversary Of The Founding of Hansboro, N.D., June 22, 1955.
- Northwood Diamond Jubilee 1957. Northwood Gleaner. Editor Dan Campbell, Pub.
- Portland, N.D., Diamond Jubilee Hist. Com. Diamond Jubilee, July 1957. 1882-1957. Portland, N.D.
- Fiftieth Anniversary, Rhame, N.D. June 26, 1958.
- Savo Finnish Hist. Socy. Hist. of Finnish Settlements In Brown & Dickey Cos. In S.D. & N.D. 1881-1955. N.Y. Mills, Minn. N.W. Pub. 1955.
- Shults, Ralph. 50th Anniversary, Hettinger Co., N.D. 1957.
- Smith, Arie N. Gackle Golden Jubilee 1904-1954. Mandan, N. D. Crescent Print. Co. 1954.
- Steffen, Bernard R., Pembina, North Dakota's Oldest Settlement. Pembina, N.D. Pub. by Pembina Community Club. 1957.
- Souvenir Program of The Frontier Cavalcade and 75th Anniversary of Dickerson, N.D., Dickinson Press. 1957.
- Streeter, N.D., Golden Jubilee. 1905-55. 1955.
- Turtle Lake Commercial Club - 50th Anniversary, Turtle Lake, N.D., 1905-1955. Sept. 12, 1955.
- Wold, Josephine - Fort Abercrombie Centennial 1857-1957. Wahpeton, N.D. Farmer Globe. 1957.

OHIO - 88 Counties

Akron
- Akron & Summit Cos. by Karl H. Grismer. Summit Co. Hist. Socy. 1952.

Allen
- Allen Co. Cent. Program & Hist. 1831-1931. Lima, News-Gazette Print. 1931.
- Miller, C.C. & Baxter, S.A., Allen Co. 872 pp. Chi. 1906.
- Rusler, W., Allen Co. 2 v. Chi. 1921.
- Warner, Beers & Co., Allen Co. 824 pp. Chi. 1885.
- W.P.A. Project Guide To Lima & Allen Co. 1931. 64 pp.

Ashland
- Baughman, Ashland Co. Clarke. 1909. 864 pp.
- Hill, Ashland Co. Williams 1880. 408 pp.
- Knapp, Ashland Co. Lippincott. 1863. 550 pp.

OHIO (Continued)

Ashtabula
- Ashtabula Co. Biog. 256 pp. Phila. 1878.
- Williams, W. W.. Ashtabula Co. Phila. 1878. 256 pp.

Athens
- Cent. Athens Co. 1905.
- Walker, C. M. Athens Co. 600 pp. Cinti. 1869.

Auglaize
- Chapman Bros. Part. & Biog. Auglaize, Logan & Shelby Cos. 592 pp. Chi. 1892.
- McMurray, W., Auglaize Co. Hist. Pub. 2 v. 1240 pp.
- Simpkins, J. D., Early Auglaize Co. 119 pp. St. Mary's 1901.
- Sutton, R. Auglaize Co. Wapakoneta. 1880.
- Williamson, C. W., West Ohio & Auglaize Co. Columbus. Linn. 1905. 860 pp.

Belmont
- Caldwell, J. A., Belmont & Jefferson Cos. 611 pp. Wheeling. 1880.
- Cent. Hist. Belmont Co. McKelvey. 1903. 829 pp.
- Cochran, Hon. J.S., Bonnie Belmont. 1907. 291 pp.
- McKelvey, A. T. Cent. Belmont Co. 833 pp. Chi. 1903.

Brown
- Brown Co. 308 pp. Chi. 1883.
- Linning, M.,Lineage of The Linning Family of Brown Co. Ohio. 1954.
- Williams, B., Clermont & Brown Cos. 2 v. Milford. 1913.

Butler
- Cent. Butler Co. 989 pp. 1905. Biog-Cyclopedia Butler Co. 666 pp. Cinti. 1882.
- Mem. Rec. Butler Co. Record Pub. Chi. 1894. 447 pp.
- McBride, J., Early Settlers of Butler Co. Clarke. 1869. 640 pp. 2 v.

Carroll
- Eckley, H. J. and Perry, W. T., Carroll & Harrison Cos. 2 v. Chi. 1921.

Champaign
- Champaign Co. 921 pp. Chi. 1881.
- Cent. Biog. Champaign Co. 724 pp. N. Y. 1902.
- Antrim, J., Champaign & Logan Cos. 460 pp. Bellefontaine. 1872.
- Middleton,.E. P., Champaign Co. 2 v. Indpls. 1917.

Clark
- Port. & Biog. Greene & Clarke Cos. 924 pp. Chi. 1890.
- Clark Co, 1085 pp. Chi. 1881.
- Clarke. Biog. Clark Co. 824 pp. 1902.
- Prince, B. F., Clark Co. & Springfield. 2 v. Chi. 1922.
- Rockel. W. M. 20 C. Clark Co. & Springfield. 1154 pp. Chi. 1908.

Clermont
- Rockey, J. L., Bancroft R. J., Clermont Co. Phila. Everts. 1880. 557 pp.
- Williams, B. Clermont & Brown Cos. 2 v. Milford. 1913.

132

Clinton — Brown, A. J., ed. Clinton Co. Bowen. Indpls. 1915. 967 pp.
         — Nelson, S.B., Clinton Co. Burs. Chi. 1882. 1180 pp.

Columbiana — Barth, H. B., Columbiana Co. 2 v. Topeka. 1926.
            — Mack, H. Columbiana Co. Phila. Ensign. 334 pp. 1879.
            — McCord, W. B., ed. Columbiana Co. Biog. Pub. 1905. 848 pp.

Coshocton — Balmer, W. J., Cent. Hist. of Coshocton Co. Chi. Clarke. 1909.
            2 v.
            — Hill, N.N. Jr., Hist. of Coshocton Co. 1740-1881. Graham 1881.
            — Hunt, W.E., Coshocton Co. 1764-1876. Cinti.Clarke. 1876. 264 pp.
            — Coshocton Co. O. Marriages & Wills. Coshocton. 1957.
            — Nicholas, S.H., Coshocton Co. Cent. Hist. Coshocton. Amer. Art
            Works. 1911. 75 pp.
            — Shaw, L. C., Our Co. Coshocton. City Schools 1935-6. 65 pp.

Crawford — Baskin & Battey. Crawford Co. 1047 pp. Chi. 1881.
          — Hopley, J.E., Crawford Co. 1254 pp. Chi. 1912.
          — Lewis, Cent. Biog. Crawford Co. 868 pp. Chi. 1902.
          — Perrin, W.H., Crawford Co. Chi. Puskin. 1881.

Cuyahoga — Coates, W.R., Cuyahoga Co. 2 v. Chi. 1924.
          — Johnson, C. Cuyahoga Co. 534 pp. Cleve. 1879.
          — Lewis. Cuyahoga Co. and Cleveland. 924 pp. 1894 Chi.

Darke — Abbott, W.S., Darke Co. Beers. 1880. 900 pp.
       — Lewis, Biog. Darke Co. 758 pp. Chi. 1900.
       — McIntosh, W. H., Freeman, H. Darke Co. Beers. Chi. 1880. 772 pp.
       — Wilson, F. E., Darke Co. 2 v. Milford. 1914.

Defiance — Defiance Co. Hist. Warner. Chi. 1883. 374 pp.

Delaware — Lewis. Delaware, Union & Morrow Cos. 501 pp. Chi. 1895.
         — Delaware Co. O. Auditors Tax List. 1955.
         — Pabst, Anna Catherine Smith. Berlin Township & Del. Co. O.
         Hist. Del. O. 1955.
         — Lyttle, J.R., ed. 20th Cent. Hist. of Del.Co. Biog. Pub. Chi.
         1908. 896 pp.
         — Perrin, W. H. & Battle, J. H., Del. Co. & O. Baskin. Chi. 1880.
         885 pp.

Erie — Aldrich, L. C., Erie Co. Mason. 1889. 653 pp.
     — Pelke, H. L., Erie Co. Lewis. 1916. 2 vol. 1232 pp.
     — Stewart & Page Pub. Erie Co. & Atlas. 1874.

Fairfield — Sanderson, G. A., Early Fairfield Co. Lancaster. Wetzler. 1851.
         32 pp.
         — Scott. H., Fairfield Co. 304 pp. Columbus. 1877.
         — Wiseman, C.M.L. Pioneer Fairfield Co. 430 pp. Columbus. 1901

OHIO (Continued)

Fayette
- Allen, F. M. Fayette Co. 756 pp. Indpls. 1914.
- Dills, R.S. Fayette Co. 1039 pp. Dayton. 1881.
- Putnam, R., Pioneer Fayette Co. 120 pp. Cinti. 1872.

Franklin
- Franklin & Pickaway Cos. Illus. Biog. 593pp. 1880.
- Hist. Pub. Co. Franklin Co. 1900. 460 pp. Columbus. 1901
- Martin, W. T., Franklin Co. Biog. 1858.
- Moore, O. Franklin Co. 3 v. Topeka. 1930.
- Taylor, W. A., Cent. Franklin Co. 2 v. Chi. 1909.

Fulton
- Aldrich, L.C., ed. Henry & Fulton Co. Syracuse. Mason 1888. 713 pp.
- Mikesell, T. ed. Co. of Fulton, Madison. N.W. Hist. Assn. 1905. 661 pp.
- Reighard, F.H., ed. Fulton Co. Chi. & N.Y. Lewis. 1920. 2 v.

Geanga
- Williams Bros. Geauga and Lake Cos. 259 pp. Phila. 1878.

Greene
- Broadstone, M. A., Greene Co. 1803-1908. 226 pp. Xenia. 1908.
- Greene Co. 1803-1908. Home Coming Assn. Aldine. Xenia. 1908. 226 pp.
- Patterson, A. M. Greene Co. 1803-1908. 226 pp. Xenia. 1908.
- Robinson, G. F., Greene Co. 927 pp. Chi. 1902.

Guernsey
- Cent. Hist. of Guernsey Co. Cambridge. Jeffersonian Pr. 1876. 11 pp.
- Sarchet, C.P.B. Guernsey Co. 2 v. Indpls. 1911.
- Wolfe, W. G., Guernsey Co. 1093 pp. Cambridge. 1943.

Hamilton
- Ford, H.A. and Kate, B. F., Hamilton Co. 432 pp. Cleve. 1881.
- Hamilton Co. O. Marriage Records 1808-20 and Wills 1790-1810. M. Dickore. Natalie Thornburgh. Cinti. 1959.
- Hamilton Co. Biog. 1920. Chi. v. 3. Memoirs of Miami Valley.
- Hamilton Co. Memoirs In The Miami Valley. v. 2. 521-670 pp.
- Howe, H., Hamilton Co. Cinti. Krehbiel. 1908. 2 vols. 866 pp.
- Olden, J. G., Early Hamilton Co. Cinti. 1882. Watkins. 294 pp.

Hancock
- Beardsley, D. B., Hancock Co. 472 pp. Springfield. 1881.
- Brown, C. R., Hancock Co. Warner. Chi. 1886. 880 pp.
- Kimmell, J.A., 20 C. Findlay & Hancock Co. 656 pp. Chi. 1910.
- Lewis Pub. Co. Cent. Biog. Hist. of Hancock Co. 595 pp. N.Y. 1903.

Hardin
- Atlas of Hardin Co. Comp. by H.G. Howland, C. Gasche. & W. Engel. Phila. Sutton. 1879. 131 pp.
- Blue, H.T., O. Cent. Hist. of Hardin Co. 1833-1933, 180 pp. Canton. 1933.
- Hist. of Hardin Co. Chi. Warner. 1883.
- Kohler, Mrs. Minnie, 20 Cent. Hist. of Hardin Co. Chi. Lewis. 1910. 2 v. 898 pp.
- Robinson, J. S. Hardin Co. Dir. Toledo. 1876.

OHIO (Continued)

Harrison — Hanna, C. A. Harrison Co. Priv. Pr. 1900. 636 pp.

Henry — Aldrich, L. C. Henry and Fulton Cos. 713 pp. Syracuse. 1888.

Highland — Klise, J. W. Highland Co. 535 pp. Madison. 1902.
— McBride, David Newton, Cemetery Inscriptions, Highland Co. O.
Ann Arbor, Edwards. 1954.
— McBride, David Newton, Wills, Administration, etc. Highland Co. O.
1954-1957.

Huron — Baughman, A. T. Huron Co. Clarke. 1909. 2 v.
— Biog. Rec. of Counties of Huron & Lorain, Beers. 1894. 515 pp.

Jackson — Aten-Jones, R. Early Jackson
▿ Williams, D. W. Jackson Co. Jackson. 1900.

Jefferson — Caldwell, J. A. Richmond & Jefferson Cos. 611 pp. Wheeling. 1880.
— Doyle, J. B. 20 C. Steubenville & Jefferson Cos. 1196 pp. Chi. 1910.

Knox — Biog. Rec. of Knox Co. Chi. 1902.
— Ellicott, Mary G. Writers of Knox Co., Mt. Vernon. 1937.
— Graham, A. A. Knox Co. & Licking Co. Newark. Graham. 1881.
— Hill, N. N. Jr. Knox Co. 854 pp. Mt. Vernon 1881.
— Norton, A. B. Knox Co. 1779-1862. 424 pp. Columbus. 1862.
— Williams, A. B. Knox Co. 2 v. Indpls. 1912.

Lake — W. P. A. Proj. Lake Co. Hist. 1941. 100 pp.

Lawrence — Atlas & Hist. of Lawrence Co. Hardesty. Chi. 1882. 223 pp.

Licking — Brister, E. M. P. Cent. Hist. of Newark & Licking Co. Clarke. 1909.
1452 pp. 2 vol.
— Hill, N. N. Licking Co. Graham. Newark. 1881. 822 pp.
— Smucker, I. Cent. Licking Co. 80 pp. Newark. 1876.

Logan — Kennedy, R. P. Logan Co. 823 pp. Chi. 1903.
— Lake, D. J. & Co. Logan Co. 66 pp. Phila. 1890.

Lorain — Boynton, W. W. Early Lorain Co. add. July 4, 1876. Elyria, O.
— Lorain Co. Illus. Biog. Phila. Williams. 1879. 373 pp.
— Wright, G. F. Lorain Co. 2 v. Lewis. Chi. 1916.

Lucas — Lucas Co. Ser. v. 1 Toledo. 1948.
— Lucas Co. Ser. vol. 4. Industrial Beginnings. By Randolph L. Downes.
Hist. Socy. of N. W. Ohio. Toledo. 1954.

Madison — Bryan, C. E. Madison Co. Bowen. Indp'ls. 1915. 942 pp.
— Hist. of Madison Co. Chi. Warner. 1883.

OHIO (Continued)

Mahoning
— Butler, E. S. Mahoning Co. Dir. 1868. 34 pp.
— Cutler, H. G. Hist. of W. Res. Mahoning Co. Mrs. H. T. Upton.
  Biog. Lewis. Chi. & N. Y. 1910. 1874 pp.
— Summers, E. Genealogy Hist. of E. Ohio, Mahoning Co.
  Lewis. Chi. & N. Y. 1903. 792 pp.
— Youngstown and The Mahoning Valley. Biog. 282 pp.
  Amer. Hist. Socy. Pub. Chi. & N. Y.

Marion
— Hist. of Marion Co. Chi. Leggett. 1883.
— Port. & Biog. Marion & Hardin Co. Chi. Chapman. 1895.
— Barker, J. Recollections of The First Settlement of Ohio.
  1958. Marietta.

Medina
— Hist. of Medina Co. & O. Chi. Baskin. 1881. 922 pp.
— Northrop, N. B. Early Medina Co. Medina. Redway. 1861. 224 pp.

Meigs
— Ervin, E. Pioneer Hist. of Meigs Co. O. 1954.
— Larkin, S. C. Pioneer Meigs Co. Columbus. Berlin. 1908. 208 pp.

Miami
— Geneal. & Biog. Rec. of Miami Co. Chi. Lewis. 1900.
— Harbaugh, T. C. Cent. Miami Co. Chi. Richmond. 1909.
— A Hist. of Miami Co., O. 1807-1953. By Leonard N. Hill, Miami Co.
  Sesquicentennial Com. Heer Printing Co. Piquace. 1953.
— Miami Co. Chi. Beers. 1880. 880 pp.
— Sterritt, F. M. Miami Co. Troy. Montgomery. 1917. 2 v.
— In Words & Pictures. Cleveland. World Pub. 1953.
— Izant, Grace (Goulder) This Is Ohio; Ohio's 88 Counties.

Montgomery
— Conover, Mrs. C. ed. Dayton & Montgomery Co. Lewis. 1932. 4 v.
— Drury, A. W. Dayton & Montgomery Co. Chi. Clarke. 1909. 2022 pp.
— Everts, L. H. Atlas of Montgomery Co. Phila. Hunter. 1875. 172 pp.
— Hist. of Montgomery Co. Chi. Beers. 1882.

Morgan
— Robertson, C. Morgan Co. Bio. Chi. 1886. 538 pp.

Morrow
— Baughman, A. J. & Bartlett, R. F. Morrow Co. Lewis, Chi. 1911.
  2 v. 1884.
— Perrin, W. H. Battle, J. H. Baskin, O. L. Hist. of Morrow Co.
  Chi. 1880. 838 pp.

Muskingum
— Everhart, J. F. Muskingum Co. Illus. Biog.
  Columbus. Everhart. 1882. 480 pp.

Perry
— Martzolff, C. L. Perry Co. Columbus. Heer. 1902. 195 pp.

Portage
— Portage Co. Chi. Warner Beers. 1885. 927 pp.
— Port. & Biog. Portage & Summit Cos. Logansport. Bowen. 1898.
  988 pp.

136

Preble
- Bib. Hist. Preble Co. Chi. Lewis. 1900. 573 pp.
- Hist. of Preble Co. Cleveland. Williams. 1881.
- Runyon, G. C. Preble Co. D.A.R. Eaton. 1945. 122 pp.

Richland
- Baughman, A. J. Cent. Biog. Hist. of Richland & Ashland Cos.
  Chi. Lewis. 1901. 831 pp.
- Graham, A. A. Richland Co. Mansfield. 1880.
- McGaw, J. F. Seymour, P. Early Richland Co. With Hist. Addenda
  By A. J. Baughman. Mansfield. 1902.
- Rothermel, H. A. Hist. & Bus. Guide of Richland Co. Mansfield.
  Wade. 1873. 64 pp.

Ross
- Evans, L. S. Ross Co. Chi. Lewis. 1917. 2 v.
- Finley, I. J. Early Cinti. Clarke. 1871. 148 pp.
- Ross & Highland Co. Biog. Cleve. Williams. 1880. 532 pp.
- Meek, B. 20 C. Sandusky Co. Chi. Richmond. 1909. 934 pp.
- W.P.A. Proj. Chillicothe & Ross Co. Columbus. Heer. 1938.
  91 pp.

Sandusky
- Broekhoven's Fremont City & Sandusky Co. Div.
- Everett, H. Earliest Sandusky Co. & Civil War Record.
  Freemont. 1878.
- Everett, H. Sandusky Co. Biog. Cleveland. Williams. 1882. 834 pp.
- Fremont City & Sandusky Co. Dir. 1899-1900.
- Proceedings At Unveiling of Soldier's Monument at Fort Stephenson.
  Freemont. Address By Maj. Geo. Croghan, Aug. 2, 1813. 1885.
- Sandusky Co. Dir. 1911.
- Wiggins' Fremont City & Sandusky Co. Dir. 1897-8.

Scioto
- Evans, N. W. Scioto Co. Portsmouth. Evans. 1903. 1322 pp.

Seneca
- Baughman, A. J. Seneca Co. Chi. Lewis. 1911. 2 v.
- Butterfield, C. W. Seneca Co. Sandusky. Campbell. 1848. 251 pp.
- Hist. of Seneca Co. Lewis. 1902. 757 pp.
- Seneca Co. Chi. Warner. 1886. 1069 pp.
- Lang, W. Seneca Co. Springfield. Trans. 1880. 691 pp.

Stark
- Heald, E. T. The Stark Co. Story. O. 1958.
- Industry Comes of Age. Vol. 3 of The Stark Co. Story. Heald.
  1952.
- Perrin, W. H. Stark Co. Chi. Baskin. 1881. 1012 pp.
- Port. & Biog. Stark Co. Chi. Chapman. 1892. 524 pp.
- Ruthermel, H. A. Stark Co. Canton. Hartfeld. 1872. 62 pp.

Summit
- Bierce, L. V. Summit Co. Akron. Canfield. 1854. 157 pp.
- Chamberlain, Gladys E. Summit Co. In War of 1812.
-       "   "   " ed. "   " Marriage Licenses 1840-65,
  1932-4. 2 v.
- Cuyahoga D.A.R. Rev. War Soldiers Buried in Summit Co. 1911.

OHIO (Continued)

Summit — W.P.A. Proj. Akron & Summit Co. 1940. 218 pp.
(Cont'd) — Grant, C. R. Summit Co. Illus. Akron Atlas Co. 1891. 184 pp.
— Hixon, W. W. " " Rockford. Pub. By. Co.
— Perrin, W. H. Summit Co. Chi. Baskin. 1881. 1056 pp.
— Portage & Summit Co. Biog. Logansport. Bowen. 1898.
— Summit Co. Honored Dead. Mil. Hist. of O. 1885. Hardesty.
320 pp.
— Atlas & Ind. Geog. of Summit Co. Rectigraph. 1910. 182 pp.

Trumbull — Trumbull & Mahoning Cos. Biog. Cleve. Williams. 1882. 2 v.

Tuscarawas — Mitchever, C. H. ed. Tuscarawas & Muskingum Valley. Odell.
Dayton. 1876. 358 pp.
— Tuscarawas Co. Warner. Chi. 1884. 1007 pp.
— Port. Biog. Tuscarawas Co. Chi. Owen. 1895. 507 pp.

Union — Union Co. Chi. Beers. 1883. 694 pp.

Van Wert — Gilliland, T. S. Van Wert Co. Chi. Richmond. 1906. 803 pp.
— Van Wert and Mercer Cos. Biog. Wapakoneta. 1882. 488 pp.

Vinton — Biggs, L. O. Vinton Co. Columbus. Heer. 1950. 184 pp.
— Organ, Lew. Hist of Vinton Co. McArthur. 1954.

Warren — Hist. of Warren Co. Beers. Chi. 1882.

Washington — Andrews, M. R. Wash. Co. Biog. Chi. 1902. 1471 pp.
— Wash. Co. Biog. Cleve. Williams. 1881. 739 pp.
— Biedel, Helen C. Davis Records. Wash. Co. Tacoma. 1952.

Wayne — Douglass, B. Wayne Co. Douglass. Indp'ls. 1878. 868 pp.

Williams — Blanchard, C. ed. Williams Co. Biog. Goodspeed. Battey.
Chi. 1882. 820 pp.
— Shinn, W. H. Co. of Williams. Madison. N. W. Hist. Assn.
1905. 611 pp.
— W.P.A. Bryan & Williams Co. Gallipolis. Down. 1941. 117 pp.

Wood — Ross, May E. ed. Wood Co. Democrat. 1910. 264 pp.
— Wood Co. Biog. Chi. Beers. 1897. 1386 pp.

Wyandot — Dir. Wyandot Co. 1877. Upper Sandusky, Gillingham &
Tallcott. 1877. 170 pp.
— Wyandot Co. Chi. Clarke. 1913. 2 v.
— Wyandot Co. Chi. Leggett. 1884. 1065 pp.

OKLAHOMA - 77 Counties

Adair
— Adair Co. Okla. John D. Benedict (In Muskogee & N. E. Okla.) 3 vol. 1922. Chi. Clarke.

Atoka
— A Hist. of Atoka Co. William H. Underwood. Thesis. Norman. 1931. 118 pp.

Caddo
— Mathvin, J. J. Anadarko In Caddo Co. 137 pp.

Cherokee
— Cherokee Co. Okla. John D. Benedict. 3 v. 1922.

Craig
— Craig Co. Okla. John D. Benedict. 1922. 3 v.

Custer
— Hist. of Custer & Washita Co. 1883-1937. Pub. 1937. By Clinton Daily News.

Delaware
— Delaware Co. Okla. John D. Benedict. 1922. 3 vols.

Garfield
— Hist. of Covington, Garfield Co. Okla. & Surrounding Territory. F. L. G. Eisele, R #1 Douglas, Okla. 1954.

Jefferson
— Hist. of Jefferson Co. Okla. by J. M. Dyer. 80 pp.

Kay
— Kay Co. Okla. Gas Co. Ponca City, Okla. 1919.

Mayes
— Mayes Co. Okla. N. E. Okla. 1922. 3 vol.

McCurtain
— Carter, W. A. McCurtain Co. & S. E. Okla. Hist. Biog. Idabel. 1923. 381 pp.
— McCurtain Co. & S. E. Okla. W. A. Carter. Idabel. 1923. 381 pp.

McIntosh
— McIntosh Co. Okla. N. E. Okla. 1922. 3 vol.

Muskogee
— Muskogee & N. E. Okla. J. D. Benedict. Chi. Clarke. 1922. 3 vol.
— Benedict, J. D. Muskogee & N. E. Okla. including Counties of Muskogee, McIntosh, Wagoner, Cherokee, Sequoyah, Adair, Delaware, Mayes, Rogers, Washington, Nowata, Craig, and Ottawa. Chi. Clarke. 1922.
— W.P.A. Survey Project No. 51 Muskogee Co. 1937. 181 pp.

Noble
— Hist. of Noble Co. Okla. Allen D. Fitchett. Thesis. U of Okla. Norman. 1938.
Hist. of Noble Co. Okla. Fannie L. Eisele, Covington. 1955.

Nowata
— Hist. of Nowata Co. Okla. N. E. Okla.

Ottawa
— Ottawa Co. N. E. Okla.

OKLAHOMA (Continued)

Pottawatomie - Pott. Co. A. Hist. of Pottawatomie Co. J. Fortson.
Shawnee. 1936.   "   " Hist. Secy.
- Fortson, J. Pottawatomie Co. Shawnee. 1936. 90°pp.
- Johnson, R. M. Okla. Hist. Has Brief Hist. of The Follow-
ing Counties: Atoka, Beckham, Bryan, Caddo, Carter,
Choctaw, Coal, Comanche, Cotton, Custer, Dewey, Garvin,
Grady, Greer, Harmon, Haskell, Jackson, Jefferson,
Johnston, Kiowa, Latimer, LeFlore, Love, McCurtain, Marshall,
Murray, Pittsburg, Pontotoc, Pushmataha, Roger Mills, Stephens,
Tillman, & Washita. Chi. Clarke. 1925.

Roger Mills - Brief Hist. of Roger Mills Co. N. M. Taylor. 1947. pp. 64.

Rogers - Rogers Co. Okla. N. E. Okla.

Sequoyah - Sequoyah Co. "   " "   "

Wagoner - Wagoner Co. "   " "   "

Washington - Washington   "   " "   "

Woods - Hist. of Woods Co. Okla. George R. Crissman. Alva, Alva, Okla.
1928.

OREGON - 36 Counties

Baker - Hialt, L. Baker Co. 1861-93. Baker City. Abbott. 1893.

Benton - Fagan, D. D. Benton Co. Portland. Walling 1885.

Clatsop - Clatsop Co. Ore. Ils. Hist. Legends & Industries. Emma G. Miller.
Binfords & Mort. Portland. 1958.

Coos & Curry - A Century of Coos & Curry. E. R. Peterson & A. Powers.
- Dodge, O. Pioneer Coos & Curry Cos. Salem. Capital Prints. 1898.

Harney - Harney Co. Ore. By George F. Brimlow. Binford & Mort.

Jackson - Tucker, W. P. Jackson Co. Thesis U. of Wash. 1931. 251 pp.
- Walling, A.G. Hist. of S. Ore. Jackson, Josephine, Douglas,
Curry & Coos Cos. Portland. Walling. 1883.

Jefferson - Jefferson Co. Ore. Reminiscences By Many Hands. Binfords &
Mort. Portland. 1957.

Klamath - Sisemore, L. ed. Good, Rachael A. Klamath Co.

OREGON (Continued)

Lane
- Walling, A. G. Lane Co. Portland. Walling. 1884.

Linn
- W.P.A. Linn Co. Albany. 1941. 174 pp.

Lincoln
- Pioneer Hist. of N. Lincoln Co. Ore. McMinnville. 1951.

Malheur
- Pioneer Days In Malheur Co. By J. R. Gregg. Pub. Morrison. Los Angeles. 1950.
- Gregg, J. R. Pioneer Days In Malheur Co. Ore. Los Angeles. Morrison. 1950.

Marion
- Steeves, Mrs. S. Marion Co. Pioneers 1840-60. Portland. Berncliff, 1927.
- Marion Co. Hist. Salem, Ore. Marion Co. Hist. Socy. 1955.

Polk
- D.A.R. Sarah Co. Polk Chap. #6. Polk Co. Pioneers. Dallas.
- Polk Co. Observer. 1927-9. 2 vols.

Sherman
- Hist. of Sherman Co. Ore. By Giles French. Pub. By The Ore. Hist. Socy. Portland, Ore. 1958.

Tillamook
- Land of Many Waters. By Ada M. Orcutt. Binfords & Mort. Portland. 1951.
- Vaughn, Warren N. Early Settlement of Tillamook Co. article written 1890.

Umatilla
- Illus. Hist. Umatilla Co. Spokane. Lever 1902. 581 pp.

Union
- Union Co. 1936.

Yamhill
- Cooper, J. C. Mil. Hist. of Yamhill Co. McMinnville. 1829.
- Illus. Hist. of Baker, Grant, Malheur & Harney Counties. Spokane, Wash. Hist. Pub. 1905.
- Illus. Hist. of Cent. Oregon, Wasco, Sherman, Gilliam, Wheeler, Crook, Lake & Klamath Co., Spokane. W. Hist. Pub. 1905.
- The Oregon Hist. Records Survey In 1938-42 Histories of:
- No. 2 Benton Co. '42 Corvallis, No. 4 Clatsop Co. Astoria '40.
- No. 6 Coos Co. Coquille '42. No. 14 Hood River Co. '39.
- No. 17 Josephine Co. '39. No. 18 Klamath Co. Klamath Falls '41.
- No. 22 Linn Co. Albany '39. No 25 Morrow Co. Heppner '37.
- No. 26 Multnomah Co. 2 v. '40. No. 29 Tillamook Co. '40.
- No. 30 Umatilla Co. Pendleton '42. No. 33 Wasco Co. The Dallas '41.
- No. 34 Washington Co. Hillsboro '40.

PENNSYLVANIA - 67 Counties

Adams
- McPherson, E. Adams Co. Inquirer. Lancaster. 1889. 50 pp.
- Reily, J. T. Hist. of Dir. of Boroughs of Adams Co. Gettysburg. 1880. 182 pp.
- Rupp, D. Hist. & Top. of Dauphin, Cumberland, Franklin, Bedford, Adams, & Perry. Gilbert Hills. Lancaster. 1816. 24 pp.
- Hist. of Cumberland & Adams Co. Warner. Chi. 1886. 512 pp.
- Pa. Archives Inventory #1 Adams Co. 1941.

Allegheny
- Allegheny Conf. on Community Dev. Pittsburgh & Allegheny Co. Pa. Pittsburgh. 1956.
- Durant, S. W. Allegheny Co. Everts. 1876. 242 pp.
- Kelly, G. E. ed. Allegheny Co. 1788-1938. Sesqui. Pittsburgh. 1938. 402 pp.
- Lambing, A. A. White, J. E. Early Allegheny Co., Pitts. Snowden & Patterson. 1888. 176 pp.
- Ruoff, N. W. Hist. of W. Pa. Top. Des. of Allegheny, Westmoreland, Washington, Somerset, Greene, Fayette, Beaver, Butler, Armstrong, etc. Kaufman. 1846. 352 pp.
- Thurston, G. H. Allegheny Co. 100 yrs. Pitts. Anderson. 1888.
- Hist. of Allegheny Co. Phila. Everts. 1876. Lippincott. 242 pp.
- " " " " Chi. Warner. 1889. 762 pp. 2 v.

Armstrong
- Armstrong Co. Biog. Chi. Beers. 1914. 995 pp.
- Smith, R. W. Armstrong Co. Chi. 1883.

Ashland
- Knapp, H. S. Ashland Co. Phila. Lippincott. 1868. 550 pp.

Beaver
- Bausman, Rev. J. Beaver Co. Knickerbocker. 1904. 1315 pp. 2 v.
- Jordan, J. W. Beaver Co. Geneol. Lewis. 1914. N.Y. 1125 pp. 2 v.
- Richard, J. F. & Levy, S. & Henry T. Beaver Co. 1888. Warner. 908 pp.
- Hist. of Beaver Co. Phila. & Chi. Warner. 1888. 908 pp.

Bedford
- Blackburn, E. H. Bedford & Somerset Cos. Lewis. 1906. 3 v.
- Early Bedford Co. Pioneer Hist. Socy. 1946. 32 pp.
- Rupp, I. D. Hist. & Top. of Bedford Co. 1846. 602 pp.
- Waterman, Walkins & Co. Bedford, Somerset & Fulton Cos. 1884. 672 pp.

Berks
- Baer, S. A. Berks Co. Reading 1877. 28 pp.
- Balthoser, F. W. Berks Co. Reading. 373 pp. 1925.
- Rec. of Aborigines. Socy. of Natl. Sciences. Reading. Book & Job Pr. 1881. 177 pp. 1897. 257 pp.
- Graeff, A. D. ed. Ind. Berks Co. 1748-1948.
- Reading: Textile Machine Works, Berkshire Knitting Mills, 1948. 35 pp.
- Blair, Beulah Hix. Some Early Lineages of Berks Co. Pa. Clauser. Hicks. Denver. Rileys Reproductions. 1959.

PENNSYLVANIA (Continued)

Berks
(Cont'd)
- Fox, C. T. Reading & Berks Co. Lewis. 1925. 3 v.
- Montgomery, M. L. Berks Co. 1774-83. Hooge. 1894. 295 pp.
-    "   " " " " " Phila. Everts. 1886. 1204 pp.
-    "   " " " " " Rodgers. 1889. 302 pp.
- Nolan, J. B. ed. S. E. Pa. Counties of Berks, Bucks, Chester,
  Delaware, Montgomery, Philadelphia & Schuylkill. Phila.
  Lewis. 1943.
- Montgomery, N. L. Berks Co. Biog. Chi. Beers. 1909. 2 v.
- Ruoff, H. W. Counties of Berks, Levanon, Lancaster, Hills,
  1844. 519 pp.
- Wagner, A. E. Balthaser, F. W. Hoch, D. K. Berks Co. Reading.
  Eagle. 1913. 253 pp.

Blair
- Africa, J. S. Huntingdon & Blair Co. 1883. 761 pp.
- Clark, C. B. Blair Co. Altoona. Clark 1896. 116 pp.
- Ewing, J. H. Slep, H. Altoona & Blair Co. 1880. 262 pp.
- Davis, T. S. Blair Co. 1931. 441 pp. 2 v.
- Hoenstine, F. G. Soldiers of Blair Co. 1940. 432 pp.
- Sell, J. C. 20 C. Hist. of Altoona & Blair Co. 1911. 972 pp.
- Wiley, S. T. & Gardiner, W. S. Biog. Cyclopedia of Blair Co.
  1892. 602 pp.
- Blair, Co. & Dir. Altoona. 1868. 24 pp.
- Wolf, G. A. & McGraw, H. A. Blair County's Postal History &
  McGraw's Blair Co. Place Names, Altoona, Pa. Blair Co. Hist.
  Socy. 1947. 94 pp.
- Hist. of Blair Co. Altoona High School. 1938. 122 pp.

Bradford
- Bradsby, H. C. Bradford Co. Biog. Chi. Nelson. 1891. 1320 pp.
- Craft, D. Bradford Co. Biog. Everts. 1878. Phila. 492 pp.
- Heverly, C. F. Bradford Co. 1615-1924. Towanda. 1926. 594 pp.

Bucks
- Battle, J. H. Bucks Co. Phila. Chi. Warner. 1887. 1176 pp.
- Buck, W. J.   "   " & Wrightstown Township By C. W. Smith.
- Buck, W. J. Legends of Bucks & Montgomery Cos. Author.
  1887. 340 pp.
- Davis, W. W. H. Early Bucks Co. To 1876. Doylestown. Dem. Bk.
  Pr. 1876. 875 pp.
- Hutton, H. A. House of Decision. Bucks Co. Pa. 1956.
- MacReynolds, George. Place Names in Bucks Co. Pa.
  Doylestown, Pa. Bucks Co. Hist. Socy. 1955.
- Michener, H. C. Bucks Co. Bi-Cent. Doylestown. Sept. 1882.
  Paschall. Intelligencer. 39 pp.

Butler
- Brown, R. C. Butlers Co. Chi. Brown. 1895. 1360 pp.
- Sesqui-Centennial Assn. Pa. Butler 1950.
- Butler Co. Brown. 1895. 1360 pp.
- Butler Co. Waterman, Watkins & Co. 1883. 454 pp.
- McKee, J. A. Butler Co. Richmond. Arnold. 1909. 1487 pp.
- Sipe, C. H.   "   " Hist. Pub. Topeka. 1927. 1343 pp.

PENNSYLVANIA (Continued

Cambria	- Caldwell, J. A. Atlas of Cambria Co. Phila. Atlas Pub. 1890. 194 pp.
	- Gable, J. E. Cambria Co. Hist. Pub. Topeka. Indpls. 1224 pp. 2 v.
	- Storey, H. W. Cambria Co. Geneal. Lewis. N. Y. & Chi. 1804 pp. 3 v.
	- Swank, J. M. Cambria Co. Pioneers. Phila. Allen. 1910. 138 pp.
	- Cambria Co. Biog. Illus. Union. 1896. 518 pp.
Cameron	- Leeson, M. A. Counties of McKean, Elk, Cameron & Potter. Chi. Beers. 1890. 1261 pp.
	- McKnight, W. J. Northwestern Penn. Counties, Phila. Lippincott. 1905. 748 pp.
Carbon	- Lacier, J. D. Mil. Hist. of Carbon Co. Mauch Chunk. 1867.
Centre	- Linn, J. B. Centre & Clinton Co. Phila. Everts. 1883. 672 pp.
	- Maynard, D. S. Centre Co. Richie. Bellafonte. Repub. 1877. 34 pp.
	- Mitchell, J. T. " " Ind. Library. 1937. 31 pp.
	- " " " " " Bellefonte. Watchman. 1942. 119 pp.
	- Rupp, I. D. Hist. of Northumberland, Juniata, Huntingdon, Mifflin, Centre, Union, Columbia & Clinton Counties. Lancaster. Hill. 320 pp.
Chester	- Futhey, J. S. Cope, G. Chester Co. Biog. Phila. Everts. 1881. 782 pp.
	- Pinowski, Edward. Chester Co. Pa. Place Names. Phila. Sunshine Press. 1955.
	- Wiley, S. T. Chester Co. Biog. Gresham. Chi. 1893. 879 pp.
	- Chester Co. Record. W. Chester. 1824. Reprint. 1894.
Clarion	- Davis, A. J. Clarion Co. Syracuse. Mason. 1887. 664 pp.
Clearfield	- Aldrich, L. C. Clearfield Co. Syracuse. Mason. 1887. 731 pp.
	- Swope, R. D. Jr. 20 Cent. Hist. of Clearfield Co. Biog. Richmond. Arnold. Chi.
	- Wall, T. L. Clearfield Co. Author 1925.
	- Biog. Rec. of Central Pa. Counties of Centre, Clearfield, Jefferson & Clarion. Beers. Chi. 1898.
Clinton	- Furey, J. Clinton Co. Towns. Biog. Williamsport, Pa. Grit. Pr. 1892. 417 pp.
	- Maynard, D. S. Clinton Co. & Townships. Lock Haven. Enterprise. 1875. 228 pp.
	- Meginness, J. F. Otzinachson: Hist. of West Branch Valley of the Susquehanna. Pioneers. Wars. Williamsport, Bull. Pr. 1889. 702 pp.
	- Rupp, I. D. Hist. & Top. of Northumberland, Huntingdon, Mifflin, Centre, Union, Columbia, Juniata & Clinton Cos., Towns, etc. Lancaster. Hills 1847. 564 pp.
	-- W.P.A. Project. Clinton Co. Com. 1942. 195 pp. Grit Pub. Co. Williamsport.

PENNSYLVANIA (Continued)

Columbia
- Battle, J. H. Hist. of Columbia & Montour Co. Warner. 1887. 894 pp.
- Barton, Edwin Michelet. Hist. of Columbia Co. Pa. & Co. Hist. Socy. 1958.
- Freeze, J. G. Columbia Co. Elwell. 1883. 572 pp.
- Walker, G. H. & Jewett, C. F. Columbia & Mountour Co. Beers. 1876. 95 pp.
- Hist. & Biog. Columbia & Montour Co. Beers. 1915. 1260 pp.

Crawford
- Bates, S. P. Crawford Co. Biog. Meadville. 1899.
- Atlas of Crawford Co. Everts. 1870. 159 pp.
- Dir. of Crawford Co. 1874.
- Crawford Co. Erie. Herald. 1883. 184 pp.
- Crawford Co. Chi. Brown. 1885. 1186 pp.

Cumberland
- Day, S. Pa. Hist. Col. Div. In Counties.
- Cumberland Co. Phila. Croton. 1843. 10 pp.
- Hist. of Cumberland Co. 1951. Pub. By Hamilton Lib. & Hist. Assn. Cumberland Co. Carlisle, Pa.
- Two Hundred Years In Cumberland Co. Pa. Pub. by Hamilton Lib. & Hist. Assn. Cumberland Co. Carlisle, Pa. 1951.
- Wing, Rev. C. P. Cumberland Co. Phila. 1731. Scott. 1879. 271 pp.
- Cumberland & Adams Co. Warner. 1886. 588 pp.
-    "   "   "   " Franklin Co. 1886-7. Chi. Warner.

Dauphin
- Donehoo, G. Harrisburg & Dauphin Co. Hist. Assoc. 1925. 2 v.
- Egle, W. H. Dauphin Co. Biog. Phila. Everts. 1883. 616 pp.
-   "   "   " Cent. of Dauphin Co. 1785-1885 & Harrisburg, 1886.
-   "   "   " Notes & Queries of Dauphin Co. Hbg. Pub. Co. 12 v.
- Everts & Stewart Comp. Dauphin Co. Atlas. Phila. 1875.
- Gough, H. Dauphin Co. Report. Hbg. Tel. Pr. 1914.
- Hamilton, A. B. Egle, W. H. Dauphin Co. Harrisburg. #1 & 2. 95 pp.
- Kelker, L. R. Dauphin Co. N.Y. Chi. Lewis. 1907. Illus. 3 v.
- Parthemore, E. W. S. Dauphin Co. Harrisburg. 1896. 16 pp.
- Robinson, T. H. Hamilton, A. B. Engle, W. H. Church & War Hist of Dauphin Co.
- Ruoff, H. W. Hist. & Top. of Dauphin, Cumberland, Franklin, Bedford, Adams & Perry Co. Lancaster. Hills Pub. 1846. 604 pp. With Hist. of Somerset, Cambria & Ind. Counties.
- Rupp, I. D. Dauphin, Cumberland, Franklin, Bedford, Adams & Perry Counties. Lancaster. Hills. 1846. 606 pp.
- Com. Biog. Encyclo. of Dauphin Co. Chambersburg. Runk. 1896. 1196 pp.
- Dauphin County Reports. 85 pp.

Davidson
- Clayton, W. W. Davidson Co. Biog. Phila. Lewis. 1880. 499 pp.

Delaware
- Ashmead, N. G. Del. Co. Everts. 1884. 767 pp.
- Broomall, J. M. Delaware Co. Media. Vernon. 1876. 24 pp.
- Cape & Ashmead.   "   " & Chester Co. N.Y. Lewis. 1904.

PENNSYLVANIA (Continued)

Delaware
(Cont'd)
- Del. Co. Hist. Socy. Some Aspects of Del. Co. Hist. Pa. 1954.
- Garner, W. S. Del. Co. Pa.
- Jordan, J. W. " " N. Y. Lewis. 1914. 1155 pp. 3 v.
- Palmer, C. Shenk. Lucile eds. Del Co. Harrisburg. Natl. Hist. Assoc. 1932. 425 pp. 2 v.
- Smith, G. & Ashmead, H. B. Del. Co. 1862. 581 pp.
- Wiley, S. T. Biog. Clclop. of Del Co. Richmond. Ind. N. Y. Gresham. 1894. 500 pp.
- Memoirs of Del & Chester Co. Cape & Ashmead, N.Y. Lewis. 1904. 1198 pp. 2 vol.
- Inv. Co. Archives Pa. Hist. Survey #23 Del. Co. 1941. 287 pp.

Elk
- Who's Who In Elk Co. St. Mary's Pa. Lenze Commercial Index. 1956.
- Kuhn's, J. F. Cemetery Records Erie Co. Pa. 1955.

Erie
- Hist. of Erie Co. Warner. Chi. 1884. 1683 pp.
- Miller, J. 20 Cent. Hist. of Erie Co. Lewis. Chi. 1909. 883 pp.
- Moorhead, I. Erie Co. (In Egle, W. H. Hist. of Pa. 1883)
- Reed, J. E. " " Pa. Hist. Pub. Topeka. Ind. 1925. 704 pp.
- Sanford, Laura G. Erie Co. Phila. Lippincott. 1862. 347 pp.
- Whitman, Bed. Nelson's Biog. & Hist. Ref. Bk. Nelson Pub. Erie. 1896. 910 pp.
- Erie Co. Warner. Chi. 1884. 239 pp.

Fayette
- Ellis, F. Fayette Co. Everts. Phila. 1882. 841 pp.
- Gresham, J. M. Biog. Cyclo. of Fayette Co. author. 1889. 602 pp.
- Jordan, J. W. Hadden, J. ed. Fayette Co. Biog. Uniontown. Lewis. N. Y. 1912. 922 pp.
- Lewis F. Veech, J. Fayette Co. Pittsburgh. 1860. 240 pp.
- Nelson's Biog. & Hist. Ref. Book of Fayette Co. 1900. Nelson. Uniontown. 1225 pp.
- Wiley, S. T. Biog. & Port. Cyclo. of Fayette Co. Chi. 1889.602pp.

Fergusson
- Our County. Bates Fergusson. 1899. 972 pp.

Franklin
- Stoner, J. H. Franklin Co. & Cumberland Valley. Chambersburg. Croft. 1947. 549 pp.
- McCauley, I. H. Franklin Co. Cent. Cel. Chambersburg. July 4, 1876. 322 pp. Harrisburg Patriot. 1878. 294 pp.

Fulton
- Greathead, E. S. Fulton Co. McConnelsburg News. 1936. 55 pp.
- Marks, W. E. Fulton Co. Biog. 1941. 68 pp.

Greene
- Bates, C. F. Greene Co. Chi. 1888. 898 pp.
- Hanna, Rev. W. Greene Co. 1682-1781. 1882. 350 pp.

Huntingdon
- Africa, J. S. Huntingdon & Blair Co. Everts. 1883. 500 pp.
- Lytle, M. S. Huntingdon Co. Ray. 1876. 361 pp.
- Rupp, I. D. Northumberland, Huntingdon, Mifflin Co. 1847.531 pp.
- Wolf, George Anderson, A Div. of Names of Inhabitants of Huntingdon Co. In 1790. U. S. Census. Altoona. Blair Co. Hist. Socy. 1951.

PENNSYLVANIA (Continued)

Indiana
- Caldwell, J. A. Indiana Co. 1745-1880. Caldwell. Newark. 1880. 543 pp.
- Stewart, J. T. Indiana Co. Biog. Beers. Chi. 1913. 1597 pp. 2 v.
- Taylor, A. W.   "   "   1876.
- Wiley, S. T. Biog. & Hist. Cyclop. of Ind. & Armstrong Co. Gresham. Phila. 1891. 636 pp.

Jefferson
- Scott, Kate M. Jefferson Co. Biog. Syracuse. Mason. 1888. 753 pp.

Juniata
- Jones, N. J. Juniata Valley. 1856. 380 pp.
- Weiser, J. G. Forts In Juniata Valley. Vol. 1. 1896.
- Nat'l. Hist. Socy.   "   "   1936. 724 pp. 3 vol.

Lackawanna
- Donehoo, G. P. ed. Hist. Resume Vol. 4. Lewis. N. Y. Chi. 1926.
- McKune, R. H. Lackawanna Co. Scranton. Walter. 1882. 115 pp.
- Munsell, W. W. Luzerne, Lackawanna & Wyo. Co. Biog. Munsell. 1880. 540 pp.
- Murphy, T. 50 Anniv. of   "   Co. Topeka. Indpls. 1928. 1267 pp.

Lancaster
- Ellis, F. Lancaster Co. Biog. Phila. Everts. 1883. 110 pp.
- Floyd, V. Lancaster Co. Pa. Towns. 1956.
- Tate Massacres In Lancaster Co. Benj. Franklin, 1764.
- Harris, A. Lancaster Co. Biog. Barr. 1872. 638 pp.
- Klein, Frederic Shriver. Lancaster Co. Pa. Since 1841. Lancaster Co. Nat'l. Bank. 1955.
- Mombert, J. ed.   "   "   Barr. 1869. 617 pp.
- Ruoff, H. W.   "   "   Hills. 1844. 524 pp.
- Port. & Biog. Rec. of Lancaster Co. Chi. Chapman. 1894. 690 pp.
- Newswange, K. C. Amishland Lancaster Co. Pa. 1954.

Lawrence
- Durant, S. W. & P. A. Lawrence Co. Phila. Everts. 1877.

Lebanon
- Engle, W. H. Co. of Lebanon. Biog. Phila. Everts. 1883. 360 pp.
- Graeff, A. D. Lebanon Co. Thru The Centuries.
- Lebanon, Lebanon Steel Foundry. 1945. 35 pp.
- Miller, Frederick K. Rise Of An Iron Community, An Economic Hist. of Lebanon Co. Pa. 1740-1865. Lebanon Co. Hist. Socy. 1950.

Lehigh
- Hauser, J. A. Lehigh Co. Times. 1901. 93 pp.
- Matthews, A. Hungerford, A. N. Counties of Lehigh & Carbon. Phila. Peck. 1884. 802 pp.
- Ohl, Albert. Hist. of The Milfords (Lehigh Co. Pa.) 1732-1947.
- Rinkenbach, W. The Allender Family & Lehigh Co. Pa. 1958.

Luzerne
- Bradsby, H. C. ed. Luzerne Co. Biog. Chi. Nelson. 1893. 1509 pp.
- Harvey, O. J. Early Luzerne Co. Wyo. Hist. Socy. Wilkes Barre Proc. 1914. v. 13. 93-123 pp.
- Pearce, S. Luzerne Co. to 1806. Phila. Lippincotts. 554 pp.
- Santee, T. Tornado of Aug. 19, 1890 In Luzerne & Columbia Co. Wilkes-Barre. 1891. 51 pp.
- Hist. of Luzerne, Lackawanna & Wyo. Co. Biog. N. Y. Munsell. 1880. Hist. Rec. Survey. Pa. No. 40, Luzerne Co.   540 pp.
- Wilkes-Barre Inv. of Co. Archives. 1938. 3 v.

PENNSYLVANIA (Continued)

Lycoming
- Collins, E. & Jordan, J. W. Lycoming Co. N. Y. Lewis. 1906.
  2 v.
- Lloyd, T. W. Lycoming Co. Indpls. Hist. Pub. Co. 1929. 2 v.
- Meginness, J. F. " " Biog. Chi. 1892.
  "   "   "   "   " 1795-1895 Lycoming Co. Williamsport.
                          Bull. Pr. 1895. 822 pp.
-     "   "   "   "   " 1795-1895, 7-4-95 Bull Pr.1896.388pp.
- Lycoming Co. Stewart. Phila. 1876. 132 pp.
- W.P.A. Project. Lycoming Co. Williamsport. Com. of Lycoming
  Co. 1939. 223 pp.

McKean
- Counties of McKean, Elk, & Forest. Beers. 1890. 970 pp.
-     "   "   "   "   " Cameron & Potter. Beers. 1890.
  1259 pp.
- Lillibridge, C.W. McKean Co. 1804-1945. Smethport Co. Schools.
  1945. 34 pp.

Mercer
- Durant, S. W. 80 Years of Mercer Co. 1796-1876. Everts. Phila.
  1877. 156 pp.
- Garvin, W. S. Hist. of Mercer Co. Brown. Chi. 1888.
- White, J. G. Mercer Co. Lewis. Chi. 1909. 2 v. 1111 pp.
- Mercer Co. Illus. Chi. Brown. 1888. 1210 pp.

Middlesex
- Fletcher, Rev. J. Middlesex Co. Illus. 1890. Roy 8 v.

Mifflin
- Bell, R. W. Heads of Families In Mifflin Co. Pa. Lewiston.1957.
- Cochran, J. Mifflin Co. Harrisburg, Pa. 1879. 422 pp.
- Counties of Mifflin, Juanita, Perry, Union & Snyder. Phila.
  Everts. 1886. 894 pp. 2 v.
- Stroup, John Martin. The Genesis of Mifflin Co. Pa. Lewiston.
  1957.

Monroe
- Keller, R. B. Monroe Co. Monroe Pub. Stroudsburg. 1927. 500 pp.
- Koehler, L. J. Monroe Co. During The Civil War. By Co. Hist.
  Socy. & Co. Com. 1950. 250 pp.
- Lantz, J. Picturesque Monroe Co. Stroudsburg. 1897. 162 pp.
- Matthews, A. Wayne, Pike & Monroe Co. Peck. Phila. 1886.1283pp.
- Rupp, I. D. Northampton, Lehigh, Monroe, Carbon & Schuylkill
  Co. Hickock, Harrisburg. 1845. 568 pp.

Montgomery
- Alderfer, Everett Gordon. The Montgomery Co. Pa. Story
  Co. Com. 1951. Norristown.
- Bean, T. W. Montgomery Co. Phila. Everts. 1884. 1197 pp.
- Buck, W. J. "   " Early Hist. Indians, Swedes &
  Others. Morristown. Ocher. 1859. 124 pp.
- Buck, W. J. Atlas of Montgomery Co. Townships. Phila. 1877.
- Harley, J. J. "   "   "
- Hobson, F. G. Buck, W. J. Dotterer, N. S. Cent. Cel.
  Montgomery Co. Morristown. Sept. 1884. 467 pp.
- Hunsiker, C. S. Montgomery Co. N. Y. Lewis. 1923. Biog.
  1133 pp. 3 v.
- Kriebel, H. W. "   " Morristown Schools. 1923.215 pp.

PENNSYLVANIA (Continued)

Montgomery
(Cont'd)
- Roberts, E. ed. Montgomery Co. Biog. N. Y. Benham. 1904.
  1086 pp. 2 v.
- Ruoff, H. W. Biog. & Port. Cyclo. Montgomery Co. Wiley.
- Stoudt, John Joseph. Montgomery Co. Pa. Narberth, Pa.
  Livingston Pub. 1958.
- Wiley, S. T.   "   "   "   "   " Phila. 1895 652
- Montgomery Co. Morristown — Herald. 1895-1900. 416 pp.
-     "   "   Scott. Phila. 1877.

Montour
- Battle, J. H. Columbia & Montour Co. Townships, Villages.
  Warren. Chi. 1887. 220 pp.
- Beers, J. H. Columbia & Montour Co. Biog. 1915. 1260 pp. 2 v.
- Bower, D.H.B. Danville,   "   "   "   Hart. Harrisburg.
  1881. 288 pp.
- Strausner, D.   Montour Co. 1936 Danville.   158 pp.
- W.P.A. Project   "   " Hist.

Northampton
- Ruoff, H. W. Northampton, Lehigh, Monroe, Carbon & Schuylkill
  Co. Hills. Lancaster. 1845. 550 pp.
- Northampton Co. Illus. Phila. Fritts. 1877. 293 pp.

Northumberland
- Bell, H. Northumberland Co. Chi. 1891. 1256 pp.
- Mickley, J. J. Massacres in Northumberland Co. Oct. 8, 1763.
  Phila. Stuckey. 1875. 37 pp.
- Ruoff, H. W. Northumberland, Huntingdon, Mifflin, Centre,
  Union, Columbia, Juniata & Clinton Co. Lancaster, Hills.
  1846. 556 pp.
- Hist. of Northumberland Co. Illus. Phila. Evarts. 1876. 161 pp.
-   "   "   "   "   "   Sketches. Chi. Brown. 1891.
  1256 pp.

Perry
- Hist. of Perry Co. New Bloomfield. 1880-2. 146 pp.
- Wright, S. "   " Lancaster. Wylie. 1873. 290 pp.

Potter
- The Ole Bull Colony In Potter Co. Pa. 1852 Centennial 1952.
  Coudersport. 1952.

Schuylkill
- Schuylkill Co. Biog. N. Y. Munsell. 1881. 390 pp.
- Wiley, S. T. Ruoff, H. W. Schuylkill Co. Biog. Phila. Ruch.
  1893. 752 pp.
- Pottsville, Pa. School Dist. Hist. of Schuykill Co. Pa. Hobbs
  Dir. of Publicity. 1950.

Snyder
- Dunkelberger, G. F. Snyder Co. Selinsgrove. Snyder Co. Hist.
  Soc. 1948. 982 pp.
- Fisher, C. A. Snyder Co. Pioneers. Fisher, Selingsgrove.
  1938. 103 pp.
- Wagenseller, G. W. Snyder Co. Annals. Middleburgh Post. 1915.
-   "   "   "   "   " Marriages. 1835-1899.
          Middleburgh. Wagenseller. 1899. 266 pp.
- Wagenseller, G. W. Tombstone Inscriptions of Snyder Co.
          Middleburgh, Wagenseller. 1904. 279 pp.
- Doyle, F. Early Somerset Co. Somerset Co. Hist. Socy. 1945
  60 pp.

PENNSYLVANIA (Continued)

Somerset
- Butler, Mary. Three Archeological Sites. Com. Bull. 1939.79 pp.
- Cassidy, J. C. Somerset Co. Memorite. Scotdale. 1932. 263 pp.
- Walkinshaw, L. C. "   " Lewis. 1906.
- Waterman, Watkins & Co. Somerset, Bedford & Fulton Co. authors. 1884. 202 pp.
- Welfly, W. H. Somerset, Bedford & Fulton Co. Lewis.1906.695 pp.
- W.P.A. Survey World War Veterans of Somerset Co. 1936.

Sullivan
- Ingham, T. J. Sullivan Co. Chi. 1899. 218 pp.
- Streby, G. Hist. of Sullivan Co.

Susquehanna
- Blackman, Emily C. Susquehanna Co. Phila. Claxton.1878. 640 pp.
- Dubois, J. T. Pike, W. J. Cent. of Susquehanna Co. Wash. D.C. Gray. 1888. 138 pp.
- Stocker, R. M. Cent. Hist. of Susquehanna Co. Phila. Peck. 1887. 851 pp.

Tioga
- Meginness, J. T. Tioga Co. Brown. 1897. Harrisburg. 1186 pp.
- Rolfe, M. O. 1787. Our County 1877. Ninety Years. Tioga. Bunnell. 116 pp.
- Sexton, J. L. & others. Tioga Co. Munsell. 1883. 366 pp.
    "   "   " Tioga Co. Elmira Gazette. 1874.
    "   "   " Tioga Co. and Bradford Co. Gazette. N. Y.
- Hist. of Tioga Co. Meginness, Meagher & Croft. Brown. 1897. 1186 pp.
- McKnight, W. J. Pioneer Outline Hist. of N. W. Pa. Counties of Tioga, Potter, McKean, Warren, Crawford, Venango, Forest, Clarion, Elk, Jefferson, Cameron, Butler, Lawrence & Mercer, Lippincott. Phila. 1905.

Union
- Counties of Mifflin, Juniata, Perry, Union and Snyder. Phila. Everts. 1886. 2 v.
- Blair, H. L. Warren Co. 1739-1950. Warren. Blair. 1950. 38 pp.

Venango
- Babcock, C. A. Venango Co. Pioneers. Beers. Chi. 1919. 1087 pp.
- Bell, H. C. Venango Co. Brown. Chi. 1890. 1164 pp.
- Eaton, S. J.   "   " Add. At Franklin, Pa. July 4, 1876. Spectator. 1876. 48 pp.
- Newton, J. H. ed."   " Caldwell. Columbus. 1879. 651 pp.

Warren
- Howden, J. A. & Odbert, A. Warren Co. Wash. 1878. 159 pp.
- Noyes, Hon. C. H. Warren Cent. Cel. July 2, 3 & 4, 1895. Lib. Assn. 1897. 244 pp.
- Schenck, J. C. Rann, W. S. Warren Co. Syracuse, N. Y. Mason. 1897. 692 pp.

Washington
- Creigh, A. Washington Co. Harrisburg. Singerly. 1871. 375 pp.
- Crumwine, B. Wash. Co. Biog. Phila. Everts. 1882. 1002 pp.
- Forrest, E.   "   " Clarke. 1926. 1164 pp.
- McFarland, J.F."   " Richmond, 1910. 1369 pp.
- Washington Cent. Cel. of Wash. Co. Sept. 7 & 8, 1881. Crumwine. Wash. 1881. 109 pp.

PENNSYLVANIA (Continued)

Wayne
- Goodrich, P. G. Wayne Co. Honesdale. Haines. 1880. 409 pp.
- Mathews, A. Wayne, Pike & Monroe Co. Phila. Peck. 1886. 1283 pp.
- Cent. & Illus. " Co. Biog. Honesdale. Haines. 1900. 152 pp.

Westmoreland
- Albert, G. D. Westmoreland Co. Phila. 1882. 727 pp.
  Wiley, S. T. Westmoreland Co. Biog. Gresham. Phila. 1890. 744 pp.

Wyoming
- Barnes, A. W. Genealogical Notes. 1945. Typed.
- Harding, G. M. Wyo. & Its Incidents.
  D.A.R. Paper. Wilkes-Barre. 1901. 23 pp.
- Peck, G. Wyoming. N. Y. Harpers. 1858. 432 pp.

York
- Carter, W. C. York Co. York. Glossbremer. 30 pp. 1834.
- "   " "   "   " Harrisburg. Aurand. 1930. 221 pp.
- Gibson, J. York Co. Chi. Battey. 1886. 772 pp.
- Prowell, G. R. York Co. Prowell. York. 67 pp. 1906.
- Ruoff, H. W.   "   " Lancaster, Hills. 1845.
- Check List of Pa. Co. Towns & Town Hist. Harrisburg. Meyers. 1892.
- Selected Bibliography of Secondary Works of Pa. Hist. Compiled
  By Dr. A. C. Bining, U. of Pa. Pr. by Pa. St. Lib. Oct. 1933.
  Pa. Lib. Notes.

RHODE ISLAND - 5 Counties

Bristol
- Arnold, J. N. Bristol Co. Births, Marriages & Deaths, Providence,
  Narragansett. 1894. Vol. 1.

Kent
- Arnold, J. N. Kent Co. Births, Marriages & Deaths. Providence.
  Narragansett. 1891
- Hist. of Kent Co.

Newport
- Arnold, J. N. Newport Co. Births, Marriages & Deaths. Providence.
  Narragansett. 1893.
- Bayles, R. M. Newport Co. 1638-1887. N. Y. 1888. 1060 pp.

Providence
- Arnold, J. N. Providence Co. Births, Marriages & Deaths.
  Providence. Narragansett. 1892.
- Bayles, R. M. Providence. N. Y. 1891.
- Atlas of Providence Co. Everts. 1895.

Washington
- Arnold, J. N. Washington Co. Births, Marriages & Deaths.
  Providence.Narragansett. 1894.
- Cole, J. R. Washington & Kent Counties. Preston, N.Y. 1889.

SOUTH CAROLINA - 46 Counties

Anderson
- Vandiver, Mrs. L. A. Anderson Co. Ruralist Press. 1928.
  Atlanta. 318 pp.

Beaufort — Hist. of Beaufort Co.
— Willet, N. L. Beaufort Co. Gazette. 1923. 30 pp.

Charleston — Hist. of Charleston Co.
— Lesesue, T. P. Charleston Co. Charleston. Cawston. 1931.
369 pp.

Chesterfield — Hist. of Chesterfield Co.

Craven — Hist. of Craven Co. F.A.P. Charleston. 1852.
— Parcher, F. A. Craven Co. Charleston. 1852. 52 pp.

Dillon — Hist. of Dillon Co.

Edgefield — Chapman, J. A. Hist. of Edgefield Co. To 1897. Biog. Mil.
Newburg. Auld. 1897. 521 pp.

Fairfield — McMaster, F. H. Fairfield Co. Columbia. State. 1946.220 pp.

Florence — Hist. of Florence Co.

Greenville — Richardson, J. M. Hist. of Greenville Co. Biog. Cawston.
Atlanta. 1930. 342 pp.

Kershaw — Hist. of Kershaw Co.

Lancaster — Floyd, Viola C. Lancaster Co. Tours. Lancaster Co. Hist.
Com. 1956.
— Hist. of Lancaster Co.

Marion — Sellers, A. Marion Co. Columbia. 1902.

Marlboro — Thomas, Rev. J.A.W. Marlboro Co. Foote. Atlanta. 1897.
292 pp.
— Hist. of Marlboro Co.

Newberry — Summer, George Leland. Newberry Co. S. C. Geneal. & Hist.
Newberry. 1950.

Orangeburg — Brookhart, Mrs. T.W.E. & Adams, Mrs. Georgie. Orangeburg
Co. Records. W.P.A.
Sally, A. S. Jr. Orangeburg Co. To 1783. Berry. 1898.572 pp.

Pickens — McFall, Pearl Smith. It Happened In Pickens Co. S.C.
Sentinel. 1959.

Richland — Green, E. L. Richland Co. 1732-1805. Bryan. 1932. 385 pp.

Spartanburg — Landrunn, J. B. O. Spartanburg Co. Atlanta. Franklin. 1900.
— 739 pp. W.P.A. Spartanburg Co. Spartanburg Bond. 1940.
304 pp.
— Hist. of Spartanburg Co.

SOUTH CAROLINA (Continued)

Sumter
- Hist. of Sumter Co. S. C. By Anne King Gregorie. Pub. by Library Bd. of Sumter Co. Sumter, S. C. 1954.
- Hist. of Sumter Co.

Union
- Hist. of Union Co.

Williamsburg
- Boddie, W. W. Williamsburg. 1923.
- Hist. of Williamsburg Co.
- McGill, Samuel Davis. Narratives of Reminiscences in Williamsburg Co. Kingstree, S. C. Lithographic Co. 1952.
- McGill, S. D. Williamsburg Co. Columbia. Bryan. 1897. 304 pp.
- Simms, W. G. Geo. of S. C. & has data of several Counties.

SOUTH DAKOTA - 67 Counties

The only County histories published in S. D. during 1955-60 are anniversary publications of certain S. D. Towns.

Beadle
- Rogers, B. Econ. & Soc. Hist. Beadle Co. McClasky. 1940.

Brookings
- Sanders, G. O. Brookings Co. M. A. Thesis. U. of S. D. 1936.

Brown
- S. D. H. S. Coll. Brown Co. v. 17. 159 pp. Andreas '84. Peterson '04.

Brule
- S. D. H. S. Coll. Brule Co. v. 23. 184 pp.

Buffalo
- Pioneer Stories of Buffalo Co. Ladies Socy. of Cong. Church.

Clay
- S. D. H. S. Coll. Clay Co. v. 13. 87 pp. Andreas '84. Peterson '04.

Codington
- S. D. H. S. Coll. Codington Co. v. 24. 194 pp. Peterson '04.

Day
- Ochsenreiter, L. G. Day Co. 1873-1926. Educ. Supply Co. 1926. 258 pp.

Douglas
- W.P.A. Douglas Co. Armour. 1938. 22 pp.

Faulk
- Ellis, C. H. Faulk Co. Record. Faulkton. 1909. 500 pp.

Grant
- Bloch, D. L. Grant Co. 1861-1937. Herald. Milbank. 1937. 98 pp.

Hamlin
- Hist. & Atlas 1936. 44 pp. Herald. Hayti. Andreas '84. Peterson '04.

Harding
- S. D. H. S. Coll. Harding Co. v. 21. 49 pp.

Hughes
- Hall, B. L. Hughes Co. 1937. 205 pp. Andreas '84. Peterson '04.
- Hist. of Hughes.

Hyde
- Perkins, J. B. Hyde Co. 1908. 300 pp. Andreas '84. Peterson '04.

SOUTH DAKOTA (Continued)

Jerauld — Dunham, N. J. Jerauld Co. 1910. 441 pp. Andreas '84. Peterson '04.

Marshall — Hickman, G. Marshall Co. 1886. 86 pp. Banbury. Britton.
Peterson '04.

McPherson — Hickman, G. McPherson Co. 1886.
— W.P.A. Homesteaders of McPherson Co. Pierce. 1941. 86 pp.

Miner — Fjellestad, L. J. Miner Co. 1931. 52 pp. Mimeo.
— Andreas '84. Peterson '04. W.P.A. Prairie Tamers of Miner Co.
1939. 36 pp.

Minnehaha — Bailey, D. R. Minnehaha Co. Brown. Sioux Falls 1899. 1091 pp.
— Ellis, F. Minnehaha Co. & Sioux Falls. Sioux Falls. 1887.
— Smith, C. A. Minnehaha Co. Educ. Mitchell. 1950. 504 pp.

Sully — Hist. of Sully Co.
— Old Settlers Assn. Sully Co. 1923. Andreas '84. Peterson '04.

Turner — Stoddard, W. H. Turner Co. 1931.

Union — Fate, W. H. H. Union Co. Perkins. Sioux City '24. 143 pp.
Andreas '84. Peterson '04.

Yankton — Kingsbury's Dakota Covers Yankton. 943 pp. '15 Clarke. Chi.
Andreas '84. Peterson '04.
— Block Hills Books Cover Counties There.
— Andreas Atlas of 1884 and Peterson's Atlas of 1904 Covers Nearly
all S. D. Counties.

TENNESSEE - 95 Counties

Foster, Austin P. Counties of Tenn. Dept. of Educ. Nashville.1923.

Anderson — Salber, R. C. Anderson Co. Knoxville. M. A. Thesis '38. U. of
Tenn. 116 pp.

Bedford — Davidson, H. L. Bedford Co. Chattanooga. Garrett. Hist. of Tenn.
339 pp.
— Cent. Cel. July 4, 1876. Shelbyville. Chattanooga. Crandall. 1877.
— Hutson, J. L. Bedford Co. Shelbyville Lions Club.

Bledsoe — Duggan, Brown & Miser. Bledsoe Co. U. of Tenn. 4 v. Apr. 1927.

Blount — Bevins, Inez E. Hist. of Blount Co. War Trails To Landing Strip.
1795-1955. Nashville Hist. Com. 1957.
— Settlement & Early Hist. of The Coves of Blount Co. By Inez
Bevins. Pub. #24: 44-67 Tenn. Tenn. Hist. Socy.
— Early East Tenn. Tax Payers, II Blount Co. 1801-1952. E. Tenn.
Hist. Socy. Pub. #24. 1952.

TENNESSEE (Continued)

Bradley
- Cleveland Adv. Co. Bradley Co. 1929.
- Hurlburt, J. S. Rebellion In Bradley Co. Indpls. Downey. 1866. 280 pp.

Campbell
- Ridenour, Dr. G. L. Campbell Co. Lafayette. 1941. 115 pp.
- The Dev. of Pub. Educ. In Campbell Co. Tenn. By R. G. Lawrence. M. A. Thesis U. of Tenn. 1950.

Cannon
- Brown, S. S. Woodbury & Cannon Co. Doak. Manchester. 1936. 234 pp.

Carter
- Early Hist. of Carter Co. 1760-1861 By Merritt, Frank. Knoxville E. Tenn. Hist. Socy. 1950.
- Selected Aspects of Early Carter Co. Hist. 1760-1861. By F. Merritt, M. A. - U. of Tenn. 1950.
- A Hist. of The Iron Industry In Carter Co. To 1860. By Robt. T. Trane. M. A. U. of Tenn. 1953.
- A Study of The Debt Hist. of Carter Co. Tenn. 1892-1952. K. W. Sharp. M. A. U. of Tenn. 1952.

Cheatham
- Hist. of Cheatham Co.

Chester
- Reed, S. E. Chester Co. Johnson. Jackson. 1924. 24 pp.

Cocke
- A Hist. of The Secondary Schools of Cocke Co. By Marie M. Knight. M. A. U. of Tenn. 1952.
- Over The Misty Blue Hills. The Story of Cocke Co. Odell. Ruth W. Newport. 1951.

Coffee
- Ewell, L. Coffee Co. Manchester. Doak. 1936. 85 pp.

Cumberland
- Krechniak, Helen B. Cumberland County's First 100 Yrs. Crossville. Cent. Com. 1956.
- Hist. of Cumberland Co.

Davidson
- Clayton, W. W. Davidson Co. Lewis. Phila. 1880.
- Marriage Record Bk. I. Jan. 2, 1789 to Dec. 13, 1837. Davidson Co. Nashville. 1952. D.A.R. French Lick Chap.

Decatur
- A Note On Decatur Co. By Hawkin, D. Tenn. Folklore Socy. Bull. Sept. 1953. v. 19.

De Kalb
- Hale, W. T. De Kalb Co. Nashville, Tenn. Hunter. 1915. 254 pp.

Dickson
- Hist. of Dickson Co.
- Corlew, Robt. E. A Hist. of Dickson Co. Tenn. Nashville. Hist. Com. 1956.
- Some Aspects of Slavery In Dickson Co. By Corlew, Robt. E. Tenn. Hist. Quart. Sept.-Dec. 1951.

Fayette
- Gray, R. H. Sebastian, Emma. Fayette In Lincoln Co. 1925.

TENNESSEE (Continued)

Fentress
- Hogue, A. R. Fentress Co. Mark Twain's Family. Nashville. Williams. 1916. 1920. 165 pp.
- Hogue, A. R. David Crockett & Others In Fentress Co. Jamestown. 1955.

Franklin
- Phonton, T. F. Franklin Co. Knoxville. M. A. Thesis. U. of Tenn. '41. 87 pp.

Giles
- Hist. of Giles Co. Tenn. By Parker, Elizabeth C. M.A. Thesis Mid. Tenn. St. Coll. 1953.
- Marriages of Giles Co. By Smith, Jean Waldrop. Elkmont, Ala.1952.
- Kellebrew, J. B. Giles Co. Nashville. Union & Amer. Bk. Pr. 1871.
- McCallum, J. Giles Co. Pulaski. Citizen. 1928.

Greene
- Peterson, Mrs. Z. R. Early Marriage Bonds of Greene Co. Detroit Socy. For General Res. Mag. 1939. 2 v.
- Some Aspects of Dev. of Pub. Educ. In Greene Co. By Roberts, Harry B. M. A. U. of Tenn. 1950.

Hamilton
- Armstrong, Zella. Hamilton Co. Chattanooga. Lookout. 1931. 1940. 2 v.
- W.P.A. Inventory of Co. Archives, Nashville No. 33. Chattanooga. 1937. 130 pp.

Hardeman
- Clifft, W. W. Early Hardeman Co. Nashville. M. A. Thesis. Peabody. 1930.

Hardin
- Brazelton, B. G. Hardin Co. Nashville. 1885. Presby Pub. Cumberland. 1885. 135 pp.

Henderson
- Bolen, N. J. Henderson Co. Murfreesboro. Journal. 1922. 14 pp.
- Powers, A.   "   " 1930. 169 pp.

Henry
- Folklore of A Negro Couple In Henry Co. By Hurdle, Virginia Jo. Ed. By H. Halpert. Tenn. Folklore Socy. Bul. Sept. 1953.
- Reynolds, E. H. Henry Co. Jacksonville . Sun. 1904. 301 pp.

Hickman
- Spence, W. Jerome, D. David, L. Hickman Co. Adv. Pub. 509 pp. 1900. Nashville.

Houston
- Hist. of Houston Co.

Jefferson
- Bell, Mrs. A. W. B. Rec. of Marriages 1792-1851. Wash. D. C. 1935. 78 pp. Typed.
- A Study of Dev. of Organized Religion In Jefferson Co. 1785-1950. By J. E. Cockrun. M. A. Thesis. U. of Tenn. 1951.

Knox
- 1850 Census Knox Co. Tenn. Hist. Socy. 1949. 201 pp.

Lauderdale
- Pub. Educ. In Lauderdale Co. 1911-50. By Taylor, O. R. M. A. Memphis St. Coll. 1953.
- Peters, Kate Johnston. Lauderdale Co. Tenn. From Earliest Days. Ripley Sugar Hill. 1957.

156

Lincoln   - Gray, R. H. Sebastian, Emma. Fayette in Lincoln Co. 1925.

McMinn   - A Hist. of Educ. In McMinn Co. Tenn. Powers, Ozelle S. M. A. U. of Tenn. 1950.

McNairy   - Wright, M. J. Early McNairy Co. Wash. D. C. Com. Pub. 1882.

Madison   - Cisco, J. G. Hist. of Madison Co. v. d.
- Kuhlman, A. F. Jackson & "   "   Jackson McKaran A.R.C. 1920.
- Williams, E. I. "   "   "   "   Hist. Socy. 1946. 553 pp..

Marion   - A Hist. of Marion Co. By Link, Gertrude Bible. M. A. Mid. Term. St. Coll. 1953.

Maury   - Century Rev. 1805-1905. Maury Co. Tenn. Pub.
- Jones, N. W. Mt. Pleasant & W. Maury Co. Nashville. McGuiddy. 1903.
- Maury Co. Cent. Cel. Address July 4, 1876. Columbia Excelsior. 1876.
- Maury Co. & The Civil War. Waller, Charlotte; Clay, M. A. Vanderbilt U. 1951.
- Turner, Williams Bruce. Hist. of Maury Co. Tenn. Nashville. Parthenon Press. 1955.

Obion   - Goodpasture, A. V. Overton Co. Address. Lexington. July 4, 1876.
- Nashville. Cumberland Presby Pub. 1877.
- Marshall, E. H. Obion Co. Towns etc. 1887-1925. Union City Messenger. 1941. 272 pp.

Overton   - Goodpasture, A. Overton Co. Address at Livingston, Tenn. July 4, 1876. Nashville. 27 pp.

Pickett   - Smith, C. G. Pickett Co. Thesis. Vanderbilt U. 1928.

Polk   - Haynes, E. R. Hist. of Polk Co. Tenn. 1937.

Putnam   - McClain, W. S. Putnam Co. Cookeville. 1925. 152 pp.

Rhea   - Campbell, T. J. Rhea Co. Rhea Pub. Co. Dayton. 205 pp.

Roane   - Welles, Emma M. Roane Co. 1801-70. Chattanooga. Lookout Pub. 1927.

Rutherford   - Mutual Realty Handbook of Murfreesboro & Rutherford Co. Journal v. d. 1923. 128 pp.
- Hughes, M. B. Rutherford Co. Homes. Murfreesboro. Mid-South. 1942. 68 pp.

Scott   - Foster, A. P. Scott Co. Tenn. 1923. 328 pp.
- Sanderson, Esther (Sharp). County Scott, Tenn. and Its Mountain Folk. Huntsville. 1958.
- A Hist. of Educ. In Scott Co. Tenn. By Sexton, Oxwell S. M. A. U. of Tenn. 1951.

<u>TENNESSEE</u> (Continued)

Sevier
— Hammer, J. Sevier Co. July 4, 1876. Photo. 1938.
— Handicrafts In Sevier Co. Tenn. Hodges, Sidney Cecil. M. A. U. of Tenn. 1951.
— Matthews, Fred. Decatur. Hist. of Sevier Co. Tenn. Knoxville, Tenn.

Shelby
— Keating, J. M. Memphis & Shelby Co. Syracuse. Mason. 1888. 2 v.
— Williams, J. R. Shelby Co. Memphis. De Garis. 1897. 96 pp.
— The Taxing District of Shelby Co. Bejach, L. D. — W. Tenn. Hist. Socy. Papers. 1950.

Smith
— Bowen, J. W. Hist. of Smith Co. Tenn. Typed. v. d.

Stewart
— Some Folkways of A Stewart Co. Community. Guerin. Wayne. Tenn. Folklore Socy. Bull. Sept. 1953.

Sullivan
— Taylor, O. Sullivan Co. Bristol. King Pr. 1909.

Sumner
— Cisco, J. G. Sumner Co. General. Nashville Folk. Keelin. 1909. 319 pp.

Tipton
— Hist. of Tipton Co.

Warren
— Hale, W. T. Warren Co. McMinnville. Standard. 1930. 59 pp.
— Hist. of Warren Co.
— U. S. Census Office — Seventh Census For Warren Co. Tenn.

White
— Seals, Rev. M. White Co. Brown Pr. 1935. 152 pp.

<u>TEXAS</u> — 254 Counties

Anderson
— Hohes, Mrs. P. B. Cent. Hist. of Anderson Co. 1936. Naylor. San Antonio. 561 pp.

Angelina
— Boone, Mrs. E. M. Angelina Co. M. A. Thesis U. of Tex. Austin. 1937. 245 pp.
— Hatton, E. B. Hist. & Des. of Angelina Co. Luflinn. 1888.

Archer
— Nance, Winnie. Archer Co. M. A. Thesis U. of Tex. Austin. 1927. 118 pp.

Armstrong
— Hist. of Armstrong Co. Woman's Dev. Club. 3 v. 942 pp.

Austin
— Hist. of Austin Co.

Bailey
— Stevens, Thelma L. Bailey Co. M. A. Thesis. Tex. Teach. Coll. Lubbock. 1939. 125 pp.

Bandera
— Hunter, J. M. Bandera Co. Baird. Star. 1949. 76 pp.
—   "   " "   "   " Bandera. Hunter. 1922. 287 pp.
— Hist. of Bandera Co.

TEXAS (Continued)

Bastrop   – Karges, W. H. Bastrop Co. M. A. Thesis. U. of Tex. Austin. 1933. 287 pp.

Bee   – Madranz, Mrs. I. C. Bee Co. & Other Co. Beeville. 1939. 135 pp.
– Schoppe, Lillian G. "   " M. A. Thesis. U. of Tex. Austin. 1939. 218 pp.
– Tex. Cent. Com. 1858–1958. Beeville, Tex. 1958.

Bell   – Atkinson, Bertha. Bell Co. M. A. Thesis. U. of Tex. 1929. 253 pp.
– Tyler, G. W. Bell Co. San Antonio. Naylor. San Antonio. 1936. 425 pp.

Brazos   – Marshall, E. G. Brazos Co. M. A. Thesis. U. of Tex. Austin. 1937. 234 pp.

Brown   – Havins, T. R. Brown Co. M. A. Thesis U. of Tex. Austin. 1931. 192 pp.

Caldwell   – O'Banion, Maurine M. Caldwell Co. M. A. Thesis U. of Tex. Austin. 1931. 259 pp.

Cameron   – Pipkin, M. S. Cameron Co. Kingsville. 1940. 123 pp. Typed.

Chambers   – Harry, J. H. Chambers Co. M. A. Thesis U. of Tex. Austin. 1940. 285 pp.

Cherokee   – Roach, Hattie J. Cherokee Co. Southwest Pr. 1934. 174 pp.

Coleman   – Gay, Beatrice G. Coleman Co. Santa Anna. 1936. 193 pp.

Collin   – Stambaugh, J. Lee. A Hist. of Collin Co. Tex. Austin. Tex. St. Hist. Assn. 1958.

Collingsworth – Brown, C. C. Hist. of Collingsworth. M. A. Thesis. U. of Colo. Boulder. 1934. 127 pp.
– Collingsworth Co. Wellington. Leoder. 1925. 107 pp.

Comanche   – Wells, E. N. Comanche Co. Wells. Blanket. 1942. 168 pp.

Cooke   – Smith, Alex Morton. The First 100 Yrs. In Cooke Co. Tex. San Antonio. Naylor. 1955.

Coryell   – Simmons, F. E. Coryell Co. Gatesville. Coryell Pr. 1936.102 pp.

Crosby   – Burgess, R. A. Crosby Co. M. A. Thesis. U. of Tex. Austin. 1927. 111 pp.

Dallam   – Mauldin, W. D. Dallam Co. M. A. Thesis. U. of Tex. Austin. 1938. 127 pp.

Dallas   – Brown, J. A. Dallas Co. 1837–87. Dallas. 1887.
– Cochran, J.H.   "   " Dallas. Mathis Pr. 1928. 296 pp.
– Stark, Owen   "   " M. A. Thesis U. of Tex. Austin. 1935. 198 pp.
– Biog. Hist. of "   " Chi. Lewis. 1892. 1011 pp.

Dawson   — Gelin, Leona M. Dawson Co. To 1917. M. A. Thesis Tex. Teach. Coll. Lubbock. 1937. 168 pp.

Delta   — Patterson, I. G. Delta Co. Dallas. Mathis. 221 pp.

Denton   — Bates, E. F. Denton Co. Denton. McNitzley Pr. 1918. 412 pp.

Donley   — Ford, W. D. Donley Co. M. A. Thesis U. of Colo. Boulder. 1932. 122 pp.

Eastland   — Cox, Edwin J. Hist. of Eastland Co. Tex. San Antonio. 1950.
— Langston, Mrs. C. L. Eastland Co. Dallas. Aldridge. 1904. 220 pp.
— Lindsey, R. Y. Jr. Eastland Co. M. A. Thesis U. of Tex. Austin. 1940. 200 pp.

Ellis   — Ellis Co. Hist. Biog. Lewis. Chi. 1892. 573 pp.

Erath   — Eoff, Vallie. Erath Co. M. A. Thesis. U. of Tex. Austin. 1937. 226 pp.

Falls   — Brown, W. W. Falls Co. M. A. Thesis. Baylor U. Waco. 1938. 167 pp.
— Old Settlers & Veterans Assn. Falls Co. Ed. R. Eddins. Marlin. 1947. 312 pp.

Fannin   — Carter, W. A. Fannin Co. Bouham. 1885. 150 pp.

Fayette   — Lotto, F. Fayette Co. Schulenburg. Author. 1902. 424 pp.
— Weyand, Leonie R. Rummel & Wade. Early Fayette Co. Jour. 1936. 383 pp.

Floyd   — Hall, C. V. Early Floyd Co. M. A. Thesis. U. of Tex. Austin. 1922. 197 pp.

Fort Bend   — Bridges, J. L. Fort Bend Co. 1822-61. M. A. Thesis U. of Tex. 1939. 220 pp.
— McMillan, S. A. Fort Bend. McMillan. 1926. 264 pp.
— Sowell, A. J. Fort Bend. Biog. Houston. Coyle. 1904. 373 pp.
— Wharton, C.   "   "   San Antonio. Naylor. 1939. 250 pp.

Freestone   — Browne, P. D. Early Freestone Co. To 1865. M. A. U. of Tex. Austin. 1925. 179 pp.

Gatlin   — Bowles, Flora. (Gatlin) A No Man's Land Becomes A County. Tex. Mills. Austin. 1958.

Gillespie   — Biesele, R. L. Gillespie Co. 1931. Jones. Austin. 139 pp.

Glasscock   — Greenwood, M. H. Glasscock Co. M. A. Thesis Tex. Teach. Coll. Lubbock. 1937. 106 pp.

Grayson   — Anderson, E. H. Guide of Sherman & Grayson Co. 1940. 75 pp.
— Lucas, Mrs. W. H. Hall, Mrs. H. E. Grayson Co. Scruggs. 1936. 209 pp.

TEXAS (Continued)

Gregg   – Levy, Hon. R. B. Gregg Co.

Grimes   – Blair, E. L. Grimes Co. Austin. 1930. 253 pp.

Guadalupe   – Moellering, M. Guadalupe Co. M. A. Thesis of Tex. 239 pp.
          – Sowell, A. J. Guadalupe Co. Seguin Record. 1884.

Hale   – Cox, Mary L. Hale Co. Plainview. 1937. 230 pp.

Hall   – Baker, Inez. Hall Co. 1940. Bk. Craft Dallas. 219 pp.

Harris   – Harris Co. Tex. Hist. Socy. Harris Co. Rep. of Tex. 1839-45.
          Huston. Jones Pr. 1950.
          – Looscan, Mrs. A. L. Harris Co. 1822-45. Hist. Assn. 78 pp.

Harrison   – Armstrong, J. C. Harrison Co. 1839-80. M. A. Thesis. U. of Colo.
          Boulder. 1930. 216 pp.

Hays   – Dobie, D. R. Hays Co. M. A. Thesis. U. of Tex. Austin. 1932. 134 pp.

Henderson   – Faulk, J. J. Henderson Co. Athens Rev. Pr. 1929. 322 pp.

Hidalgo   – Scott, O. R. Hidalgo Co. 1749-1852. M. A. Thesis. Tex. Christian
          U. Fort Worth. 1934. 113 pp.

Hill   – Johnson & Hill Co. Lewis. 1892. Chi. 735 pp.

Hood   – Ewell, T. T. Hood Co. Granbury News. 1895. 161 pp.

Hopkins   – Fleming, E. B. Early Hopkins Co. Biog. 1902. 183 pp.
          – St. Clair, Gladys A. Hopkins Co. M. A. Thesis. U. of Tex. Austin.
          1940. 164 pp.
          – Wright, Celia M. Heritage From The Past, Sketches From Hopkins
          Co. Tex. Hist. 1959. Sulphur Sprgs. Path Pr.

Houston   – Armistead, A. A. Houston Co. Naylor. San Antonio. 1943.
          – Kennedy, W. Houston Co. From Terrell Kaufman Co. To Sabine Pass
          on The Gulf of Mexico, Austin, Hutchins Pr. 1892. 125 pp.

Hunt   – Cassles, Anne E. Hunt Co. M. A. Thesis. U. of Tex. Austin. 1935.
          172 pp.

Hutchinson   – Garner, L. Hutchinson Co. M. A. Thesis. S.W. Metho. U. Dallas.
          1930. 90 pp.

Jack   – Huckabay, D. Jack Co. 1854-1948. Jacksboro. 513 pp.

Jackson   – Horton, T. F. Jackson Co. Pioneers. Jacksboro Gazette Pr. 1932.
          166 pp.
          – Taylor, I. T.   "   " San Antonio, 1938. Naylor. 471 pp.

Jim Wells   – Pollard, N. V. Jim Wells Co. Kingsville. 1945. 106 pp. Typed.

TEXAS (Continued)

Johnson
- Abernathy, F. D. Johnson Co. & E. Mo. 1936. 330 pp. Vol. 1.
- Byrd, A. J. Johnson Co. Marshall. 1879.
- Johnson & Hill Co. Biog. Chi. Lewis. 1892. 735 pp.

Kaufman
- Butler, R. R. Kaufman Co. M. A. Thesis. U. of Tex. Austin. 1940. 172 pp.

Kerr
- Bennett, Bob. Kerr Co. Tex. 1856-1956 Vandruff. San Antonio. Naylor. 1956.

Kleberg
- Boss, S. W. Kleberg Co. M. A. Thesis. U. of Tex. Austin. 1931. 254 pp.

Lamar
- Neville, A. W. Lamar Co. Paris. U. Tex. Pub. 1931. 246 pp.
-    "   " "   "   " 1937 "   "   "   -   262 pp.

Lampasas
- Elaner, Jonnie (Ross). Lamplights of Lampasas Co. Tex. Austin. 1951. Firm Foundation.

Leon
- Leathers, F. J. Leon Co. Oakwood. 1946. 218 pp.

Liberty
- Fincher, Rosalie. Liberty Co. M. A. Thesis U. of Tex. Austin. 1937. 99 pp.
- Pickett, Arline.   "   " Dallas. Tardy Pub. 1936. 117 pp.

Limestone
- Steele, H. Limestone Co. 1833-60. Mexia News Pub. 1926. 37 pp.
- Biog. Hist. of Navarro, Henderson, Anderson, Limestone, Freestone, and Leon Co. Chi. 1893. Lemos. 908 pp.

Lavaca
- Boethel, Paul Carl. Hist. of Lavaca Co. Tex. Austin. Von Boeckmann. 1959.
- Boethel, Paul Carl.   "   "   "   " Naylor. San Antonio. 1936. 151 pp.

Marion
- McKay, Mrs. A. & Spellings, Mrs. R. A. Jefferson & Marion Co. Jefferson. 1936. 77 pp.

Mason
- Eilers, Mrs. K. Mason Co. M. A. U. of Tex. 1939. Austin. 260 pp.

McCulloch
- Barfoot, Jessie L. McCulloch Co. M. A. Thesis U. of Tex. 1937. Austin. 165 pp.

McLennan
- McLennan, Falls, Bell and Coryell Counties. Biog. Chi. Lewis. 1893. 999 pp.
- Sleeper, J. I. Hutchins, J. C. Waco & McLennan Co. Waco Pr. 1876. 170 pp.
- Biog. Hist. of McLennan, Falls, Bell & Coryell Co. Chi. Lewis. 1893. 999 pp.

Menard
- Pierce, N. H. Menard Co. Menard Press. 1946. 213 pp.

Milam
- Batte, Lelia McAnally. Hist. of Milam Co. Tex. San Antonio. Naylor. 1956.

TEXAS (Continued)

Mitchell — Bradford, G. E. Mitchell Co. M. A. Thesis. U. of Texas. Austin. 1937. 178 pp.

Montague — Potter, F. C. B. Montague Co. Austin. Steck. 1913.
— Potter, Fannie Cora (Bellows) Hist. of Montague Co. Tex. St. Jo 1957.
— Donnell, G. R. Montague Co. M. A. Thesis. U. of Tex. Austin. 1940. 191 pp.

Nacogdoches — Brown, N. E. Nacogdoches Co. Author. 1927. 96 pp.
Haltom. R. W.   "   " Nacogdoches. Author. 1880. 73 pp.

Navarro — Love, Mrs. Annie C. Navarro Co. Dallas. S.W. Pr. 1933. 278 pp.
— Biog. Hist. of Navarro, Henderson, Anderson, Limestone, Freestone & Leon Counties. Chi. Lewis. 1893. 980 pp.

Nolan — Bradford, Louise. Nolan Co. M. A. Thesis U. of Tex. Austin. 1934. 131 pp.

Nueces — Deviney, M. L. Nueces Co. To 1850. M. A. Thesis. U. of Tex. Austin. 1935. 134 pp.
— Taylor, P. S. Nueces Co. Chapel Hill. U. of Car. Pr. 1934. 337 pp.

Oldham — Israel, T. C. Oldham Co. M. A. Thesis. U. of N. Mex. Albuquerque. 1934. 91 pp.

Panola — Hooker, Mrs. V. D. Panola Co. Carthage Bk. Club. 1935. 52 pp.
— Sharp, L. R. Panola Co. To 1860. M. A. Thesis U. of Tex. Austin. 1940. 212 pp.

Parker — Grace, I. S. & Jones, R. B. Parker Co. Weatherford. Democrat Pub. 1906. 206 pp.
— Smythe, H. Parker Co. & Weatherford. St. Louis. Lavat Pr. 1877. 476 pp.
— Farrant & Parker Co. & Tex. Biog. Chi. Lewis. 1895. 658 pp.

Polk — Haynes, Emma R. Polk Co. Livingston. 1937. 160 pp.

Potter — Shearer, E. C. Potter Co. M. A. Thesis. U. of Colo. Boulder. 1933. 153 pp.

Presidio — Gregg, J. E. Presidio Co. M. A. Thesis. U. of Tex. Austin. 1933. 231 pp.

Rains — Hebison, W. O. Early Tex. & Rains Co. Emory. Leader. 1917. 55 pp.

Randall — McClure, C. B. Randall Co. & T. Anchor Ranch. M. A. Thesis. U. of Tex. Austin. 1930. 156 pp.

Red River — Clark, P. B. Clarksville & Old Red River Co. Dallas. Mathis. Van Mort & Co. 1937. 259 pp.
— Kewbow, Mrs. B. Early Red River Co. 1817-65. M. A. Thesis. U. of Tex. Austin. 1936.

TEXAS (Continued)

Refugio	– Huson, Hobart. Refugio Co. Tex. From Aboriginal Times. Woodsboro Rooke. 1953-6.
	– Moore, R. L. Refugio Co. M. A. Thesis U. of Tex. Austin. 1937. 110 pp.
Robertson	– St. Clair, L. W. Robertson Co. Thesis U. of Tex. Austin. 1931. 187 p.
Runnels	– Self, N. B. Runnels Co. M. A. Thesis. Tech. Col. Lubbock. 1931. 116 pp.
Rusk	– Farmer, Garland Roscoe. The Realm of Rusk Co. Tex. Henderson Times. 1951.
	– Watkins, Myrtis & Watkins, P. Old Rusk Co. Henderson. 1940. 54 pp.
San Augustine	– Crockett, G. L. N. Cent. In E. Tex. San Augustine Co. From 1865 To Present. Dallas. S. W. Press. 1932. 372 pp.
San Patricio	– Early San Patricio Co. Sinton. Martin. 1934. 12 pp.
San Saba	– Hamrick, Mrs. A. W. San Saba Co. San Antonio. Naylor. 1941. 331 pp.
Schleicher	– Holt, R. D. Schleicher Co. 80 Yrs. of Dev. In S. W. Tex. Eldorado. Success. 1930. 110 pp.
Scurry	– Cotten, Kathryn, Saga of Scurry, Tex. & San Antonio. Naylor. 1957.
Smith	– Green, L. M. Smith Co. Tyler. 1917. 30 pp.
	– Henderson, Adele. Smith Co. M. A. Thesis U. of Tex. Austin. 1926. 118 pp.
	– Woldert, A. Smith Co. San Antonio. Naylor. 1948. 165 pp.
Somervell	– Ewell, T. T. Hood Co. & Somervell Co. Granbury. 1895. 161 pp.
Stephens	– Hartsfield, L. W. Stephens Co. M. A. Thesis. U. of Tex. Austin. 1929. 271 pp.
Sterling	– Watkin, Ira L. Sterling Co. M. A. Thesis. Tex. Tech. Coll. Lubbock. 1939. 128 pp.
Stonewall	– Whitmore, J. R. Stonewall Co. M. A. Thesis. Tex. Tech. Coll. Lubbock. 1936. 156 pp.
Tarrant	– Berrong, Verna E. Tarrant Co. 1875. M. A. Thesis. Tex. Christian U. Fort Worth. 1938. 80 pp.
	– Tarrant & Parker Co. Hist. of Tex. Biog. Chi. Lewis.1895.658pp.
Titus	– Pierce, B. C. Titus Co. M. A. Thesis U. of Colo. Boulder. 1932. 122 pp.

Travis   — Hardy, Mrs. A. Hist. of Travis Co. 1832-65. M.A. Thesis.
              U. of Texas. Austin. 1938. 256 pp.

Trinity   — Bowles, Flora G. Trinity Co. M. A. Thesis U. of Tex. Austin.
              1928. 188 pp.

Uvalde   — Getzendaner, Dillard. Family & Uvalde Co. Tex. 1956.

Van Zandt   — Manning, W. Van Zandt Co. Des Moines. Homestead. 1919. 220 pp.

Victoria   — Rose, V. M. Settlement of Victoria. 1883. Laredo. Daily Times
              Pr. 215 pp.

Waller   — White, F. E. Early Waller Co. 1821-1884. M. A. Thesis. U. of
              Tex. Austin. 1936. 154 pp.

Washington — Crane, W. C. Wash. Co. 1876. Brenham. Re-Print. 1939.

            — Dietrich, Wilfred O. The Blazing Story of Wash. Co. Tex.
              Brenham.

            — Pennington, Mrs. R. E. Brenham & Wash. Co. Houston. Stan.
              Pr. 1915. 123 pp.

            — Schmidt, C. F. Wash. Co. San Antonio. Naylor. 1949. 146 pp.

Western Falls — St. Romain, Lillian Schiller. Western Falls Co. Austin. 1951.
              Tex. St. Hist. Assn.

Wharton   — Graham, J. O. Wharton Co. Rich. 1926. 234 pp.

Wheeler   — Perkins, W. C. Wheeler Co. M. A. Thesis. U. of Tex. Austin.
              1938. 129 pp.

Wilbarger   — Ross, C. P. & Rouse, T. L. Early Wilbarger Co. Vernon Times.
              1933. 208 pp.

            — Wilson, T. B. Wilbarger Co. M. A. Thesis U. of Tex. Austin.
              1938. 122 pp.

Williamson — Hinds, W. W. Williamson Co. 1716-1870. M. A. Thesis. S. W.
              Univ. Georgetown. 1928. 115 pp.

Winkler   — Study Club. Winkler Co. Wink. Bull. 1942. 52 pp.

Wise
- Cates, C. D. Pioneer Wise Co. 20 Yrs. Hist. Decauter. 1907. 471 pp.
- Johnson, C. A. Wise Co. Intro. J. N. Hillman. Morton Pr. 1938. 416 pp.
- Moore, Mary Cates. Cent. Hist. of Wise. Co. 1853-1953. Dallas Story Book. 1953.

Young
- Crouch, Carrie J. Young Co. Biog. Dallas. 1937. 339 pp.
- Crouch, C. J. Hist. of Young Co. Tex. and Local Hist. Vol. 2. 1956.
- Crouch, Carrie (Johnson) Hist. of Young Co. Tex. Austin. Texas Hist. Assn. 1956.
- Fulmore, J. T. Hist. & Geo. of Tex. As Told In County Names, pub. by S. R. Fulmore. 1926. 225 pp.

Zapata
- Tott, V. N. Kingdom of Zapata Co. Tex. 1953.

UTAH - 29 Counties

Box Elder
- Hist. of Box Elder Co. D. U. P. 1948.
- Box Elder Lore of The Nineteenth Century. Sons of Utah Pioneers 1951.

Beaver
- A Hist. of Beaver Co. D. U. P. 1948.

Cache
- The Beginnings of Settlement In Cache Valley. Ricks, Joel E. Logan. 1953.
- Ricks, Joel E. & Cooley, Everett L. editors "Hist. of A Valley, Cache Valley, Utah & Idaho" Logan. Utah Cent. Com. 1956. Cache Co.

Carbon
- Centennial Echoes From Carbon Co. D. U. P. 1948.

Daggett
- A Hist. of Daggett Co. Dunham, Dick & Vivian. 1947.

Davis
- Hist. of The First Fifty Years of Davis Co. D. U. P.

<u>UTAH</u> (Continued)

<u>Duchesne</u>	– Early Hist. of Duchesne Co. 1948. D. U. P.
<u>Emery</u>	– D. U. P. McElprang, Mrs. S. Emery Co. 1949.
<u>Garfield</u>	– A Hist. of Garfield Co. 1949.
	– Pioneer Garfield Co.
	– A Hist. of Garfield Co. Panguitch, Utah. 1949.
<u>Iron</u>	– Iron Co. Cent. Larson, Gustave O. 1951. Cedar City.
<u>Juab</u>	– McCune, A. P. Juab Co. Nephi. D. U. P. 1947. 301 pp.
<u>Kane</u>	– D. U. P. Hist. of Kane Co. Kanab. 1959.
<u>Llogan</u>	– Curtis, A. J. Early Logan & Cache Valley. 1946.
<u>Millard</u>	– 100 Yrs. of Millard Co. 1951. D. U. P.
<u>Morgan</u>	– Fine Arts Study Group. Mountains Conquered. Story of Morgan with Biographies.
	– Morgan Co. Utah News Pub. 1959.
	– Pioneering Morgan Co. 1947. Epperson, Albert W.
<u>Salt Lake</u>	– A Hist. of Salt Lake County. 1847-1900. 1947. D. U. P.
<u>San Juan</u>	– Board of Co. Com. San Juan Co. Monticello. 30 pp.
	– D. U. P. Saga of San Juan. Blanding, Utah. 1957.
<u>Sanpete</u>	– D. U. P. Cent. Hist. Sanpete Co. These Our Fathers. 1849-1947. 1947. Springville Art City. 253 pp.
	– Halvorson, F. D. County Histories of The U. S. Contains Name of County, Parent Co. date org. Salt Lake City. 1937.
	– Lever, W. H. Sanpete & Emery Co. 1898.
	– Tullidge, E. E. Vol. II, Containing the history of all the Northern, Eastern & Western Counties of Utah. Prop. Pub. Salt Lake City. Press of Juvenile Instr.

UTAH (Continued)

Sevier   – Sevier Co. Cent. Hist. 1947. D. U. P.

Summit   – Summit Co. Cent. Hist. 1947. D. U. P.

Uintah   – A Cent. Hist. of Uintah Co. 1947. D. U. P.

Utah   – D. U. P. Memories That Live. Utah Co. Cent. Hist. By
N. Brown, E. B. Jones, E. C. Beardall. Provo. 1947.

     – Huff, E. N. Utah Co. Cent. D. U. P. 1947. Art City.
Springville.

Wasatch   – A Hist. of Wasatch Co. 1854-1900. 1954. D. U. P.

Washington   – A Hist. of Wash. Co. 1950. D. U. P.

Wayne   – A Hist. of Wayne Co. 1953. D. U. P.

Weber   – Census Weber Co. Deseret. 1850. W. P. A. Ogden. 1937. Type.

     – Weber Co. 1824-1900. D. U. P. Hunter. 1945.

     – A Hist. of Weber Co. 1824-1900. 1945. D. U. P.

     – Beneath, Ben. Lomond's Peak. Weber Co. 1824-1900.

     – D. U. P. ed. by M. R. Hunter Desert News Press. Salt Lake City.
1945. 606 pp.

     – W. P. A. Project. Weber Co. & Ogden City. Ogden Hist. Socy.
1938. 27 pp.

VERMONT – 14 Counties

No County Histories were published in Vt. during 1955-60.

Addison   – Child, N. Dir. of Addison Co. 1882-3. Syracuse. 1882. 551 pp.
     – Smith, H.P. Addison Co. Syracuse. Mason. 1886. 852 pp.
     – Swift, S. Co. of Addiscn. Middlebury Copeland. 1859. 132 pp.

Bennington   – Aldrich, L. C. Bennington Co. Syracuse. Mason. 1889.
     – Brownell, E. E. Bennington Co. Phila. 1941. 207 pp.
     – Bennington Co. Vt. Genealogy. Brownell, Elijah Ellsworth.
Phila. 1941.

VERMONT (Continued)

Caledonia   – Child, H. Caledonia & Essex Co. Syracuse Jour. 1887. 492 pp.

Chittenden   – Child, H. Dir. Chittenden Co. 1882-3. Syracuse. 1882. 584 pp.

              – Homenway, A. M. Chittenden Co. Albany. Munsell. 1863. 616 pp.

              – Rann, W. S., A. M. Chittenden Co., Illus. Biog. Syracuse. Mason. 1886. 867 pp.

Essex   – Child, H. Caledonia & Essex Co. Syracuse. Journal. 1887. 492 pp.

Franklin   – Aldrich, L. C. Franklin & Grand Isle Co. Syracuse. Mason. 1891. 821 pp.

           – Child, H. Bus. Dir. of Franklin & Grand Isle Co. 1882-3. Syracuse. 1883. 612 pp.

Lamoille   – Child, H. Bus. Dir. of Lamoille & Orlean Co. Syracuse. Journal. 1883.

Orange   – Child, H. Orange Co. Syracuse. Journal. 1888. 214 pp.

Orlean   – See Lamoille Co.

Rutland   – Child, H. Bus. Dir. of Rutland Co. 1881-2. Syracuse Journal. 1881. 643 pp.

         – Hemenway, A. M. Rutland Co. White River. 1882. 1245 pp.

         – Redington, L. W. 1781. Rutland Co. 1881. Montpelier.

         – Rutland Co. Vt. Genealogy. Brownell, Elijah Ellsworth. Phila. 1942. 317 pp.

         – Smith, H. P. Rann, W. S. Rutland Co. Syracuse. Mason. 1886. 958 pp.

         – Spargo, Mary. Rutland Co. Pamphlet 20. Herald. 1931.

Washington   – Child, H. Washington Co. Syracuse. Journal. 1889. 544 pp.

             – Hemenway, A. M. Wash. Co. Montpelier. Press. 1882. 932 pp.

Windham   – Child, H. Bus. Dir. of Windham Co. Syracuse. Journal. 1884.

Windsor   – Aldrich, L. C. ed. Windsor Co. Syracuse. Mason. 1891.

         – Child, H. Bus. Dir. of Windsor Co. "   1884. 666 pp.

There is a Child's Gazetteer For Addison, Bennington, Chittenden, Franklin, Grand Isle, and Rutland Counties.

VIRGINIA — 98 Counties

Accomack
- Nottingham, S., Marriage License Bonds 1774-1806, Accomack Co. 1927. 49 pp.
- Nottingham, S., Certificates & Rights 1663-1709, Accomack Co. 1929.
- Nottingham, S., Land Causes. Accomack Co. 1727-1826. 1930
- Nottingham, S., Rev. Soldiers & Sail rs, Accomack Co. 1927. 100 pp.
- Nottingham, S., Tax Lists. 1663-95. 1931.
- Nottingham, S., Wills & Administrations. 1663-1800 Accomack. 1931.

Albemarle
- Coddington, Mrs. Anne Barlett. Geneological Index. Albemarle Co., Va. Phila. Magee. 1936
- Col. Dames of Amer. Hist. Guide to Albemarle Co. Va. Charlottesville. Michie. 1924.
- Marriages of Albemarle Co. & Charlottesville, Va. 1781-1929. Norford. Jarman. 1956. 279 pp.
- Rawlings, Mary. Ante-Bellum Albemarle Co., Va. Charlottesville. 1935.
- Rawlings, Mary. Albemarle, Charlottesville. Michie. 1925. 145 pp.
- Seamon, W. H., Albemarle Co. Prout. Charlottesville. 1888.
- St. Clairo, Mrs. Emily (Entwisle). Beautiful & Historic Albemarle. Richmond Appeals. 1932.
- Woods, Edgar. Albemarle Co. In Va. Charlottesville. Michie. 1901.
- Woods, E. Albemarle Co. Charlottesville. Michie. 1901. 412 pp.

Alexandria (Arlington)
- Bd. of Supervisors - A Brief Hist. of Alexandria Co. Va. Falls Church. Newell. 1907. 56 pp.

Alleghany
- Covington Chamber of Comm. Alleghany Co. Va. 1907
- Morten, Orem Frederic. Cent. Hist. Alleghany Co. Va. Dayton. Ruebush. 1923. 226 pp.

Amherst
- Lynchburg. Bell. 1937. 102 pp.
- Sweeney, Lenora (Higginbotham) Amherst Co., Va. In The Revolution. Lynchburg. 1951.
- Sweeney, W. M. Marriage Records. 1763-1800.

Arlington
- Lee, Dorothy (Eli) Hist. of Arlington Co. Va. Richmond. Dietz. 1946.
- Nat'l. Retail. Inst. Book of Arlington Co. Va. Wash. 1928.

Augusta
- Peyton, J. L. Augusta Co. Staunton. Yost. 1882. 387 pp.
- Peyton, John Lewis. Hist. of Augusta Co. Va. Bridgewater. 1953.
- Waddell, Joseph Addison. Annals of Augusta Co. Va. 1726-1871. Bridgewater. Carrier. 1958.
- Waddell, J.A., Augusta Co. Staunton. Caldwell. 1902. 545 pp.

VIRGINIA (Continued)

Bath — Morton, O. F., Bath Co. Staunton. McClure. 1917. 208 pp.

Bedford — Bedford Co. 1753. Lynchburg. Bell. 1907. 121 pp.
— Morton, O.F., Bedford Co. Bedford City. Hubard. 1907. 121 pp.
— Parker, Lula Eastman (Jeter) Hist. of Bedford Co. Va. Bicentennial. 1754-1954. Bedford.

Botetourt — Bell, Mrs. A.W.B. Census. 1810. Wash. 1934.
— Worrell, Anne Lowry. Early Marriages, Wills & Some Rev. War Records. Botetourt Co. Va. Hillsville. 1958.

Bridgeland — Fothergill, Augusta. Bridgeland Co. Va. Marriage Records. Richmond. 1953.

Brunswick — Bell, Mrs. A.W.B., Census. 1810. Wash. 1934.
— Bell, Edith Rathburn. Hist. of Brunswick Co.Va. Lawrenceville. Brunswick Times Gazette. 1957.
— Marriages of Brunswick Co. Va. 1750-1810. Catherine L. Knorr. Pine Bluff, Ark. Perdue. 1953. 138 pp.
— Knorr, Catherine Lindsay. Brunswick Co. Va. Marriage Records 1750-1810. Pine Bluff, Ark. 1953.

Buckingham — Bell, Mrs. A.W.B., Census 1810. Wash. 1934.

Campbell — Early, Miss Ruth N. Campbell Co. 1915. 250 pp.

Caroline — Bell, Mrs. A.W.B., Census. 1810. Wash. 1934.
— Campbell, Thomas Elliott. Colonial Caroline. A Hist. of Caroline Co. Va. Richmond. Dietz. 1954. 561 pp.
— Collins, H. R., Hist. & Geneology of The Collins Family of Caroline Co. Va. 1954.
— Wingfield, M. Caroline Co. Richmond. 1924. 528 pp.

Charlotte — Bell, Mrs. A.W.B., Census. 1810. Wash. 1934.
— Carrington,J.C.,Charlotte Co. Richmond. Hermitage Pr. 1907. 142 pp.

Chesterfield— Bell, Mrs. A.W.B., Census. 1810. Wash. 1934.
— Burns, Annie (Walker) 3rd Census of U.S. 1810, Co. of Chesterfield, Va. Wash' 1931.
— Chesterfield: An Old Virginia Co. by Frances Earle Lutz. Richmond. Byrd Press. 1954. 385 pp.
— Clarke, E.C., Chesterfield Co. Rec. Richmond. 1937.
— Cox, T. B., Chesterfield Co. Richmond. Williams Ptg. Co. 1907.

Clarke — Gold, T.D., Hist. of Clarke Co. Berryville. Hughes. 1914. 332 pp.

VIRGINIA (Continued)

Culpeper
- Bell, Mrs. A.W.B. Census 1810. Wash. 1934.
- Culpeper Co. Va. Will Book A. 1749-1770. Abstracted & Compiled by John Frederick Dorman. Wash. D.C. 1956. 155 pp.
- Finnell, W.-Daniel Brown of Culpeper Col Va. 1954.
- Green, Raleigh Travers-General & Hist. Notes. Culpeper Co. Va. Balto. Southern. 1959.
- Green, R. T. Culpeper Co. & Dr. Slaughter's Hist. of St. Mark's Parish. Culpeper. Green. 1900. 305 pp.
- Raleigh, T.G., Geneological & Historical Notes of Culpeper Co. Va. 1958.
- Culpeper Co. Va. Courts. County Court Will Book. 1956.
- Culpeper Co. Va. Marriages of Culpeper, Va. 1781-1815. 1954.

Dickinson
- Meet Virginia's Baby: A Brief Pictorial History of Dickinson Co. Va. Ed.by Elihu Joseph Sutherland, Clintwood: Dickinson Co. Diamond Jubilee Comm. 1955
- Sutherland, Elihu Jasper. Brief Pictorial Hist. of Dickinson Co. Va. 1880-1955. Clintwood. 1955.

Dinwiddie
- Bell, Mrs. A.W.B. Census. 1810. Wash. 1934. WPA
- Dinwiddie Co. Richmond. Whittet. 1942. 302 pp.
- Glick, J.P. Dinwiddie Co. Sch. Bd. 1926. 38 pp.
- WPA Country of The Apamatica. Dinwiddie Co. Pub. by Sch. Board. 1942.

Elizabeth City
- Starkey, M. L., Hampton & Elizabeth City Co. 1607-1887. Houston. 1936. 95 pp.
- Tyler, L.G., Hampton & Elizabeth City Co. Bd. of Supv. 1922. 56 pp.

Essex
- Dorman, John Frederick. Essex Co. Va. Records 1717-22. Dorman, Wash. 1959.
- Showell, Va. Essex Sketches. Balto. Thomas Pr. 1924. 85 pp.
- Warner, Pauline P. & Warner, T.H., Essex Co. 1607-1692. Dubsville. Urbanna. Sentinel Pr. 1926. F.F.V. Ser.

Fairfax
- Bd. of Sup. Fairfax Co. Falls Church. Newell. 1907. 95 pp.
- Warner, Pauline P. & Warner, T.H., Fairfax Co. Bd. Supvs. 1907.

Fauquier
- Maps & Notes Pertaining To The Upper Section of Fauquier Co. Va. Comp. By B. Curtis Chappelear- Notes by Meade Palmer. Warrenton. Antiquarrian. 1954.
- Evans, Marie Louise. An Old Timer In Warrenton & Fauquier County. Va. Warrenton. 1955.

Frederick
- Bell, Mrs. A.W.B., Census. 1810. Wash. 1934.
- Cartwell, T. K., Frederick Co. Winchester. Eddy Press. 1909. 587 pp.

VIRGINIA (Continued)

Giles — Bell, Mrs. A.W.B. Census. 1810. Wash. 1934.

Gloucester — Gray, Mary W., Gloucester Co. Richmond. 1936. 243 pp.
— Mason, P. C. Gloucester. Col. Rec. Newport. 2 v. 1946-8.
— Robins, Mrs. S.N., Gloucester. Richmond. West. 1893. 21 pp.
— Assn. for Preservation of Va. Antiquities. Epitaphs of Gloucester & Matthews Cos. Va. 1959. St. Lib.
— U.S. Nat'l. Park Service. Excavations at Green Spring Planation, Va. 1955.

Goochland — Wight, R. C. Goochland. Richmond Press. 1935. 51 pp.

Grayson — Nuckolls, B. F., Pioneer Grayson Co. Bristol. King Pr. 1914. 206 pp.

Halifax — Knorr, Catherine Lindsay. Marriage Bonds and Ministers Returns of Halifax Co. 1753-1800. Pine Bluff, Ark. 1957.
— Carrington, W. J., Halifax Co. Richmond. Appeals Pr. 1924. 525 pp.

Hanover — Page, R., Hanover Co. Author. 1926. 153 pp.
— Coche, William Ronald. Hanover Co. Va. Taxpayers St. Paul's Parish 1782-1815. 1956. St. Lib. Columbia.
— A Sketch of The Early Hist. of Hanover Co. R.B. Lancaster. Ashland: Assn For Preservation of Va. Antiquities. 1957. 31 pp.

Henrico — Henrico Parish 1730-73. Richmond, 1874.
— Moore, J. S., Henrico Parish. Richmond. Williams 1904. 221 pp.
Warner,Pauline(Pearce) The County of Henrico, Va. 1959.

Henry — Hill, Gudith P.A. Henry Co. Martinsville. Aurhot. 1925. 332 pp.

Highland — Morton, O. F. Highland Co. Monterey. Author. 1911. 419 pp.

King — Bagby, A. King & Queen Co. Neale. 1908. 402 pp.

King William — Clarke, P.N., King William Co. Louisville. Morton. 1897. 211 pp.
— Elizabeth Hawes Ryland. Richmond: Dietz Press. 1955. 137 pp.
— Ryland E. H. King William Co. Va. 1955.

Lancaster — Abstracts Lancaster Co. Va. Wills 1653-1800 Ed. by Ida Johnson Lee. Richmond. Dietz. 1959. 240 pp.
— Nottingham S.Marriages. 1701-1848. Onancock. 1927. 106 pp.
— Nottingham, S.Rev. Veterans. Onancock. 1930.

Lee — Burns, Annie Walker. S.W. Va. Hist. Records Lee Co. Jonesville.

VIRGINIA (Continued)

Loudoun
- Nichols, Joseph Van Devanter. Loudoun Valley Legends. Purcellville, Va. 1955.
- Sweeney, William M. Marriage Bonds & Records. Lynchburg. Bell. 1937.
- Head, J. W., Loudoun Co. Wash. D.C. Park View Pr. 1909. 186 pp.

Louisa
- Harris, M. H. Louisa Co. Richmond. Dietz. 1936.
- Williams, Kathleen Booth. Marriages of Louisa Co. 1766-1815. Alexandria. 1959.
- McKay, H.B., Marriages In Louisa Co. Va. 1766-1815.

Lunenberg
- Bell. L. C., Lunenberg Co. Richmond. Byrd Press. 1927. 2 v.

Madison
- Yowell, C. L., Madison Co. Strasburg. Shenandoah Pub. 1926. 203 pp.

Mecklenburg
- Alexander, C., Mecklenburg Co. 1907.

Middlesex
- Register of Christ Church. 1653-1812. Richmond. Jones. 1897. 341 pp.

Montgomery
- The Montgomery Co. Story. 1776-1957. Comp. & ed. by C. W. Crush. Christiansburg: Montgomery Co. (Jamestown) Festival Com. 1957. 167 pp.
- Crush, Charles W. The Montgomery Co. Va. Store. 1776-1957.

Nausemond
- Dunn, Jos. B. Nausemond Co. Herald. 1907. 71 pp.

Nelson
- Claiborne, J.G., Nelson Co. Lynchburg. Brown. 1925.
- Co. of Nelson by Creasy, Giannisci, Jones, Maupin, U. of Va. Pub. by Co. Sch. Board. 1929.

Norfolk
- Porter, J. W. H. Norfolk Co. Apr. 19, 1861. May 10, 1862. Hist. of Those Who Served In Confederate Army & Navy. Fiske. 1892. 366 pp.
- Stewart, W. H., Norfolk Co. Chi. Biog. Pub. 1902. 1042 pp.
- West, Alma H., Norfolk Co. 1920. 25 pp.

Nottoway
- Turner, W. R., Families In Nottoway. Blackstone. 1932. 105 pp.

Orange
- Scott, W.W., Orange Co. 1734-1870. Richmond. Waddy. 1907. 292 pp.
- Newman,H.F., Newman Story. Orange Co. Va. Will Bk. I.
- Brockman, W.E., Orange Co. Va. Families. Brockman Family. 1949.
- Brockman, William Everett. Orange Co. Families & Marriages. Rev. War Claims. 1956.

VIRGINIA (Continued)

Orange (Con't)
- Dorman, John Frederick. Orange Co. Va. Will Book. Abstracted & Compiled 1735-43. 1958. 72 pp.
- Knorr, Catherine Lindsay. Marriages of Orange Co. 1747-1810. Pine Bluff, Ark. 1959.
- Strickler, Harry Miller. Short Hist. of Page Co. Dietz. Richmond. 1952.

Patrick
- Conner, M. C., King, W.K., Patrick Co. U. of Va. 1937. 102 pp. Pedigo, Virginia G. Patrick & Henry Co. Roanoke. Stone Pr. 1933.

Pittsylvania
- Knorr, Catherine Lindsay, Marriages Pittsylvania Co. 1767-1805. 1956.
- Clement, Maud C. Pittsylvania Co. Lynchburg. Bell. 1929. 340 pp.

Powhatan
- Powhatan Co. Va. Courts. Marriage Bonds & Minister's Returns of Powhatan Co. 1957.
- Knott, Catherine Lindsay, Marriage Bonds of Powhatan Co. 1777-1830. Pine Bluff, Ark. 1957.

Prince Edward
- Burrell, C.E., Prince Edward Co. Richmond. Williams Pr. 1922. 408 pp.
- Hist. of Prince Edward Co., H.C. Bradshaw 1754-1954. Richmond. Dietz. 1955. 934 pp.
- Eggleston, J. D., Prince Edward Co. Herold. 1927. 16 pp.

Prince George
- Geol. Survey. Prince George Co. Va.

Prince William
- Clark, A. B., Prince William Co. Manassas Co. School Bd. 1933. 79 pp.
- Prince William Co. Will Book C. 1734-54. J.F. Dorman. Wash. D.C. 1956. 135 pp.

Roanoke
- McCauley, W., Roanoke Co. 1734-1900. Chi. Biog. 1902. 556 pp.
- Jack, G. S., Roanoke Co. Roanoke. 1912. 255 pp.

Rockbridge
- McClung, J. W., Rockbridge Co. Staunton. McClure. 1939. 276 pp.
- Morton, O.F., Rockbridge Co. Staunton. McClure. 1920. 574 pp.
- Tompkins, Edmund Pendelton. Rockbridge Co. Richmond. Whittet. 1952.

Rockingham
- Wayland, J. W., Rockingham Co. Dayton. Ruebush. 1912. 467 pp.

Scott
- Addington, R. M. Scott Co. Kingsport Press. 1932.

Shenandoah
- Wayland, J. W., Shenandoah Co. Strasburg. Shenandoah Pub. 1927. 874 pp.

Smyth
- Wilson, G., Smyth Co., Kingsport Press. 1932.

VIRGINIA (Continued)

Southampton — Knorr, Catherine Lindsey. Marriage Bonds. Southampton Co. 1750-1910. Pine Bluff, Ark. 1955.

Surrey — Surrey Co. Wills & Administration Courts of Surrey Co. 1671-1750. 1955.
— Stephenson, M. A., Homes In Surrey & Sussex, Richmond. Dietz. 1942. 130 pp.
— Davis, Eliza Timberlake. Wills & Administrations of Surrey Co. 1671-1750. Smithfield. 1955.

Sussex — W.P.A. Sussex Co. Richmond. Whittet. 1942. 324 pp.
— Burns, Annie (Walker) Third U.S. Census of 1810. Sussex Co. Va. 1934.
— Knorr, Catherine Lindsay. Marriage Bonds. Sussex Co. 1754-1810. Pine Bluff, Ark. 1952.
— Register of Albemarle Parish Surrey & Sussex Cos. 1739-78. Transcribed & ed by Gertrude R. B. Richards. Richmond, Va. U.S.C.D.A. 1958.
— Foster, T. D. Sussex County.

Tazewell — Bickley, G.W.L. Tazewell Co. Cincinnati. Morgan. 1852. 267 pp.
— Harman, J. N., Tazewell Co. Richmond, Hill, 1922. 457 pp.
— Pendleton, W.C., Tazewell Co. & S.W. Va. Hill Pr. 1920. 700 pp.

Washington — Sumners, L. P. Washington Co. 1777-1870. Richmond Hill. 1903. 921 pp.

Westmoreland— Westmoreland Co. Com. of Safety. Proc. of Co. Com. of Safety. 1774-6. Com. of Safety. Westmoreland. Fincastle. 1956. St. Lib.
— Bell, Mrs. A.W.B., Census. 1810. Wash. 1934.
— Nottingham, S. Marriages 1786-1850. Onancock. 1928.
— Wright, T.R.B., Westmoreland Co. Richmond. Whittet Pr. 1912.

King William — Ryland, Elizabeth H., King William Co. Va. Richmond. Dietz. 1955.

Wise — Addington, Luther F., The Story of Wise Co. Cent. Com. & School Bd. 1956.
— Johnson, C.A. Wise Co. Norton. 1938. 416 pp.

Wythe — Bell, Mrs. A.W.B., Census 1810. Wash. 1934.

York — Bradshaw, Ura Ann. York Co., Hampton, Va. 1957.

Bull. of Va. State Library Vol. 8, No. 204 entitled "A Bibliography of Virginia, Part I" by Earl J. Swem. Contains additional material referred to in the index under the names of the various counties.

WASHINGTON - 39 Counties

The Book of the 39 Counties in Washington, Pub. 1953 by the
Washington State Assn. of Co. Com. & Co. Engrs. with State
College of Washington; Seattle First National Bank, Standard
Oil of Calif., Weyerhauser Lumber Co.

Asotin
- Historic Glimpses of Asotin Co., Wash. by Judge Elgin V.
  Kuykendall. Pub. by the Clarkstone Herald. 1954.

Clark
- Hist. of Clark Co. Biog. Wash. Pub. Walling. Portland. 1885.
- Clark Co. Hist. Fort Vancouver Hist. Socy. Vancouver, Wash. 1960.

Columbia
- Gilbert, F. T. Walla Walla, Whitman, Columbia & Garfield Cos.
  Portland. Walling. 1882. 66 pp.

Ferry
- Putnam, Mrs. Van B., A Hist. of Ferry Co. Inchelium.

Garfield
- Gilbert, F. T., Walla Walla, Whitman. Columbia & Garfield Cos.
  Wash. Ter. & Umatilla Co. 1882.

King
- Bagley, C. B., Kings Co. Clarke. 1929. 4 v.

Kitsap
- Kitsap Co. Bremerton-News. Jan. 1933.

Pacific
- Herald, R. ed. Pacific Co.

Pierce
- Bonney, W. P., Pierce Co. Pioneer Hist. Pub. Co. 1927. 3 v.

Skagit
- Skagit & Snohomish Cos. Interstate. Chi. 1906. 1117 pp.

Snohomish
- Whitfield, W., Snohomish Co.

Spokane
- Edwards, J. Spokane Co. 1900. Lever. 726 pp.
- Hist. Records Survey. Inv. Co. Archives of Wash. Spokane Co.
  Seattle. 1941. 620 pp.
- Rockford, Washington Years Ago. (A Hist. of Spokane Co.)
  Stand. Reg. 1953. 23 pp.

Thurston
- Blankenship, Mrs. G. E., Thurston Co.
- Rathburn. Thurston Co.

Walla Walla
- Ankeny, Nesmith. The West As I Knew It. Walla Walla Co.
  Lewiston, Ida. R. G. Bailey Ptg. Co. 1953. 148 pp.
- Lyman, W. D., Walla Walla Co. San Fran Lever. 1901. 510 pp.
- Lyman, W. D., Walla Walla Co. Columbia, Garfield & Asotin
  Cos. Chi. Clarke. 1918. 2 v.

Whatcom
- Bellingham Herald. Cent. ed. Whatcom Co. 4-26-1953. Bellingham.
- Roth, Lottie R., Whatcom Co. 2 v. Pioneer Pub. Chi. Seattle 1926.

Yakima
- Klickitot, Yakima & Kittitas Cos. Chi. Interstate.1904.941 pp.

Brief County histories have been written of Adams, Asotin, Chelay,
Columbia, Douglas, Ferry, Franklin, Jefferson, Lewis, Okanogan,
Shagit, Stevens & Whitman.

WEST VIRGINIA - 55 Counties

Barbour — Maxwell, Hu Barbour Co. Morgantown. Acme. 1899. 517 pp.

Berkeley
- Aler, F. V., Berkeley Co. Mail. 1888. 438 pp.
- Aler, F. V., Martinsburg & Berkeley Co. Hagerstown. 1888. 452 pp.
- In Hardesty's Historical & Geog. Encyclo.
- Cartmill, T. K., Berkeley Co.
- Evans, W. Hist of Berkeley Co., W.Va. 1928.
- Norris,J.E., Berkeley Co.

Braxton
- Jacob, J. G., Brooks Co. Wellsburg. Herald. 1882.
- Sutton, J.D., Braxton Co. Sutton. 1919. 458 pp.

Cabell
- Smith, W. Guyandotte Cent. 1810-1910. Cabell Co. Huntington. 1910.
- Wallace, G. S., Cabell Co. Richmond. etc. 1935. 589 pp.

Fayette
- Darlington, L. N., Early Loup Creek. Fayette Co. 1798-1865. Fayetteville Tribune. 1933. 68 pp.
- Donnelly, Clarence Shirley. Hist. notes on Fayette Co. W.Va. Oak Hill. 1958.
- Holliday, Robert Kelvin. Politics In Fayette Co. W.Va. Montgomery Herald. 1956.

Hardy & Grant — Hist. of Hardy & Grant Cos. by E. L. Judy. Petersburg. 1951.

Greenbrier — Cole, J. R., Greenbrier Co. Lewisburg. 1917. 347 pp.

Hampshire
- Cartnell, T. K., Hampshire Co.
- Maxwell, Hu. Hampshire Co. Morgantown. Boughner. 1897. 744 pp.

Harrison
- Clarksburg & Harrison Co. Clarksburg Telegram. 1875. 123 pp.
- Haymond, H., Harrison Co. Morgantown Acme. 1909. 451 pp.

Jefferson — Bushong, M. K., Jefferson Co. Charles Town. Jefferson 1941. 438 pp.

Kanawba
- Atkinson, G. W., Kanawba Co. Charleston. Journal 1876. 338 pp.
- Kanawba Spectator. 2 vols. by Julius A. DeGruyter. Charleston. 1953.
- Hale, J. P., Kanauba Co.
- Hardesty, Kanawba Co.
- Laidley, W.S., Kanawba Co.
- Laidley, W.S., Charleston & Kanawba Co. Chi. Richmond-Arnold. 1911. 1021 pp.

Lewis
- Cook, R. B., Lewis Co. In The Civil War. Charleston. Jarrett. 1924. 155 pp.
- Cook, R. B., Lewis Co. In The Span. Amer War. Charleston. Jarrett. 1925. 30 pp.
- Hardesty. Lewis Co.
- Smith, E. C. Lewis Co. Western. 1920. 427 pp.

Lincoln
- Lambert, F. B., Lincoln Co. Hamlin, Carroll High. 1925. 65 pp.

Logan
- Swain, G. T. Logan Co. 1927. 383 pp.
- Ragland, H. C., Logan Co. Logan. Banner, 1949. 123 pp.

Marion
- Dunnington, C.A., Marion Co. Fairmont. 1880. 162 pp.
- Watson, J. O. Marion Co. In The Making. Fairmont High School. 1917. 362 pp.

Marshall
- Boyd, P. Ohio, Marshall, Brooke & Hancock Co.
- Powell, Scott. Marshall Co. Moundsville. 1927. 334 pp.

McDonnell
- DAR McDonnell Co. W. Va. Hist. Fort Worth. Tex. Univ. Supply. 1959.

Mercer
- The Story of Mercer Co. W. Va., by Kyle McCormick. Charleston. Print. 1957. 132 pp.

Mineral
- Sesqui Frankfort.Mineral Co. 1787-1938. Mineral Co. Hist. Socy. 79 pp.

Monongalia
- Baker, G. C., Monongalia Co.
- Monongalia Hist. Socy. Morgantown, W. Va. 175th Anniv. of Monongalia. 1954. Morgantown.
- Wiley, S. T., Monongalia Co. Kingwood. Preston. 1883.

Monroe
- Morton, O. F., Monroe Co. Staunton. McClure. 1916.

Nicholas
- Brown, William Griffee. Hist. of Nicholas Co. Richmond. Dietz. 1954. 425 pp.

Ohio
- Crammer, G. L. Wheeling City & Ohio Co. Chi. Biog. Pub. 1902. 853 pp.
- Newton, J. H., Ohio. Brooke, Marshall & Hancock Co. Caldwell. Wheeling. 1879. 450 pp.

Pendleton
- Morton, O. F., Pendleton.

Pleasants
- Pemberton, R.L., Pleasants Co. St. Mary's. Oracle Press. 1929. 272 pp.
- Hardesty. Pleasants Co.

WEST VIRGINIA (Continued)

Pocahontas   - Price, W. T., Pocahontas Co. Marlinton. 1901. 622 pp.

Preston   - McRae, D., Preston Co. Kingwood, Journal. 1891. 50 pp.
             - Morton, O. F., Preston Co. Kingswood Journal, 1914. 2 v.
             - Wiley, S. T., Preston Co. Kingswood Journal. 1882. 529 pp.

Randolph   - Maxwell, H. Randolph Co. Morgantown. Acme. 1898. 531 pp.
             - Bosworth, Dr. A.S., Randolph Co. Elkins. 1016. 448 pp.

Ritchie   - Harsty,   Ritchie Co.
             - Lowther, M. K. Ritchie Co. Wheeling. News. 1911. 681 pp.

Roane   - Bishop, W. H. Roane Co. 1774 -1927. Spencer. 1927. 710 pp.

Summers   - Miller, J. H., Summers Co. Hinton. 1908. 838 pp.

Tucker   - Maxwell, H. Tucker Co. Biog. Kingwood. Preston. 1884. 574 pp.

Upshur   - Cutright, W. B. Upshur Co. Buckhannon. 1907.

Webster   - Thompson, R. L., Webster Co. Webster Spgs. Star. 1942.
             199 pp.

Wetzel   - McEldowney, J.C., Jr., Wetzel Co. 1901. 181 pp.

Wood   - Gibbons, A.F. Cent. Wood Co. 1799-1899. Acme. Morgantown.
             1899.
             - Shaw, S.C., Early Wood Co. Parkersburg. Job Printer, 1878.
             65 pp. Johnston, R. B., W. Va.

WISCONSIN - 71 Counties

Ashland   - Hist. of Ashland Co.

Barron   - Gordon, M. Curtiss, W. Barron Co. Copper. Minneapolis 1922.
             1165 pp.

Brown   - Martin, Deborah B. Brown Co. Chi. Clarke. 1913. 358 pp.

Buffalo   - Hist. of Buffalo Co.

Burnett   - Peet, E. L. Burnett Co. 1902.

Chippewa   - Handbook of Chippewa Co. 48 pp.
             Chippewa Co. Chi. Clarke. 1913. 924 pp.

WISCONSIN (Continued)

Clarke
- Biog. Clarke & Jackson Co. Chi. Lewis 1891. 387 pp.
- Curtiss-Wedge, F., Clark Co. Cooper. 1918. 348 pp.

Columbia
- Jones, J. E. ed. Columbia Co. Lewis. Chi. N.Y. 1914. 773 pp.
- Turner, J. A., Columbia Co. Wis. State Reg. Portage. 1904. 142 pp.
- Columbia Co. W. Hist. Co. Culver, Chi. 1880. 1095 pp.

Crawford
- Crawford & Richland Cos. Springfield. Union 1884. 1308 pp.
- Hist. of Crawford Co.

Dane
- Barton, A. O., Dane Co. Clarke. 1932. v. 2 701-1132 pp.
- Keyes, E. W., ed. Dane Co. Madison, W. Hist. Assn. 1906. 423 pp.
- Dane Co. Stat. Madison, Carpenter. 1852. 15 pp.
-   "   " & Surrounding Towns. Madison. Park. 1877. 664 pp.
-   "   "   Growth & Dev. Chi. W. Hist. Co. 1880. 1289 pp.
-   "   "   Biog. & General. Madison W. Hist. Assn. 1906. 974 pp.

Dodge
- Dodge Co. Chi. Western. 1880. 766 pp.
- Hist. of Dodge Co.
- Hubbell, H. B., Dodge Co. Chi. Clarke. 1913. 2 v.

Door
- Holand, H. R., Old Peninsula Days. Ephraim. Pioneer. 1932. 285 pp.
- Holand, H. R., Door Co. Chi. Clarke. 1917. 2 v.
- Martin, C.I., Door Co., Sturgeon Bay. Exposition. 1881. 136 pp.

Douglas
- Hist. of Douglas Co.

Dunn
- Wedge, F. C., Jones, G. & Others. Dunn Co. Cooper, Jr. 1925. 966 p.
- Bailey, W. F., ed. Eau Claire Co. Chi. Cooper. 1914. 920 pp.

Eau Claire
- Eau Claire & Chippewa Co., Oshkosh Photo Co. 1901.
- Atlas of Eau Claire Co. Chi. Ogle. 1910.

Florence
- Hist. of Florence Co.

Fond du Lac
- Glaze, A. T., Early Fond du Lac Co. Haber Prtg. 1905. 368 pp.
- McKenna, M. ed. Fond du Lac Co. Clark. Chi. 1912. 715 pp.
- Mitchell, M. Co. of ed. Fond du Lac Co. Smith. Fond du Lac, Smith. 1854. 96 pp.
- Hist. of Fond du Lac Co. W. Hist. Co. Chi. 1880. 1063 pp.

Grant
- Holford, C.W., Grant Co. Lancaster. Tellar. 1900. 782 pp.

Green
- Bingham, Helen M. Green Co. Milwaukee. Author. 1877. 310 pp.
- Port. & Biog. Album of Green Lake, Marguette & Wayshara Co. Acme. Chi. 1890.

WISCONSIN (Continued)

Iowa   - Butterfield, C. W., Iowa Co. Biog. W. Hist. Socy. 970 pp.

Jefferson   - Ott, J. H., Jefferson Co. Clarke. Chi. 1917. 674 pp.
            - Jefferson Co. W. Hist. Co. Chi. 1879. 733 pp.

Juneau   - Hanson, J. T., Juneau Co. Manston. 1888. 60 pp.

Kenosha   - Hist. of Kenosha Co.
            - Lyman, F. H., Kenosha Co. Chi. Clarke. 1916. 2 v.

Kewaunee   - Hist. of Kewaunee Co.

La Crosse   - Bryant, B. F., La Crosse Co. Madison, W. Hist. Assn. 1907.428 pp.
            - Pammel, L. H., La Crosse Co. & Vicinity. La Crosse.
              Liesenfeld Pr. 1928.
            - Hist. of La Crosse Co. W. Hist. Co. Chi. 1881. 862 pp.
            - Biog. Hist. of La Crosse Co. Treypleleau Co. & Buffalo Co.
              Lewis. 1892. Chi. 794 pp.
            - Inventory of Co. Archives. Wis. Hist. Records Survey #32.
              La Crosse. 1939. 324 pp.

La Fayette - Butterfield, C. W., La Fayette Co. Chi. 1881. 799 pp.

Langlade   - Dessereau, R., Langlade Co. Antigo. 1922.

Lincoln   - Jones, G. A., Lincoln, Oneida & Vilas Co. McVean. 1924.
              Cooper. Minneapolis.

Manitowoc   - Anderson, J.S., Manitowoc Co. Pilot. 1922. 134 pp. Illus.
            - Falge, L. ed. Manitowoc Co. Chi. Goodspeed. Hist. Assn.
              1138 pp.
            - Foote, C. M. Manitowoc Co. & Calumet Co. Minneapolis. 1893.
              83 pp.
            - Plumb, R. G. Manitowoc Co. Manitowoc. Brandt. 1904. 316 pp.
            - Plumb, R.G. Manitowoc Co. Brandt. 1940. 111 pp
            - Atlas of Manitowoc Chi. Ogle. 1921.
            - Atlas of Manitowoc. Sheboygan. Donohue. 1936. 38 pp.
            - Manitowoc Co. Dir. Manitowoc. Johnson Pub. 1942. 100 pp.

Marathon   - Hist. of Marathon Co.

Marinette   - Hist. of Marinette Co.

Milwaukee   - Gregory, J. G., ed. Old Milwaukee Co. 1932. 4 v.
            - Milwaukee Co. Employees Assn. 1923. 96 pp.
            - Watrous, J.A. Early Milwaukee Co. Biog. 1909. 3 v.

Monroe   - Richards, R. H. ed. Monroe Co. 1912. 946 pp.

Oneida   — Hist. of Oneida Co.

Outagamie   — Ryan, T. H. ed. Outagamie Co. Goodspeed Hist. Assn. 1390 pp.

Pierce   — Lowater, C. T., Pierce Co. Spring Valley Pub. Co. 1937.

Polk   — Hist. of Polk Co.

Portage   — Ellis, A. G., Portage Co. Cent. Stevens Point. July 4, 1876.
146 pp.
— Rosholt, Malcolm Leviatt. Our County, Our Story. Portage Co. Wis..
Stevens Point, Wis. Portage Co. Bd. of Supervisors. 1959.

Racine   — Brown, W. E., Racine Co. Clarke. 1932. c. 405-520 pp.
— Butterfield, C. W., Racine Co. & Kenosha Co. Chi. W. Hist.
Co. 1879. 738 pp.
— Dwyer,   C. E., Racine Co. Add. Feb. 22, 1871. Racine. Sanford,
1871. 84 pp.
— Haight, W. L., Racine Co. In World War. Racine, W. Pr. 1920.
607 pp.
— Leach, E. W. Racine Co. Militant. Author. Racine. 1915. 394 pp.
— Stone, Mrs. F.S., Racine City & Co. Clarke. 1916. 2 v. 1135 pp.

Richland   — Miner, Hon. J. ed. Richland Co. W. Hist. Assn. 1906. 698 pp.

Rock   — Brown, W. F., Rock Co. Chi. Cooper. 1908. 2 v.
— Willard, J. F. Guernsey, O. Rock Co. Janesville. Doty. 1856.
— Rock Co. Agri. Socy. Janesville. 1856.
— Rock Co. Chi. W. Hist. Co. 1879. 898 pp.

Rusk   — Maloney, Lt. G. Rusk Co. In World War I. Ladysmith. Journal. 1920.

St. Croix   — Hist of St. Croix.

Sauk   — Butterfield, C.W. Sauk Co. Chi. W. Hist. Co. 1880. 825 pp.
— Caufield, W. H. Sauk Co. To 1861. Baraboo. 1871.
— Caufield, W. H. Sauk Co. 1891. Baraboo. 1891. 53 pp.
— Cole, H.E. Sauk Co. Chi. Lewis. 1918. 1128 pp.
— Derlith, A.W., Sauk Co. Baraboo. Cent. Com. 1948. 100 pp.

Shawano   — Hist. of Shawano.

Sheboygan   — Buchen, G.W., Sheboygan Co. Sheboygan. 1944. 347 pp.
— Donohue, J. Atlas of Sheboygan Co. Sheboygan Press. 1941. 104 pp.
— Geschichte von. Sheboygan Co. Franklin Pub. Co. Sheboygan.
Demokrat. 1898. 297 pp.
— Hesslink, J. F., Sheboygan Co. Evanston. 1938. 101 pp. N.W.
Univ. MA Thesis.
— Joerns, Bros. Atlas of Sheboygan Co. Sheboygan. Joerns. 1902.
61 pp.

WISCONSIN - (Continued)

Sheboygan - Randall, G. A. Atlas of Sheboygan Co. Oshkosh. Randall.
(Con't.)   1875. 88 pp.
           - Ziller, C. ed. Sheboygan Co. Chi. Clarke. 1912. 2 v. 1096 pp.
           - Biog. Rec. of Sheboygan Co. U.S. Pres. & Wis. Govs. Chi.
           - Hist. Rec. of Survey. Inv. of Co. Archives of Wis. #59.
             Sheboygan. 1937. Madison. 113 pp.

Trempealeau - Curtiss-Wedge. F. Trempealeau Co. Chi. Cooper. 1917. 922 pp.
            - Hist. of Trempealeau Co.

Vernon   - Hist. of Vernon Co.
           - Vernon Co. Springfield. Union. 1884. 826 pp.
           - MacFarland-Carters of Vernon, Wis. 1958.

Vilas   - Hist. of Vilas Co.

Walworth   - Beckwith, A.C., Walworth Co. 1912. Bowen. 2 v. 1494 pp.
           - Walworth Co. W. Hist. Socy. 1882. 967 pp.

Washington - Quickert, Wash. Co. Clarke. Chi. 1912. 633 pp.
           -    "   "   "   Banto. Menasha. 1923. 203 pp.
           - Wash. & Ogankee Co. W. Hist. Co. 1881. 764 pp.

Waukesha   - Flower, F.A., Waukesha Co. Author. Chi. 1880. 1006 pp.
           - Haight, T.W., Waukesha Co. Madison. W. Hist. Assn. 1907.
             701 pp.
           - Gregory, J. G., Lacher, J.H.A., Waukesha Co. S.E. Wis. Hist.
             Old Milwaukee Co. Chi. Clarke. 1932. 4 v.
           - Williams, I. J., Welsh. In Waukesha Co. Columbus, Hann &
             Adair Ptg. 1926. 334 pp.
           - Waukesha Co. W. Hist. Co. Chi, 1880. 1006 pp.
           - Waukesha Co. Biog. Port. with U.S. Pres. & Wis. Gov. Chi.
           - Waukesha Co. Excelsior Pub. 1894. 910 pp.
           - Waukesha Co. Cent. & 75 Anniv. ed. of Maukesha Freeman.
             May 1934. 120 pp.

Waupoca   - Dewey, D. Early Waupoca Co. 1855. 96 pp.
           - Wakefield, J. Waupoca Co. Stinchfield. 1890. 219 pp.
           - Ware, J.M. Waupoca Co. Lewis. Chi. 1917. 866 pp. 2 v.

Waushara   - Kent, H. J. ed. Early Waushara Co. Wautoma. 1939.
           - Sorenson, J. P. Pioneer. Waushara Co. Red. Granite Times.
             Wautoma. 1932.
           - W.P.A. Inv. Co. Archives of Wis. #69. Waushara Co. 1941.

Winnebago - Harvey, R. J., Early Winnebago Co. & N.W. Oshkosh. 1880. 348 pp.
           - Lawson, R. V., Winnebago Co. 1908. 2 v.
           - Thwaites, R. G., Winnebago Co. Oshkosh. 1876.

184

Wood   - Jones, G. A., McVean, U.S. & Others. Wood Co. Cooper, Jr. Minneapolis. Winona. 1923. 795 pp.

WYOMING - 24 Counties

In Wyoming no County Histories were published during 1955-60 but several County History College Thesis were written.

- Nelson, Dick, Jr.   Only a Cow Country At One Time; Wyo. Counties of Crook, Weston, & Campbell 1875 to 1951. San Diego 1951.

Natrona   - Mohler, A. J., Natrona Co. 1888-1922. Pub. in 1923.

Uinta   - Stone, Elizabeth A.   Uinta Co. Pub. In 1924.

- Hebard, Grace R. Teaching Wyo. Hist. By Counties. Wyo. Dept. of Education. Bull. #9. Ser. B. Cheyenne, Wyoming. 1926.

- Several Wyo. Counties were Featured in The Midwest Review some years ago, One each month.

MISCELLANEOUS

- Catawba Co. Hist. Assn.- Hist. of Catawba Co. 1954.

- Clarke, Peyton Neale - Old King William Homes & Families - Louisville. J. P. Morton. 1897.

- Chase Co. History Sketches. Vol. II 1948.

- Curti, Merle Eugene. The Making of An American Community, A Case Study of Democracy In A Frontier County, Trempesleau County. Stamford Univ. Press. Calif. 1957.

- Dodd, V. A. - Henry Co. Marriage Bonds 1778-1849. 1953.

- Ervin, E. - Pioneer History of Meigs & Co. 1949.

- Ellsberry, E. P. - Marriage Records, Sullivan Co. 1959.

- Edson, Lelah (Jackson) The Fourth Corner; Highlights From The Early Northwest. Whatcom Co. Bellingham. Author. 1953.

MISCELLANEOUS (Continued)

- Eastern Shore Va. In The 17th C. Richmond, Va. Ball Book and Stationery Co. Accowmache. 1911. 406 pp.

- Freel, M. W. - Our Heritage, Cherokee Co. 1956.

- Freeman, I. S. - History of Monteguma Co. 1958.

- French, G. - Golden Land, Sherman Co. 1958.

- Groome, H. C. - Fauquier During The Proprietorship. Richmond, Va. Old Dom. Pr. 1927. 255 pp.

- Gloucester. - Robins, Sally Nelson. Richmond. West Johnson & Co. 1893. 21 pp.

- Goss, H. R. - Life & Death of A Quick Lake Co. 1958.

- Guthrie, J. M.- Thirty Three Years of Hist. of Lawrence Co. 1958.

- Gronert, T. - Sugar Creek Saga, Montgomery Co. 1958.

- Havins, T. R. - Something About Brown Co. 1958.

- Hunter, Lillie May - The Moving Finger Castro Co. 1956.

- Holliday, R. K.,- Politics In Fayette Co. 1956.

- Hands, M. - Jefferson Co. Reminiscences. 1957.

- Johnston, David E. - A Hist. of Middle River Settlement - Huntingdon, W. Va. Standard.

- Johnson, T. C. - Story of Kinston & Lenoir Co. 1954.

- Kercheval, Samuel - Hist. of The Valley of Va. 4th ed. Strasburg, Va. Shenandoah Pub. House. 1925. 405 pp.

- Klapthor - Hist. of Charles Co. 1958.

- Keleher, W. - Violence In Lincoln Co. 1957.

- Kinder, W. R. - Historic Notes of Miami Co. 1953.

- McMahon, H. - Chautauqua Co. A History. 1958.

- Morgan, V. - Folklore of Highland Co. 1946.

- McDowell County History - by Col. Andrew Donnally Chap. DAR. 1959. 132 pp.

- McCormick, K. - The Story of Mercer Co. 1957.

MISCELLANEOUS (Continued)

- Peters, Kate (Johnston) Lauderdale Co. From Earliest Times; Tours & Communities, Families and Famous People. Ripley Tenn. Sugar Hill Lauderdale Co. Library 1957.

- Prince William - Landmarks - Harrison, Fairfax. 2 vols. Priv. Print. Old Dom. Pr. 1924. 724 pp.

- Ricks, Joel E. - Hist. of Coche Co. Valley. 1956.

- Ritchie, A. - Sketches of Rabun Co. History.

- Smith, A.M. - First One Hundred Years In Cooke Co. 1955.

- Stovall, Allan A. - Nueces Headwater Co. 1959.

- Sanderson, E. - Scott Co. and Its Mountain Folk. 1958.

- Sumners, Mary Floyd - "Tishomingo County, 1836-1860". A Thesis prepared at the Univ. of Miss. 1957. 154 pp.

- Scott Co. - Addington, Robert Milford. Hist. of Scott Co. Va. Kingsport, Tenn. 1932.

- Toole, G. - Ninety Years In Aiken Co. 1959.

- Terrill, H. - History of Stewart Co. 1958.

- Van Ness, E. - Wm. Opie of Somerset Co. 1958.

- Weathers, L. B. - Living Past of Cleveland Co. 1956.

- Wise, Jennings Cropper - Ye Kingdome of Accawmache.

- Yagoo Hist. Assn. - Yagoo County Story. 1958.